The Disappearance of Introspection

The Disappearance of Introspection

William Lyons

A Bradford Book
The MIT Press
Cambridge, Massachusetts
London, England

This book was set in Palatino by The MIT Press Computergraphics Department and
printed and bound by The Murray Printing Co. in the United States of America.

Library of Congress Cataloging-in-Publication Data

Lyons, William E.
    The disappearance of introspection.

    "A Bradford book."
    Bibliography: p.
    Includes index.
    1. Introspection. 2. Consciousness. I. Title.
BF316.L96   1986   153   86-182
ISBN 0-262-12115-8

To Liam and Ailsa

To study Metaphysics, as they have always been studied appears to me to be like puzzling at astronomy without mechanics.—Experience shows the problem of the mind cannot be solved by attacking the citadel itself.—the mind is function of body.—we must bring some stable *foundation to argue from.*
Charles Darwin, "N Notebook"

Contents

Preface

Thus my paper might even be called "What Became of Introspection?"
One common answer to that question would be that introspection was
not viable and so gradually became extinct. Another answer, however,
is that introspection is still with us, doing its business under various
aliases, of which verbal report *is one.*
—Edwin G. Boring

In philosophy, and in psychology since behaviorism, there have rarely
been extended studies of introspection, and it is no longer a topic
treated in psychology textbooks. If the word "introspection" appears
in the index of a textbook, the reference will be to introductory pages
where introspectionism is summarily dismissed. There have been holistic
theories in philosophy about the relation between mind and body where
the proponents have felt the need to explain or explain away the "difficult case" of introspection in terms of the new theory. There have
been ground-level radical theories about the nature and scope of psychological explanation where the exponents have explored the efficacy
of the new methodology in explaining the nature of introspection. But
introspection has rarely been approached as a topic worthy of investigation in its own right. Further it can be safely said that in both
psychology and the brain sciences, theorizing about the nature of introspection is at a rudimentary stage in comparison with, say, theorizing
about the nature of perception or memory.

My aim in this book is to examine the nature of introspection because
to do so is an interesting and worthwhile task in itself and because to
understand something that is usually considered to be at the heart of
consciousness will be an important step in our understanding of the
nature of the mind in general. At present introspection is a central topic
in philosophy of mind and theoretical psychology only in the sense
that to attempt an explanation of it is to reveal a great deal about one's
view of the mental. To attempt even a by-the-way account of intro-

spection forces one's hand in a way that few other theoretical enterprises do. I have set out to study introspection initially by way of paying close critical attention to the crucial debates about the nature of introspection that have been more or less forced on both philosophy of mind and psychology because of the radical changes that have taken place at the theoretical level in both subjects. Besides the inherent interest in tracing the transformation in our theorizing and modeling in regard to introspection, it is very instructive to do so. A reasonable case could be made out that the history of these theoretical debates has been a history of progress at least in the sense that it has shown that certain accounts of introspection are untenable, and, in the light of this negative knowledge, I have gone on to produce a new account of introspection.

Parts I and II of this book, then, are regular academic campaigning with the battle lines clearly drawn. Part III is more irregular theoretical skirmishing with probes, speculative thrusts, and some long-range shots being the order of the day. Parts I and II document in some detail the four theories or models of introspection that have emerged from the debates of the philosophers and theoretical psychologists from the rise and fall of introspectionism to the present. These four theories are put in chronological order, though it is a smoothed-out and rounded-off chronological ordering, with overlaps and residues tidied away. These theories and their theorists are the revered ancestors of my own theorizing on the subject of introspection, as well as being for the most part still active rivals to it. I have been not merely absorbed by the struggle to understand and get clear about their arguments and viewpoints but also deeply influenced by the implications in regard to introspection of the traumatic debates by which behaviorism displaced introspectionism and how in turn various forms of physicalism displaced or are in the process of displacing behaviorist accounts of the mental. In a sense my account of introspection in part III emerges out of the debates documented in parts I and II and makes sense only when seen against the background of those debates. In wider terms, the last hundred years have been exciting times in theorizing about the nature of mind, and more or less parallel changes of a profound kind have occurred at about the same time in philosophy and psychology. I hope that some of the excitement has filtered through into my account.

Contrary to current fashion in this area, I have not given this book a subtitle such as *Essays in Philosophy of Mind* or *From the Standpoint of Philosophical Psychology* or *An Essay in Philosophy of Psychology* or *A Study in Cognitive Science* or *A Study in Theoretical Psychology*, for part of my reluctance is due to the fact that I am no longer confident that I can clearly delineate or separate what might be referred to by the labels "philosophy of mind," "philosophical psychology," "philosophy of psychology," "cognitive science," and "theoretical psychology." On the other hand part of my reluctance is due to my realization that I have already crossed or even erased boundaries that are sometimes drawn and to my suspicion that it is a good thing that I have done so, for it is arguable that it would be difficult, if not impossible, to produce anything of value on the nature of introspection without taking account of not merely the debates of philosophers but also relevant work in psychology and the brain sciences.

Finally I have attempted to present my research in a lucid and, as far as is feasible given that it strays into technical areas, a jargon-free manner. As a consequence I hope that it will be accessible to and of interest to psychologists, and maybe even some brain scientists, as well as philosophers, and to beginners as well as seasoned professionals, though I realize that a price may have to be paid for such disregard of traditional demarcations.

Acknowledgments

I would like to record my gratitude to Robert Farr of the London School of Economics for his kind and practical encouragement over a number of years and to the trustees of the Nuffield Foundation for their award to me of a fellowship for the 1983–1984 academic session.

In preparing various drafts of this book, I have profited from the judicious comments of my former colleagues at Glasgow University— Jim Edwards, Flint Schier, and Janet Sisson—as well as from those of the publisher's advisers and readers—Ray Jackendoff, Alan Millar, Terence Penelhum, and Elizabeth Valentine.

I have made use of material I previously published in the journals *Analysis, Behavioral and Brain Sciences, British Journal of Social Psychology, Canadian Journal of Philosophy*, and *International Philosophical Quarterly*. I would like to make formal acknowledgment of the permission (where required) granted by the editors and publishers of those journals.

Anne Burke typed the final version of the manuscript, and Paul Bagley checked the references and quotations. To both of these I am very grateful.

PART I

The Dethronement of Introspection

Chapter 1
Noticing with the Inner Eye

1 Introspection from Augustine to the Seventeenth Century

The Concise OED defines "introspection" as the "examination or observation of one's own mental processes" and explains that the term is derived etymologically from two Latin words *spicere* ("to look") and *intra* ("within"). It has been suggested recently that "in our culture, we take it for granted that each of us knows his own mind directly and can describe its operations."[1] I think that this is a fair suggestion. Those untouched by philosophy or psychology would take it as incontrovertible that we have direct awareness, at least on occasion, of what is going on in our mind and that this private access is so direct and immediate as to be outside the possibility of error.

Things may not always have been so. It has been argued that the ancient Greeks did not have any concept of introspection, or at least the Greeks up to and including Aristotle,[2] though there is a section in *De Anima* where Aristotle may be saying that we can reflect on our own mental states.[3] The earliest account of introspection that could lay claim to be a classical account—though neither the term "introspection" nor any equivalent technical term is employed—is probably to be found in Augustine's *De Trinitate*. He there remarks, "What then can be the purport of the injunction, Know thyself? I suppose it is that the mind should reflect upon itself."[4] Also in the *De Trinitate*, there is the famous passage foreshadowing Descartes' *cogito*, though Descartes claimed not to have known of this passage before propounding the *cogito*.[5]

> We are concerned now with the nature of mind; and we have to exclude from our consideration everything which enters our acquaintance from outside by the bodily senses, and concentrate our attention upon the points which all minds know with certainty about themselves. . . . No one can possibly doubt that he lives and remembers, understands, wills, thinks, knows, and judges. For even if he doubts, he lives.[6]

Augustine is suggesting something that became the orthodox view from roughly the end of the Middle Ages to the beginning of our century and the basis for the allegedly scientific technique of introspection in nineteenth-century psychology: that we can discover the nature of mind by a process of bracketing out the external world in order the better to perceive internal mental events or contents and then by engaging directly or indirectly in some process of inner perception or inner observation. Second, there is in Augustine also perhaps the earliest version of the claim that such a process produces or procures indubitable knowledge.

In arguing in the *Summa* that "the mind perceives itself," Aquinas quotes Augustine's *De Trinitate* in support of his claim.[7] Unlike Augustine, however, Aquinas did not consider introspection as a fundamental source of knowledge on a par with ordinary perception or inspection. He did not build a psychology or philosophy of mind on the basis of introspection because for him introspection was, ordinarily, a mere concomitant mental perception of the basic exercise of mind, which was to sort and understand the data provided by ordinary external perception. Introspection was peripheral in importance and also in a more literal sense. It was, so to speak, "seeing" out of the corner of the mind's eye rather than with it.[8]

Arguably the beginning of the golden age of introspection was the seventeenth century, and this age lasted at least until the first decade of the twentieth century. In 1637, in his *Discourse on the Method of Rightly Directing One's Reason and of Seeking Truth in the Sciences*, Descartes proposed explicitly what has since been called a "foundationalist epistemology,"[9] when he suggested that the first rule for securing true and incontrovertible knowledge was "never to accept anything as true if I had not evident knowledge of its being so . . . and to embrace in my judgment only what presented itself to my mind so clearly and distinctly that I had no occasion to doubt it,"[10] and to build all subsequent science on a foundation of facts secured in accordance with this principle. This foundation was, Descartes believed, that "from the mere fact that I thought of doubting . . . about other truths it evidently and certainly followed that I existed," and, further, from this it followed that it was a human's nature to be conscious.[11] Consciousness came to be indubitable reality and everything else a fragile by-product of it. The chief means of producing or deriving other facts from the fact of consciousness was reflection—that is, self-reflection or introspection.

Even the archenemy of Cartesian dualism in the seventeenth century, Thomas Hobbes, enthroned self-reflection as the chief means of gaining knowledge of human psychology; indeed he made it the chief means of gaining knowledge in politics and social science in general. Hobbes produced Augustine's tag, *nosce teipsum* ("know thyself")—or as Hobbes translated it, read thyself—as his maxim when urging us to discover the nature and variety of human thought and passion: "Whosoever looketh into himself, and considereth what he doth, and when he does *think, opine, reason, hope, feare,* &c, and upon what grounds; he shall thereby read and know, what are the thoughts, and Passions of all other men, upon the like occasions."[12] So it is not at all surprising that it is generally held that the first appearance of the word "introspection" was in the second half of the seventeenth century.[13]

Despite the heavy use made at this time of the terms "introspection," "inner sense," and "reflection," it was not made clear whether these terms were to be taken synonymously. What is certain is that if they were not, they were not clearly distinguished from one another at this time, and no clear model of introspection had yet been proposed as a subject of critical discussion.[14] It was taken for granted that introspection, or one of its more or less indistinguishable cognate processes, was the basic method for gaining knowledge of the mind. Locke, for example, believed that by reflection, "the mind comes to reflect on its own *operations* about the *ideas* got by *sensation* and thereby stores itself with a new set of *ideas*, which I call *ideas* of *reflection*."[15] Thus, in the manner described, one could gain direct knowledge, for example, of the fundamental acts of understanding and willing. Locke claimed that one was directly aware of the exercise of these mental powers.[16] Hume, of course, was skeptical that one had direct knowledge of any such exercises of mental powers though he was not skeptical about whether we had direct knowledge of what was in our mind. Indeed it was probably Hume, as much as Descartes, who left us with the legacy of the mind as a receptacle with contents.[17]

2 Inner Observation versus Inner Perception: The Birth of Experimental Psychology

A direct heir to this empiricist tradition, and one of the progenitors of the science of psychology, was Franz Brentano. In his book *Psychology from an Empirical Standpoint*, first published in 1874, Brentano wrote of psychology that "there is no branch of science that has borne less fruit for our knowledge of nature and life, and yet there is none which holds greater promise of satisfying our most essential needs. There is no area of knowledge, with the single exception of metaphysics, which the great mass of people look upon with greater contempt. And yet there is none to which certain individuals attribute greater value and which they hold in higher esteem."[18] Brentano went on to proclaim that the proper and sui generis objects of psychology were mental phenomena and that its chief method lay in employing what he called "inner *perception*" (*Wahrnehmung*), which he carefully distinguished from "inner *observation*" (*Beobachtung*).[19] We could not, he said, directly focus on or observe our inner mental life because, in doing so, we would thereby draw away the attention necessary for the existence of the first-order mental life of thoughts, feelings, and volitions. To attempt direct inner observation therefore was ipso facto to diminish or destroy what one was attempting to observe. The best one could hope to do was to notice or perceive indirectly, out of the corner of one's "mental eye," mental phenomena as they went about their business. In short, Brentano endorsed a seventeenth-century view of introspection in respect of the central place he gave it regarding our knowledge of human psychology and because he saw it as amounting to reflection or concomitant by-the-way noticing of mental events. One did not actively focus on mental events—mental events by their very nature forced themselves into our notice—and this was the only way of ever finding out about them.

Wilhelm Wundt attempted to make Brentano's version of introspection scientific and systematic and in doing so to make it integral to the day-to-day business of academic, scientific psychology. Although Wundt endorsed Brentano's distinction between inner perception and inner observation[20] and endorsed his preference for inner perception over inner observation, he felt that inner perception was of no value for a scientific psychology as it stood because by its very nature it must be unsystematic, for the first-order mental phenomena—the thinkings, feelings, and volitions—clearly make the pace. The perceiving subject must wait until these phenomena come to its notice. Any attempt to concentrate on it or focus on it or force the pace in any way will turn the process into inner observation and so remove the possibility of success.

On the other hand, Wundt believed that one could mold inner perception into a scientific method by so ordering and controlling the conditions that the process of inner perception came to resemble in all important respects external, ordinary perception while steering clear of becoming overblown and useless internal observation. So experimental psychology was born.[21] The first psychological experiments were inner perception under experimental conditions. Wundt so arranged his laboratory that he could control the stimuli that were to cause the first-order mental phenomena, which in turn were to be noticed in a passive, unforced way by inner perception. In practice this usually turned out to be the presentation to the subjects of simple colored shapes or objects that were presumed to cause internal sensations of color, which in turn were presumed to be noticed by the passive process of inner perception more or less immediately. Wundt also cut down as far as possible on the time allowed between the subject's inner perception and his or her report on it. Third, he believed that publishable, strictly scientific data from introspection could be obtained only from experienced subjects. E. G. Boring observed that "thus it is said that no observer who had performed less than 10,000 of these introspectively controlled reactions was suitable to provide data for published research from Wundt's laboratory."[22] It has also been suggested that the reason for this preference for seasoned inner perceivers was that "the advantage of the experienced observer lies in the fact that his acts of observation have become automatic habits and therefore are marked by speed and attentiveness with a lack of self-consciousness."[23] Fourth, by and large Wundt limited the reports of these experienced perceivers to questions of size, intensity, and duration. Finally, as was the case with experiments in physics and chemistry, his experiments with inner perception could be, and indeed had to be, replicated. This latter requirement in particular led William James to observe that

> within a few years what one may call a microscopic psychology has arisen in Germany, carried on by experimental methods, asking of course every moment for introspective data, but eliminating their uncertainty by operating on a large scale and taking statistical means. This method taxes patience to the utmost, and could hardly have arisen in a country whose natives could be *bored*. . . . There is little of the grand style about these new prism, pendulum and chronograph-philosophers. They mean business, not chivalry.[24]

The reference to prism, pendulum, and chronograph is William James's way of referring to the apparatus, the first psychological apparatus, that came to birth with the first psychological laboratories. There were, for example, the tachistoscope, a machine for presenting visual stimuli for very brief and accurately timed periods, and the metronome or its more sophisticated relative, the chronograph, an apparatus for accurately recording reaction times, such as between, say, the presentation of the stimulus and the introspective report on the ensuing sensation.

Wundt believed that he had so hedged in and controlled introspection that it could be admitted into psychology as scientific inner perception. It might be more accurate to say that he had reduced introspection to inner perception, for he believed that the more robust and complex mental phenomena, such as thoughts, volitions, and feelings, were not sufficiently amenable to experimental control to be the object of scientific inner perception.[25] One could not be sure, for example, that the presentation of a certain stimulus—say, a written word or a picture—would produce the same thought when the experiment was repeated with other subjects or even with the same subject. In short, one could not be sure of what internal phenomenon one was producing in the subject. In making psychological investigation scientific and experimental, Wundt was accused of trivializing it and making it impossibly boring. Further it could be argued that Wundt had so hedged in and reduced introspection and introspective reports that it was no longer clear how they differed from simply reporting on ordinary perception.

In defense of Wundt against the charge of making psychology trivial and boring, it should be made clear that he held that by far the greater part of what falls under the science of psychology could not be studied by this experimental method of introspection. Wundt wrote a ten-volume work on social psychology, for he believed that the higher mental phenomena were essentially social in character and were best studied in connection with the study of language, customs, religion, myth, and magic.[26] In defense of Wundt against the second charge—that he reduced introspective reports to ordinary perception reports—it can be pointed out that, regarding color, in ordinary perception one notes the color, if at all, only as one of many reportable aspects of an object embedded in a medley of other objects, while in scientific inner perception, the reporter is so constrained that he or she must concentrate on aspects normally missing from ordinary conscious perception or barely noticed, aspects such as the size or shape of some simple color phenomenon, how long it is presented to consciousness, and how intense it is in comparison with other similar phenomena.

At this stage, then, in regard to the two classical models of introspection—on the one hand, passive inner perception and, on the other, active inner observation—few would have doubted that both models accurately pictured real psychological processes. The debate was about which sort of introspection could and should be adopted as a method by the newly emerging science of psychology. Wundt settled on passive inner perception, but he believed that this could be engaged in with confidence—with confidence in the worth of its scientific results—only if the range of objects to which it should be and could be applied was very narrow. In other words, inner perception as a tool of psychology narrowed alarmingly the scope of psychological investigation. It was chiefly for that reason that this method was not the one that came to be adopted in the United States, which became the main proving ground for psychological methodology.

3 William James and Introspection as "Retrospection"

In the preface to volume 1 of *The Principles of Psychology*, William James wrote that "in this strictly positivistic point of view consists the only feature of it [*The Principles*] for which I feel tempted to claim originality."[27] James wrote and spoke French and German fluently and knew intimately the work of such positivists as Auguste Comte and Ernst Mach, as well as the work of British positivists or quasi-positivists such as John Stuart Mill. This, together with his own scientific training, made it unsurprising that James should endorse the central tenets of nineteenth-century positivism: that the only genuine knowledge was empirical or scientific knowledge, that the only valid method of gaining knowledge was the scientific method, and that, insofar as we can know anything about humans and their behavior, it can only be by the employment of the scientific method in the study of humans.

After James's initial paean to positivism, it may still come as something of a shock to modern readers of *The Principles* to read that James glossed the phrase "science of psychology" as "science of the mental life," by which he meant quite unequivocally "the description and explanation of states of consciousness as such."[28] Further, James goes on to assert that regarding the method of psychology, "*Introspective Observation is what we have to rely on first and foremost and always. The word introspection need hardly be defined—it means, of course, the looking into our own minds and reporting what we there discover. Every one agrees that we there discover states of consciousness.*"[29] By introspection James meant not Wundt's inner passive perception but the other variety mentioned by Brentano: inner active observation. But why did someone so wedded to positivism as was James, and someone so familiar with Peirce's pragmatism, cling to introspection as the preeminent method for psychology? Part of the answer lies in the fact that, besides being influenced by the European positivists, he was also influenced by the heirs to British empiricism, such as John Stuart Mill, and particularly the Scottish philosophical psychologists, James Mill and Alexander Bain. These nineteenth-century empiricists took for granted, assuming rather than arguing, that introspection was the method for studying anything to do with the mind.[30] The other reason lay in the fact that at least at the time of writing *The Principles*, James was a committed mind-body dualist. As he put it, "Nature in her unfathomable designs has mixed us of clay and flame, of brain and mind, [such] that the two things hang indubitably together and determine each other's being, but how or why, no mortal may ever know."[31] James believed that what was distinctive of human life was the fact that human behavior was guided by goals, which in turn were purposes conceived in consciousness. The proper object of psychology, and what alone clearly distinguished its subject matter from that of the sciences of physiology and neurology, was the stream of consciousness in humans, particularly the action-guiding denizens of that stream. Although James was a positivist in that he believed in the preeminence of scientific method in the pursuit of knowledge, he did not endorse the determinist or materialist views of positivists like Comte. He believed, correctly, that neither determinism nor materialism followed logically from an adherence to positivist views on epistemology.

So given James's dualism and his consequent view about the proper object of psychology, it is not at all surprising that James should turn to introspection as the method for conducting psychological investigations. James believed that there were two parts to the science of psychology: description and explanation. The descriptive part involved a careful—introspectively obtained—account of the mental events in our stream of consciousness, for these were deemed to be the subject matter of psychology. On the other hand, the explanation of these events was to be found only at the physiological and neurological level. This was central in James's approach to psychology and what he believed had the real healing power in his injection of positivism into psychology. At the end of the nineteenth century, most psychologists would have agreed with James that the proper object of psychology was conscious states, but then they would have gone on to explain the origin of any particular conscious state according to the Laws of Association.

The Laws of Association, first suggested by Aristotle (in *On Memory and Reminiscence*),[32] were canonized by the British empiricists, reaching their apotheosis in the work of Hartley, John Stuart Mill, and Bain. These laws were generalizations about how humans come to associate ideas or string thoughts together in the way they do. In his *System of Logic*, Mill describes psychology in the following way: "The subject, then, of Psychology, is the uniformities of succession, the laws, whether ultimate or derivative, according to which one mental state succeeds another: is caused by, or at least, is caused to follow, another."[33] Thus, for example, it was claimed that we recall an event or object in memory because it is either similar to, directly contrasted with, or was found originally to have been spatially or temporally (or both) contiguous with another item prior to it in our conscious stream of thoughts or ideas. In other words, most psychologists in the last quarter of the nineteenth century were associationists.

James rejected associationism, arguing that it merely plotted the "dance of ideas" and gave no real explanation of their choreography, because from the Laws of Association one could not predict the all-too-frequent exceptions to those laws. One had to look to the physiological and neurological bases of our conscious ideas—and James held that there was a one-to-one correspondence between brain states and conscious ones—in order to explain, for example, why old age or hypnosis can enhance memory but illness or excitement hinder it. This account also furnished James with the distinction between psychology and philosophy. While psychology shared with philosophy of mind the same object of study—the stream of consciousness—it parted company with philosophy in seeking explanations at the neurophysiological level by means of scientific investigation and experiment.

James's objection to associationist psychology is not quite the demolition that he sometimes seemed to imply. To produce a correct score for "the dance of ideas" would be to produce important knowledge that we did not have before, for it would tell us of the constant conjunctions, if there were any, or at least the sequential ordering of items in our mental life. If correct, and sufficiently comprehensive, and if any constant conjunctions were indeed revealed, then with such a score in hand, one could predict from the appearance of idea or mental phenomenon x that idea or mental phenomenon y would probably follow. James is right to suggest that such a score could not predict a breakdown in the whole mental system or even in part of it, or predict interference by events of another order. But to point that out is merely to indicate that such a score could hope at most only to be a partial account, which would have to be mapped on to accounts of other systems, such as the physiological, which obviously can play a causal role in the genesis of ideas or, in general, mental events. It is not to point out that the whole approach is misconceived.

What is really wrong with associationism is that its laws were never laws and showed little hope of ever being so. An individual's hopes, feelings, thoughts, and volitions were hardly ever, if at all, predictable by the Laws of Association, because few, if any, constant conjunctions ever emerged. One possible way of mapping human mental events so as to produce a map of genuine predictive power might well be achieved, as James suggested, by turning directly to the task of correlating mental events with brain events and then plotting the causal connections at the level of brain events. But there are other ways that might turn out more feasible, at least in the short run. Such a way might be to try to elaborate a precise, detailed theory of personality types such that, by sorting particular individuals into the correct personality grouping, one could begin to predict what they believe, hope, want, and are most likely to do.

In propounding his own view of the object and methods of psychology, James was well aware of the objections to it, most of which centered on his employment of introspection as the chief method in psychology. In *The Principles*, James himself brings forward the two classical objections to the employment of introspection in psychology. James introduces the first, appropriately, by quoting Comte, who had no place for psychology in his positivist map of science and always spoke of it with contempt. The study of mental phenomena had a place in Comte's general schema only as a branch of physiology:

> As for observing in the same way [as one observes something external to the organs of observation] *intellectual* phenomena at the time of their actual presence, that is a manifest impossibility. The thinker cannot divide himself into two, of whom one reasons whilst the other observes him reason. The organ observed and the organ observing being, in this case, identical, how could observation take place? This pretended psychological method is then radically null and void.[34]

The first of Comte's objections to introspection is the radical one that it cannot really occur in the way it is alleged to occur because that would involve an implausible split in consciousness. James's response is to quote Mill's response to this objection:

> A fact may be studied through the medium of memory, not at the very moment of our perceiving it, but the moment after: and this is really the mode in which our best knowledge of our intellectual acts is generally acquired. We reflect on what we have been doing when the act is past, but when its impression in the memory is still fresh. Unless in one of these ways, we could not have acquired the knowledge which nobody denies us to have, of what passes in our minds. M. Comte would scarcely have affirmed that we are not aware of our own intellectual operations. We know of our observings and reasonings, either at the very time, or by memory the moment after; in either case, by direct knowledge.[35]

So Mill's response, which James endorsed and adopted, is that (1) given that "nobody denies" that we have knowledge of what passes in our minds, (2) then our "best knowledge" of our conscious states is by directly observing them suspended in memory—that is, by retrospecting them.

The Mill-James view is that the difficulties or alleged difficulties in employing the full-blooded concept of introspection—introspection as positive active observation of our conscious states—are avoided if the mental states, so observed, are not moving quickly through the stream of consciousness but are suspended in vitro and carefully scrutinized at leisure through our mental microscope. Wundt's worries—about such direct observation disturbing the stream of mental impressions produced by stimuli in the external world and thus distorting if not destroying them—would also be avoided by such a move.

4 Difficulties with James's "Retrospection" Model of Introspection

On closer inspection, it is not at all clear how James thinks this endorsement of Mill avoids what seems central to Comte's objection: that any account of introspection will involve the inconceivable, and so incomprehensible, process of consciousness being split into the observer and observed at the same time. Is James saying, "Yes, introspection does involve a split in consciousness, but it doesn't matter. There's nothing wrong with that," or is he saying, "Introspection conceived as retrospection does not involve any split in consciousness"? James, I think, is advocating the latter response, arguing that if what is introspected is not part of the present stream of consciousness, then it is not part of consciousness. The observed mental state or process, suspended in memory, is not conscious; only the observing process, introspection, is, so the split is avoided. What is observed—say, an act of thinking—is frozen in memory into nonconsciousness, or it is abstracted from the stream of consciousness and suspended statically in memory.

Before examining what I have suggested is the most likely interpretation of the Mill-James model of introspection as retrospection, it will be useful to look at the reply to Comte that James passed over and why he did so. This reply, which might seem to be both the strongest and most obvious response, is that introspection does involve a split in consciousness, but so what? By reference to other views of James, it seems clear enough that James rejected this response because he went along with Comte in thinking that such a splitting of consciousness was impossible, though his reasons for thinking it impossible were different from Comte's. Comte appears to have thought that it was a priori impossible—that is, that it is conceivable that it could exist; it is like a square circle. James appears to have thought it a posteriori, or as a known-matter-of-fact, impossible. In chapter 11 of volume 1 of *The Principles*, James seems to be arguing that consciousness involves a single, focused, unsplittable act of attention. For example, you might have a toothache while taking an examination. Your attention can be transferred back and forth from the pain to the problems set by the examiners, but it cannot be split equally or unequally between them. Attention is like a single torch beam.

James himself refers to the experiments of the French psychologist Paulhan, who attempted to recite one poem aloud while at the same time writing down another, finding that it was possible only if one or the other, or both, of the attempted performances were so habitual as to proceed more or less automatically—that is, without needing attention from the performer. These experiments resemble the parlor game often introduced when children's parties are threatening to disintegrate. One asks the children to draw a circle counterclockwise on their foreheads with the index finger of their right hand and then draw a square, clockwise, on their chests with the index finger of their left hand. Then one asks them to try to perform both actions at the same time. There is also some support for the unsplittable nature of attention in more recent psychological work. Woodworth and Schlosberg write that "the conclusion [from the most convincing of recent experiments into the possibility of dividing attention] is that simultaneous performance of two attentive acts of cognition did not often if ever occur."[36] What does seem to happen, they report, when a person attempts to divide attention is a rapid alternation between the different objects of attention.

It might be objected, however, that an inability to recite a poem aloud and write one on paper at the same time, and an inability to draw a circle clockwise on one's forehead and at the same time a square on one's chest with the other hand, may not be evidence of the impossibility of splitting consciousness so much as evidence that you cannot overload the language center of the brain, or the motor response area of the brain, or, in general, specific regions of the brain connected with tasks that require attention. If the tasks concerned are of a different sort, one does seem to be able to split attention.[37] One can quite easily garden and converse, or ride a bicycle and sing, or play patience and listen to music. Apparent counterexamples to this interpretation, such as the difficulty of concentrating on an examination if one has a toothache or headache, can be given a different sort of explanation, for although they involve two different sorts of attention-grabbing events, and so involve events which should not block the ability to concentrate on both of them at once, one of the attention-grabbing items is of an overwhelming sort. It might be claimed that the reason why one cannot attend to both the pain and the examination is to be found in terms of the overwhelming nature in regard to attention of pains such as headache and toothache. If one changes the example slightly, perhaps to a case of a person with a pain in the knee (a dull arthritic pain) who has to take an examination, then one would be surprised if the candidate was unable to concentrate in such a context.

Woodworth and Schlosberg—or the psychologists working on attention—seem to have been alive to such countermoves, for they refer to an experiment in which the tasks or events to be concentrated on were clearly different and nothing like an overwhelming attention-grabbing pain was involved, yet it still seemed in such cases that attention could not be split. For example,

In one experiment . . . weak pressure was applied to one finger of each hand, and the subject had to say which pressure was stronger;

at the same time there was a brief visual exposure of 3–6 short lines to be counted. Either task was so easy that, when presented alone, it gave nearly 100 percent of correct responses; but, when the two tasks were presented simultaneously, both responses were correct in only 12 percent of cases.[38]

Still there is a doubt that such an experiment demonstrates that no splitting of attention had taken place. It could still have been the case, as the subject had to report verbally, that while both the finger pressures and the written lines were attended to, the subjects could not in the time allowed store anything very much in memory, even short-term memory, and so have much to report. It seems too strong a demand to stipulate that if one cannot report correctly about something, one has not attended to it. The ability to report may be a sufficient condition for attributing attention, but it seems unfair to say that it is a necessary condition. In the circumstances, the link between the attending and memory and the channels for the reporting are, by the very construction of the experiment, overloaded. Admittedly a splitting of attention that blocks the ability to report on what is attended to will be of little use to a theory of introspection based on the splitting of attention. Perhaps Comte could have rephrased his objection as not that introspection involves an impossible split in conscious attention but that introspection based on a split in attention would not allow for useful reports to be made on the targets of attention.[39]

At the more basic level one might question the equation of consciousness and attention that gave support to the view that a split in consciousness made introspection impossible or useless. There do seem to be cases where we are aware "out of the corner of our consciousness," so to speak (and this might be revealed in nonverbal behavior at the moment or later), but we do not realize that we are aware. We are not attending in any positive sense to it. Such a conceptual splitting of attention from consciousness—such that attention is to be defined as a species of consciousness, a kind of consciousness that is active, positive, and focused—again will not give much comfort to a theory of introspection that posits a split in consciousness. If one side of the split is now described as involving passive, nonattentive consciousness, then it is either the introspective act that is so described, or it is the target mental process. If the former, then it will be useless as a source of reportable data, for how could such an unfocused, nonattentive process produce accurate data? If it is the target mental process that is so described, then it will mean that only mental processes thus downgraded into passive nonattentive conscious processes can be the target of introspection. More robust, full-blooded conscious processes will not be open to inner observation.

'oes emerge clearly is that any experimental work in psychology
ssibility of splitting attention would need to be based on a
'heoretical treatment of what is to count as attention.
 ఎejected an explanation of introspection in terms of a split in
ఎonsciousness and believed that he did so on good empirical grounds.
He rejected such an explanation in favor of one that did not involve
such a split. The explanation he endorsed still involved a split but not
a split in consciousness. There was a split between the observer and
observed, but only the observing process, introspection, was conscious.
The observed mental process—say, an act of thinking—was no longer
part of the stream of consciousness but suspended nonconsciously in
memory.

There are still some residual doubts as to whether James has in fact
swept aside Comte's objection. Let us say that I engage in an act of
thinking. Let us say that I try to work through Pythagoras's theorem.
This process of thinking passes from the present into short-term or
"buffer" memory. I then introspect, in the Jamesian sense of actively
scrutinizing in a conscious mental act, this process of thinking. For
James, this process of thinking through Pythagoras's theorem must
first pass from the stream of consciousness into memory and then
remain hidden in the storage place of memory unless and until it is
recalled (or else deteriorates and fades away). But for a dualist, does
not this recalling or actively remembering amount to a recalling of the
remembered content (fact or method or whatever), from cold storage
into the warm flow of consciousness? Would it not have to be thus
inserted once again into the stream of consciousness? If not, how could
it be a process that was being scrutinized by introspection rather than
just a static flowchart of a process? If it were just a static flowchart,
then the retrospective model of introspection would have achieved only
a pyrrhic victory over Comte. Comte's objection to splitting consciousness is avoided only at the cost of squeezing consciousness out of the
object or target content of introspection, such that processes or anything
else of a dynamic streaming nature could not as such be the object of
introspection. One cannot introspect the stream of consciousness but
only a static flowchart of that stream.

James might not have worried too much over this objection to retrospection. He might simply have replied, if such an objection had
been put to him, that one cannot introspect mental processes as processes
but only as transformed into static representations of them. The nearest
we can get to rebuilding the procession aspect of the process is to
follow consecutively, in introspective scrutiny, the original chronological
order of the steps in the process. Of course, even to refer to steps in

a process is to admit that the object of scrutiny has been distorted out of its original form.

There are further difficulties with this model. If the static flowchart retrieved from memory storage is not conscious in any way, how can it even be the object of introspection? Introspection is alleged to be a conscious process having as its proper object mental phenomena, according to James, so how can mental phenomena exist as the object of wholly inner conscious attention unless they are themselves conscious? How could an inner conscious process inspect a nonconscious inner item?

James presumably would and could reply that a nonconscious mental phenomenon is, admittedly, an odd sort of phenomenon—perhaps it is better termed a mental item—it is nonetheless not to be equated with a nonmental item. It is invalid, James might reply, to infer from the fact that the flowchart is nonconscious that it is nonmental, only ultra-Cartesian dualists would want to equate the mental with the conscious. Better still, James could say that the mental was anything that can be the target content of a second-order mental process such as introspection, plus those second-order processes themselves. In introspection (that is, retrospection for James), only the process of introspection has the attribute of being conscious. Its target content—what is introspected—although it must be said to be enveloped within or processed by this conscious process, is not itself conscious. When separated from the act of introspection, it would not be a conscious process. Only mental acts or processes or events—live dynamic mentality—James might have said, are conscious. Their enveloped or processed targets are not.

Another difficulty with the Jamesian model of introspection as retrospection is that it begins to look as if in avoiding Comte's objection to any model of introspection that posits a splitting of consciousness, James has reduced retrospection to memory. What, if anything, can be the difference between consciously introspecting something held statically and nonconsciously in memory and simply remembering in a very attentive manner? What evidence would make one believe that the former is not reducible to the latter, in the sense that the ordinary explanation in terms of memory ought to take precedence over an extraordinary explanation in terms of a highly controversial process of introspection? The upshot of both processes seems indistinguishable: that one gains access to what is held in memory. After all, ordinary remembering provides just as flexible an access to what is in memory as does the putative process of introspecting the contents of memory. One can run backward and forward over events while engaged in remembering, and one can do so just as easily as one can pan (if one

ward and forward with the alleged apparatus of introspection,
mably this applies equally to gaining access to past mental
ɔ nonmental ones. I am inclined to suggest that the burden
ᵤₗ in this matter lies with the controversial theory. It is up to the
introspectionists of the retrospective persuasion to demonstrate the
difference between retrospection and memory. If the only difference
is in the existence of an alleged piece of apparatus for introspecting,
let them produce neurophysiological or other appropriate evidence for
its existence.

Admittedly it seems awkward and odd to speak of remembering
mental events as mental events rather than remembering what one
thought or believed or hoped for or remembering how one solved a
particular problem or formulated a plan. But there is no need to claim
this sort of access on behalf of memory, for it evidently seemed awkward
and unconvincing to William James himself to speak of introspecting
mental events as mental events. James asserted that "introspection is
no sure guide to truths *about* our mental states," only to truths concerning
what mental states are about, which is a very different matter, and to
think otherwise is to commit the "psychologist's fallacy."[40] This ad-
mission on the part of James sits uneasily with his initial claim in *The
Principles* that "psychology is the Science of Mental Life," for it seems
that he believed that scientific knowledge about our mental states would
be gained by discovering correlations between such states and brain
states.[41] If so, it becomes unclear how introspection can assist in this
task if it cannot tell us anything about mental states but only about
their contents. In this particular context there is the suggestion that
James himself may have undermined the whole introspectionist
program.

5 Death of Introspectionism in Psychology

Difficulties over the possibility of splitting consciousness, and with the
retrospection model of introspection that was designed to avoid these
difficulties, were not what led to the breakdown of introspection as
the basic methodology in psychology. The breakdown occurred, rather,
in connection with Comte's second objection to introspection: that even
if introspection is possible, the claimed data from introspection are so
conflicting as to be useless as data in psychology.

> The results of so strange a procedure [as that of the alleged operation
> of introspection] harmonize entirely with its principle. For all the
> two thousand years during which metaphysicians have thus cul-
> tivated psychology, they are not agreed about one intelligible and

established proposition. "*Internal observation*" gives almost as many divergent results as there are individuals who think they practise it.[42]

William James's immediate response was to try to disarm his critics by making it clear that, according to his account, the data of introspection are by nature reports and, like all other reports, fallible. It would be as foolish to claim infallibility for introspective reports as for ordinary observational ones. James went further. He agreed that not merely is introspection not infallible; we can all too easily fail to furnish reports or furnish only confused and confusing reports. For example,

> Who can compare with precision the *quantities* of disparate feelings even where the feelings are very much alike. For instance, where an object is felt now against the back and now against the cheek, which feeling is most extensive? Who can be sure that two given feelings are or are not exactly the same?[43]

Has James chosen the wrong example here?[44] The fairest test of the accuracy of introspection, according to James's model of it, would be in seeing whether different people with more or less the same neurophysiology or, better still, the same person on different occasions, gives the same reports about feelings resulting from the same stimulus. The divergence of reports about the quantity of feelings resulting from placing an object first on the subject's back and then on his or her cheek may only mirror the difference in the neurophysiological connections between brain and back, and brain and cheek.

James suggested that such difficulties in gaining reliable reports should not lead us to conclude that introspection (retrospection) is useless or that it could not be the main method for psychological research. The balanced view is that it is neither more nor less useless than ordinary perceptual inspection or observation, and neither more nor less reliable. So, says James,

> Our general conclusion [is] that *introspection is difficult and fallible; and that the difficulty is simply that of all observation of whatever kind*. . . . The only safeguard is in the *consensus* of our farther knowledge about the thing in question, later views correcting earlier ones, until at last the harmony of a consistent system is reached.[45]

In other words the safeguards against error in regard to introspection, suggested James, are much the same as the safeguards we employ against error in ordinary perception. If I think I see a ship at sea but wonder whether what I see might be in fact the result of some trick of the light or a haze over the sea, I check my observation by asking others to look and see whether they see what I claim to see. It is the same with introspection; one observation is checked against another. If, to supply James with the right sort of example, I introspect and report that the sensation resulting from your touching my back with a hairbrush is, say, of a series of small pricking sensations, then I check this by getting you to do the same when the same brush is pressed against your back. The two checking operations are much the same; both presume that the physiology of two healthy normal persons is much the same, such that the same stimulus applied to these similar physiological systems will produce the same results in the stream of consciousness, and the reports of these results, if carried out quickly and with due care, ought to be much the same as well (for such reports are also based on similar physiological mechanisms which make possible such reports).

In *The Analysis of Mind* Bertrand Russell emerges as an unequivocal supporter of William James on introspection.[46] He pointed out that feelings—a good example of the sort of thing that introspectionists introspect—are always of something going on inside our body and dependent on our body. If, to adapt his example, I have a cavity in my left incisor tooth, almost certainly I will experience pain. If I do, you can know how it feels only if you are me, which is impossible, or if you also have a cavity in your left incisor, which is quite possible. The underlying fact that makes my introspective report on my pain to be a report on how you also feel is that human physiology is roughly the same for all normal, healthy persons.

With such methods of checking, the more checks one makes, the better, and the results of such checking should be couched in terms of statistical averages. This, James pointed out, had already been going on in the laboratories of the experimental psychologists in Germany, the most famous example being the work of Wundt and his colleagues at Leipzig. But there is an important difference between Wundt's model of introspection as inner passive perception and James's model of introspection as active retrospection of what was preserved in memory. Wundt could justify to some extent his claim that the reliability of inner passive perception—since it was immediate and direct perception of the immediate and direct result of external perception—was much the same as that accorded to external perception. But James could not justify the same claim to the same extent given his model of introspection, for he interposed memory between the products of external perception and the process of internal observation. Memory is notoriously unreliable. We often imagine or invent when we believe we are remembering. Much perceptual information eludes the grasp of memory. As James himself pointed out, it seems unusually susceptible to the vagaries of age and health (though generally this would apply only to long-term memory).

Up to a point, one can offset the unreliability of memory by the arrangement of the laboratory conditions surrounding the attempt to introspect. One presents known stimuli to the subjects in the experiments. If their reports differ from what was presented or differ too widely, one rejects such subjects as unreliable introspectors. This ploy works well enough when the stimulus is simple, brief, and visual or auditory but not otherwise. If the stimulus is one designed to produce such mental phenomena as feelings, emotions, beliefs, imaginings, and volitions, then it is not easy to produce evidence that the subject's report is the unreliable product of mistaken memory rather than, say, an interestingly different approach from the expected or usual response.

There is another way in which both Wundt's and James's models of introspection differ importantly from ordinary external perception. Ordinary perception or observation is based on the organs of sight and the other senses, and these can be checked easily to see that they are in working order. This is not the case with introspection. There is as yet no agreement as to what are the equivalent organs of introspection, let alone agreement as to how they might be checked so as to see whether they are in working order. This objection would be obviated if someone did discover the or a mechanism for introspection such that, at least in experimental laboratory conditions, it or they could be checked to ensure that they are in working order.

E. B. Titchener was much more of an experimenter than William James; in fact James was bored by the experiments of his day, and although he set up one of the first psychological laboratories in the United States, he engaged someone else to run it. Titchener made considerable effort to make retrospection reliable and scientific while avoiding reducing it and psychology to the scrutiny of trivia. So although he allowed that thinking, volition, and emotion could and should be the proper object of introspective study, he devised a long list of rules as to how one should go about introspecting them. He built the scientific conditions into the attitude of the introspector rather than into the laboratory conditions themselves, as Wundt had done. These rules were elaborated by his disciples and in effect point to a further nagging doubt about how one can be sure—leaving aside the unreliable aspects of memory itself—that in the acts of inner perception or observation and the reporting on them, one is not going beyond pure observation and slipping into invention, imagination, or fancy. How, for example, can one be sure one is just engaging in inner observation and then description and not also evaluating, guessing, forecasting, elaborating, or projecting? A good example of these detailed rules for introspection, which emerged around this time in the effort to make introspection reliable and scientifically respectable, are the following:

Our first rule, therefore, is: *As far as possible, describe the constituent features of the experience in terms that resist further analysis. Describe in terms of part-processes which cannot be thought of as being themselves made up of smaller or simpler part-processes, or of part-processes found in other contexts.* [In short, make sure that you have penetrated to the basic elements or atoms of consciousness.] . . .

A second rule: *In addition to analytic description, experiences which are rapidly changing should be characterized or communicated by descriptive appellations, laying stress upon the sequences and order of the part-processes.* [It is also important to map the sequence or chains in which these atoms occur.] . . .

Rule 3 . . . *Include interpretation sparingly and always label it carefully as such.* . . ..

Rule 4: *Avoid the "stimulus error", make no attempt to estimate the stimulus; confine your report to your consciousness, to your experiences. Nothing else is introspection; it is merely physical observation under difficulties.* [Concentrate on internal conscious states and avoid all reference to what external event or internal physiological occurrence you think may have caused the conscious state.]

Rule 5: *Ordinarily describe experiences in their temporal order. But sacrifice this if necessary to catch some fleeting and elusive experience.* . . .

Rule 6: *The experience or part of an experience selected for observation should not be too long, only a few seconds at the most.* [Otherwise one will forget the details of the experience and so be unable to report on it.] . . .

Rule 7: *Avoid "putative recollection."* [Confine oneself strictly to what in fact you introspected and avoid any inference to what you think you must or should have introspected.][47]

It is interesting to note that there is no rule stating how quickly one ought to report or for how long the report should go on. In fact, it was not unknown for a report about an inner mental phenomenon, allegedly caused by a stimulus presented for only a few seconds, to go on for as long as twenty minutes.

When one tries to introspect scientifically something like a thought, belief, emotion, or feeling, a basic problem arises as to how one can isolate the target of introspection. One cannot get very far (as on the other hand one might, say, when introspecting a sensation) in isolating the target of introspection by coordinating it with the presentation of some external stimulus to a sense organ. In the case of thoughts, beliefs, or emotions, there seems to be too much going on to be able to do this with any confidence. The whole matter is too complex. George Humphrey brings forward a good example of the sort of experiment that used to be attempted.

Okabe confronted his observers with sentences expressed visually or orally, or with pairs of such sentences. The observers were requested to note whether the single sentences aroused belief or disbelief, and after this practice to report introspectively upon the belief- and disbelief-consciousness.[48]

When I have tried this experiment—on admittedly untrained and inexperienced subjects—the experiment did not really even begin. The subjects seemed at a loss to know when and whether they were focused on "belief- and disbelief-consciousness."

Introspection in its classical form (or forms) may be said to have reached its zenith and nadir at the same time in the school of Titchener in the United States. Introspection had become highly elaborated by this time and, to the growing number of outsiders, bizarre. It was so hedged in with rules and regulations and so distant from anything any ordinary person might label as introspection that it appeared like some curious rite to the uninitiated, but the increasingly complex liturgy did not bring compensating gains in faith. The most notorious, indeed scandalous, dispute among the different schools of experimental introspection arose at about this time. Titchener and his disciples at Cornell believed that their scientific introspections had demonstrated that nonsensory conscious thought was impossible. All conscious thinking, they believed, involved sensations, images, or feelings. The Würzburg school—whose best-known figures were probably Külpe, Ach, and Bühler—on the contrary, believed that their experiments showed the opposite to be the case: that there could be nonsensory conscious thought.[49]

In one way or another, scientific introspective psychology could be said to have brought itself into disrepute. While it had been accepted, more or less, that Comte's first objection—that introspection involved an impossible split in consciousness—had been obviated by the new model of introspection as retrospection, introspective psychology foundered on his second objection: that even if the concept made sense and the process was feasible, in fact introspection proved to be an unreliable source of psychological data. The way was open for the acceptance of behaviorism.

William James himself came to doubt the whole business of consciousness and introspection and voiced these doubts in a paper entitled

"Does 'consciousness' exist?" first published in 1904,[50] though he did not give up dualism.[51] He wrote that

> "consciousness" . . . is the name of a non-entity, and has no right to a place among first principles. Those who still cling to it are clinging to a mere echo, the faint rumor left behind by the disappearing "soul", upon the air of philosophy. . . . For twenty years past I have mistrusted "consciousness" as an entity; for seven or eight years past I have suggested its non-existence to my students, and tried to give them its pragmatic equivalent in realities of experience. It seems to me that the hour is ripe for it to be openly and universally discarded.[52]

He went on to suggest (in what I take to be vintage James tongue-in-cheek) that "breath moving outwards, between the glottis and the nostrils, is, I am persuaded, the essence out of which philosophers have constructed the entity known to them as consciousness."[53]

Chapter 2
Editing the Home Movie

1 Behaviorists' Dethronement of Introspection in Psychology

Although John Broadus Watson is the most famous and systematic of the early proponents of psychological behaviorism, he was not the first. Walter Pillsbury, for example, was one of the first psychologists to propose that psychology should be defined as the "science of human behavior" (though Pillsbury was hardly a behaviorist),[1] and Watson's dedication of his masterpiece, *Psychology from the Standpoint of a Behaviorist*,[2] to James McKeen Cattell and Adolf Meyer gives further clues to some of the origins of behaviorism. One might add to the list Max Meyer.[3] In his paper, "The Conceptions and Methods of Psychology," Cattell wrote, "It seems to me that most of the research work that has been done by me or in my laboratory is nearly as independent of introspection as work in physics or in zoology. . . . It is usually no more necessary for the subject in a psychology experiment to be a psychologist than it is for the vivisected frog to be a physiologist."[4] Behaviorism, or the ideas inherent in it, was in the air from about the turn of the century onward. It was in the air not merely because introspective psychology had become so bizarre but because psychologists were becoming interested in and successful at measuring and evaluating behavioral performance. A subject might be given some behavioral task to do such that, by carefully varying the conditions under which he or she was asked to perform, the limits on accurate performance or even on performance itself could be observed.[5] The science of behavior was launched.

In 1913, Watson stated quite firmly that "psychology as the behaviorist views it is a purely objective experimental branch of natural science. Its theoretical goal is the prediction and control of behavior. Introspection forms no essential part of its methods, nor is the scientific value of its data dependent upon the readiness with which they lend themselves to interpretation in terms of consciousness."[6] Initially Watson did not state that consciousness did not exist or that introspection was a myth, though probably he would not have minded if someone had made such claims; he merely claimed that they could play no part in a genuinely scientific psychology. From his point of view also, psychology had as much use for introspection as did physics and zoology.[7] But seven years after his manifesto of 1913, Watson was even more bracing in his dismissal of consciousness. He aired the view that explanations in terms of the mental (including those that made mention of consciousness) were spurious in the way that an alchemist's explanations are spurious when placed alongside those of the chemist:

> It is a serious misunderstanding of the behaviouristic position to say, as Mr. Thomson does—"And of course a behaviourist does not deny that mental states exist. He merely prefers to ignore them." He "ignores" them in the same sense that chemistry ignores alchemy, astronomy horoscopy, and psychology telepathy and psychic manifestations. The behaviourist does not concern himself with them because as the stream of his science broadens and deepens such older concepts are sucked under, never to reappear.[8]

Watson's position was that one ignored introspection and consciousness not because consciousness was not amenable to scientific investigation but because the concepts of consciousness and introspection were groundless and unscientific. Watson's friend of Chicago days, the pragmatist or social behaviorist G. H. Mead, suggested that Watson's attitude to consciousness and introspection "was that of the Queen in *Alice in Wonderland*—'Off with their heads!'—there were no such things."[9]

Watson's behaviorism was also influenced by the work on reflexes and on animal behavior in general of the Russians Pavlov and Bekhterev.[10] It was considerable success in the field of animal behavior, achieved by himself and others, that emboldened Watson to ask, "Why cannot we study his [a human's] behavior in the same way that we study the behavior of other animals, modifying our methods to suit this new genus?"[11] In studying animals one was forced to be a behaviorist and to make no use or mention of introspection, Watson pointed out. If such objective methods had been so successful in the study of nonhuman animals, why should we doubt that they will be equally successful in the study of humans? Watson believed that there were no theoretical difficulties or doubts in regard to the behaviorist method being applied to humans, though admittedly there were practical ones.

> One can scarcely blame the human subject for objecting to being kept for long stretches of time in a home box the door to which opens from time to time permitting him to pass to the right or left of a partition, and ultimately to reach one or other of two differently colored surfaces below which he finds a food trough. That which

makes the situation still more humiliating to him is the fact that if he has "backed" the wrong colour he receives a stone in the guise of an electric shock, in place of the bread which he seeks.[12]

In our own day B. F. Skinner, Watson's most famous disciple, might be said to have extended the use of the home box or problem cage to humans; he did place one of his own children into what might be called a modified Skinner box, but it seems that most likely this was not done for experimental purposes.[13] On the other hand, for a behaviorist, the obvious bridge between studying animals and studying humans was the study of the reactions of infant humans.

2 Early Behaviorist Attempts at Giving Some Account of the Nature of Introspection

The upshot of Watson's manifesto, after the initial backlash from the introspectionists, was that for a long time psychology by and large ignored introspection and consciousness altogether.[14] There were tentative suggestions or hints as to what a behaviorist might say if asked to give an account of what, if anything, might be going on when people claimed to introspect conscious states. In 1915, A. H. Jones wrote of a "relational interpretation of consciousness," wherein a conscious state is to be interpreted as "an *attribute* or *function*" of the "physical organism"—the human person—in relation to some external object that caused or stimulated that attribute or function.[15] This seems to mean that one should interpret the alleged Cartesian experience of seeing red resulting from seeing a tomato as undergoing a brain process, which in turn usually gives rise to specifiable behavior because of an external object, the tomato, causing changes in the sense organ system of the human organism. Jones went on to suggest that "the conception of introspection is similarly clarified" for it is "just a special form of ordinary knowing."[16] Although it is by no means clear exactly what his account of introspection is, it appears to be the special case whereby an attribute or function of the physical organism—again this presumably is to be interpreted as a brain state plus typical behavior—is caused by another first-level brain state plus typical behavior. Just as objects in the world give rise to brain states plus behavior, so a first-level brain state plus behavior can give rise to a second level of brain state plus behavior, such that the latter set will be what we normally refer to as introspection.

But such an account is at best a bare sketch, which raises many more questions than it answers. One brain process and its associated typical behavior, pattern A, giving rise to another brain process plus its associated typical behavior, pattern B, does not isolate the peculiar relationship of monitoring such as, it is claimed, goes on in introspection. A causing B is compatible with a noncognitive relationship between A and B. For example, it is compatible with A, an activation of some sense organ, giving rise to B, some change in the septo-hippocampal system of the brain, which in turn gives rise to emotional arousal and behavior. Nor will it do to add that the B set of brain processes plus behavior must be found in the introspective part of the brain, for this adds nothing in explanation. It does not tell us how a causal relationship becomes a cognitive intentional one.

Another way of seeing how sparse is Jones's account is to reflect that his account, as it stands, would also fit subliminal seeing giving rise to behavior, which causes a second set of brain processes plus behavior. For example, I might see subliminally—that is, without being aware that I do, for what I see is, say, inserted on frames in the film *Casablanca* at intervals that ensure that they do not register consciously— an advertisement in the form of a written message that says "Buy Tindall's Soap. It's medically safe and sure." This causes me to go out and buy several bars of Tindall's soap the next time I am in the supermarket. Moreover the subliminal perception plus behavior causes changes in my brain memory bank and probably in my language center as well, because when asked by a market researcher which soap is medically best, I reply that I know that Tindall's is medically safe and sure, but I could not vouch for other soaps.

E. C. Tolman in 1922 gave an even sparser treatment of introspection. He suggested that Watson's behaviorism—whereby psychological items, such as emotions, were to be defined in terms of patterns of physiological responses in relation to specifiable stimuli—was on the wrong track. He suggested that a new and better behaviorism would always seek definitions in terms of relations between external stimuli and patterns of (purposive) behavior (operant behavior as Skinner later termed it). Tolman claimed that "such a non-physiological behaviourism seems to be capable of covering not only behaviourism proper but introspectionism as well. For, if there are any such things as private mental 'feels' they are never revealed to us (even in introspection). All that is revealed are potentialities for behavior."[17] Tolman admits that he can only "throw out a suggestion or two" in explanation of this account of consciousness and introspection. In place of introspection and consciousness there are simply internal "behavior-acts," which are a substitute for grosser forms of behavior, though it is not clear how such internal "behavior-acts" or "potentialities for behavior" are revealed to us.

In general it is unclear what account of introspection emerges from Tolman's hints. There is the denial of the existence of internal mental events and a substitution for them of "potentialities of behavior" or internal "behavior-acts." There is the denial of any mental process of "looking" inward at mental events but presumably the substitution for it of another sort of "behavior-act." But what "behavior-act"? How exactly does a "behavior-act" differ from ordinary (and presumably gross?) behavior? What subtle "behavior-act" could perform the task of revealing other "behavior-acts" or "potentialities of behavior"? What exactly are "potentialities of behavior" in concrete discoverable form? Are the terms "behavior-acts" and "potentialities of behavior" strict synonyms? In short, it could be argued that Tolman's account raises more difficulties than those of a Cartesian sort, which it seeks to avoid. Others attempt to fill out Tolman's hints and give accounts of "covert," "reduced," and "unemitted" behavior and how we come to know of them. So rather than speculate further, we shall discuss these matters when we examine the views of Lashley, Ryle, and Skinner.

3 Lashley and the Classical Behaviorist Account of Introspection

Karl Lashley, in his celebrated two-part article in the *Psychological Review* of 1923, "The Behaviouristic Interpretation of Consciousness," in characteristic fashion tackled head-on the problems posed for behaviorism by consciousness. He suggested that we think of human consciousness in the same way as we might if asked to construct as best we could a "conscious machine." Let us grant that a machine is so constructed that it can perform all of the internal neuroglandular and muscular activities of humans, as well as engage in all the external motor activities. One need not add anything else such as some mysterious "psychic stuff," Lashley suggests, in order to make the machine conscious. Consciousness is just a certain subset of the machine's actions and reactions—those that involve its "dominant system," that is "the organized system which at the moment is most closely integrated with the speech and gestural mechanisms," and this account of consciousness can be labeled the "motor or laryngeal theory of consciousness."[18]

So Lashley—and Watson also, when confronting a similar problem of giving a behaviorist account of thinking to oneself (as distinct from thinking out loud or on paper)[19]—explained his behaviorist account of consciousness in terms of the activation of the mechanisms employed in speech, such that reading to oneself or engaging in mental arithmetic, paradigms of internal conscious events, are just the activation of those muscles, such as laryngeal ones, and other physiological mechanisms employed in speech. But in the case of internal conscious events, the activation of the speech mechanisms stops short of producing speech or gestural substitutes for it. It is truncated or "stopped-short" speech. This account turned out to be false, though for some time it was allegedly the practice in some U.S. military hospitals, on the basis of such theories, to prohibit patients with neck and throat wounds reading in bed. As Woodworth and Schlosberg report,

> Early records obtained from tambour or lever systems applied to the tongue gave rather baffling results, since slight speech movement occurred during some but not all silent speech and since the pattern of a whispered phrase was not duplicated by the pattern of the same phrase when merely "thought". But these recording systems were not sensitive or quick acting enough to catch the rapid succession of actual speech movements—and silent speech is still more rapid.[20]

Yet while "action currents led off from a muscle, amplified and recorded by means of a rapid galvanometer, are a much more sensitive indicator of slight motor activity" than those relying on purely mechanical effects, it proved difficult to separate electrical activity due to other causes (due, for example, to "currents leaking in from neighboring muscles" or to the normal state of "continued but variable tension" in the muscle under investigation) from that due to the activation of the muscles in internal subvocal speech.[21] Woodworth and Schlosberg concluded that "as to speech *movements*, the evidence for their always being present during thinking is not convincing."[22]

It might seem unnecessary for Lashley to give a behavioristic account of thinking to oneself, or in general consciousness, in terms of actual movements of the speech mechanisms. He could have suggested that consciousness was activity of an electrochemical sort in the speech area (Broca's area) of the left hemisphere of the brain. This would seem to be a much better candidate for a nonmental substitute for Cartesian conscious silent thought, though there would remain the difficulty of separating activity in this area of the brain, which is not normally associated with consciousness, from that which is—for example, the reticular formation in the region of the brain stem (though consciousness is associated in speculation with a variety of cortical and subcortical areas).

The desire to seek explanations in terms of movements in the speech mechanisms themselves was probably connected, as was Tolman's general dissatisfaction with Watson's formula for behaviorism, with the basic desire to give all behavioristic explanations in terms of literal behavior. In turn underlying this desire, most probably, was the still more fundamental desire current at this time to separate off psychology,

the "science of behavior," from physiology, including the neurophysiology of the brain. To give an explanation of something as central to
most people's conception of the psychological as consciousness in terms
of brain states or events, without mention even of truncated behavior,
would seem like handing over psychology to the physiologists.

Such was Lashley's account of consciousness. Allied to it was his
equally iconoclastic account of introspection. Introspection was in the
same relation to the behaviorist's account of such putative mental processes as astigmatism was to normal sight:

> I am exceedingly astigmatic. To my uncorrected vision the moon
> appears as seven dim and overlapping moons. . . . To the normal
> man it would be of interest only as an account of the effects of
> astigmatism. As soon as I obtain adequate correction, my former
> account becomes for me also only a pathology of the eye.
>
> The parallel holds for introspection and behaviourism. The sub-
> jective view is a partial and distorted analysis. Behaviourism pre-
> sents the possibility of a more nearly complete analysis of the
> same data. It presents, therefore, a more nearly adequate solution
> of the problem and relegates introspection (except as a method of
> verbal reaction) to a subordinate place as an example of the pa-
> thology of scientific method. The subjective and objective descrip-
> tions are not descriptions from two essentially different points of
> view, or descriptions of two different aspects, but simply descrip-
> tions of the same thing with different degrees of accuracy and
> detail.[23]

The introspectionist does not give an alternative or rival account of
internal events to that of the empirical behaviorist psychologist; he
gives a hazy, inaccurate account of what the scientist of behavior describes accurately. To introspect what one is saying in one's head or
to oneself is like examining language mechanisms through a distorting
microscope—and about as useful.

Curiously Lashley does not give a nonanalogical account of what
exactly is happening when one introspects. One can give an accurate
scientific account of astigmatism, but Lashley does not give an accurate
scientific account of the distortion called "introspection" or why it must
be held to be a distorting view of internal processes. For how does
introspection provide even a hazy macroscopic view of internal events?
To use one of Lashley's own analogies, how does introspection describe
the "form and pattern of clouds" but fail to give a "statement of the
laws of condensation, of the interplay of temperature, water vapor,
atmospheric dust, and air currents, elements which are not defined by
cloud form"?[24] Besides, to give the form and pattern of something is

to give accurate, though admittedly macroscopic, information and is hardly to be equated with astigmatism in regard to microscopic details of water droplets and dust. Lashley, in other words, is inexplicit and ambivalent about his behaviorist account of introspection. But his account did herald a slight softening in the attitude of behaviorists to the use of introspection in psychology. It could be used as a rough way of identifying problems in psychology, but the solution of them must be left to empirical investigation of the "complex physiological organisation of the human body":

> Behaviourism has a place for introspection, but it must be a vastly different form of introspection from that which now burdens the literature. Its avowed aim must be the discovery of cues to physiological problems and its final appeal for verification to the results of objective methods. Such introspection may make the preliminary survey, but it must be followed by the chain and transit of objective measurement.[25]

One result of this softening on the part of behaviorists toward introspection, even if it was still consigned only a peripheral role in psychology, was that the need to give some account of what introspection was and how it worked became a little more pressing.

4 Ryle's Philosophical Behaviorism and Introspection

The philosopher Gilbert Ryle has frequently been called a behaviorist even though he came to give behaviorist analyses of mental items for very different reasons than did the followers of Watson. Psychological behaviorists wished to found a science of behavior as an alternative to a psychology viewed as the science of the mental life because they felt that the latter had produced little of worth, since it had been based on a misconception about the nature and scientific value of introspection. Ryle arrived at his behaviorist analyses of mental concepts because of his views about the nature of philosophy. Along with so much other English-speaking philosophy at the time, Ryle saw philosophy as concerned mainly with language and believed that philosophical achievement lay in correcting conceptual mistakes perpetrated by philosophers when they mishandled ordinary language in the course of propounding and defending philosophical theories. The most common sort of conceptual error was the category mistake whereby one explained a concept in terms of one sort of category or logical type when in fact it should have been consigned to another. Indeed Ryle felt that philosophy of mind was bedeviled by one large category mistake, the Cartesian concept of mind, which he lampooned as the "ghost in the machine" because it conceived of the mind as a special nonphysical substance that inhabited the body and directed its operations. This concept also conceived of the mind as composed of special mental faculties—the will, intellect, imagination, and so on—with their proprietary operations and products. Ryle, on the other hand, contended that the correct category or logical type for most of such alleged mental items, operations, and products was behavioral dispositions of the person alleged to be inhabited by such items. Of course, Ryle and the psychological behaviorists often ended up giving similar accounts of many traditional mental concepts. If anything, Ryle was more behaviorist than the behaviorists. He did not shirk the problem of attempting to give a strict behaviorist analysis of most, if not all, mental concepts, and he was reluctant to give an account of a psychological concept in terms of anything inner, even in terms of such non-Cartesian inner events as brain processes or covert muscular activity. He preferred, where possible, to say that what philosophers and others explain as conscious items can always or nearly always be cashed out as dispositions to behave—that is, to engage in overt behavior.

In chapter 6 of his masterpiece, *The Concept of Mind*, Ryle turned his weapons on the very heart of the Cartesian dogma of the ghost in the machine: the belief that we have direct evidence for the existence of the ghost by means of self-consciousness and introspection. After attacking these notions in a way that is often reminiscent of Comte's objections to introspection—by pointing out that introspection leads to an unconvincing postulation of myriad splits in attention and that its alleged data are notoriously unreliable—Ryle puts forward his own account of introspection.[26] He gives his account the tag "retrospection," though his use of this term is very different from Mill's and James's use of it. They saw introspection as an internal mental process of directing one's attention back to items in the stream of consciousness, which had been frozen and so rendered static by being preserved in memory. By "retrospection" Ryle meant the inspection with our ordinary senses of our own overt behavior in passing or the recall for consideration from memory of our past behavior (again as previously inspected by our ordinary organs of perception). Thus Ryle argued:

> States of mind such as these more or less violent agitations [such as, for example, occur with panic and great amusement] can be examined only in retrospect. Yet nothing disastrous follows from this restriction. We are not shorter of information about panic or amusement than about other states of mind. If retrospection can give us the data we need for our knowledge of some states of mind, there is no reason why it should not do so for all. And this

is just what seems to be suggested by the popular phrase "to catch oneself doing so and so". We catch, as we pursue and overtake, what is already running away from us.[27]

Such a scrutiny of our own behavior will lead us to realize our own behavioral dispositions or tendencies. We might realize that we are lazy by suddenly realizing that we are always missing deadlines, being unable to finish what we have started, and putting off until tomorrow what we know should be done today. That is, we learn about our own personality in much the same way as we learn about that of others.

> I learn that a certain pupil of mine is lazy, ambitious and witty by following his work, noticing his excuses, listening to his conversation and comparing his performance with those of others. Nor does it make any important difference if I happen myself to be that pupil. I can indeed then listen to more of his conversations, as I am the addressee of his unspoken soliloquies; I notice more of his excuses, as I am never absent, when they are made.[28]

Regarding discovering a person's dispositions, the only advantages a person has in making discoveries about himself or herself as compared to making them about others is that the person is constantly in his or her own presence but not in that of others. This will be counterbalanced, however, by an understandable tendency on the part of someone to be biased in favor of himself or herself. I might believe that I am a particularly open and honest person when others may interpret my behavior as tactless and insensitive. We inspect the behavior of others intermittently and objectively; we retrospect our own constantly and less objectively. In both cases the process is the same: ordinary inspection of ordinary behavior giving rise to the discovery of patterns in that behavior, which in turn leads us to impute dispositions to the person behaving. There is no need to invent a special inner nonphysical arena to house the array of personality traits and dispositions that we impute to people nor is there any need to invent a special process called "introspection" by which one can inspect the inhabitants of that arena.

Ryle's suggestion that we have no need to invent a special Cartesian process of introspecting with the mind's eye is convincing enough for character traits and tendencies like laziness, wit, honesty, and vanity. It is less convincing when one tries to apply it to the alleged introspection of such purely inner and covert items as thought processes and the images of imagination. But Ryle has a gloss to his account to cover these troublesome cases. My knowledge of my own thoughts is gained in much the same way as my knowledge of your thoughts. The test of whether I followed your argument or thought is whether I am able to paraphrase or discuss it in a way that shows I understand it. The test of whether I followed my own reasoning lies in whether I could now paraphrase it for you. But our doubts are hardly stilled by this move, for it appears to conflate how knowledge of my own thoughts is gained with how it might be shown to be genuine.

Besides, hidden in this gloss lies an oblique reference to the old bogey of behaviorism: the need to refer to some internal process that can be recalled and run over again while avoiding postulating anything that smells like a Cartesian mental item or process.

> And exactly the same sorts of tests [as would satisfy me that you had understood an argument] would satisfy me that I had understood it perfectly; the sole differences would be that I should probably not have voiced aloud the expression of my deductions, illustrations, etc., but told them to myself more perfunctorily in silent soliloquy.[29]

Ryle's references to "silent soliloquy" and "talking to oneself" have to be explicated in non-Cartesian terms. Generally the favorite behaviorist tactic at this point has been to wheel on stage subvocal talk, which is explained as real inner behavior associated with vocalized talk—the activation of the muscles associated with talking (the laryngeal ones, for example)—but in a reduced or truncated way such that talking out loud or even muttering does not ensue. Although he made use of such locutions as "saying things to himself," "going through in his head phrases and sentences," "subvocal," "sotto voce," "rehearsing an imaginary conversation," and "preparing remarks in solitude," Ryle was never explicit about what exactly is going on inside *Le Penseur's* head—a reference to Rodin's statue—when he is thinking but keeping his thoughts to himself.[30]

No doubt Ryle realized that an anti-Cartesian was faced with a major problem once he granted that thinking in one's head was an occurrent happening and not something that could be analyzed away into dispositions to do future things of a certain type or pattern. The most likely and plausible possibilities open to the anti-Cartesian seem to be to reduce silent reflecting or introspection or anything kindred to some subtle internal muscular activity or to a brain process. To commit oneself to the former laid oneself open to being refuted by experimental evidence, as happened in the case of the claim that all cases of internal silent thought involved muscular activity associated with the organ of speech or, as in the case of the mute, some manual substitutes for it. To commit oneself to the latter involved one in giving up a cherished source of behaviorism: the desire to interpret most, if not all, alleged higher mental activities in terms of behavior. Besides, to give an account in terms of brain states or processes lands one with an unappetizing paradox. If thinking to oneself is just brain activity, how is it that we are aware of our thoughts but not of our brain activity? Or to put it another way, if thinking is just brain activity, then it follows that we are never aware of our own thoughts as thoughts and so cannot introspect and report on them as they are. Such an account begins to look not like a behaviorist account of introspection but a dismissal of it as illusory because it is part of the Cartesian myth, which can be completely discarded. To give an account of introspection in terms of brain processes and states is to make a convincing explanation of introspection very difficult.

Almost certainly, if forced to be explicit, Ryle would have given an account of thinking in terms of some sort of inner behavior that would enable him to maintain his claim that introspection, including the introspection of silent thinking, is just the retrospection of behavior. But in doing so he would have increased the gap between introspection of such inner activity and introspection in regard to personality traits and dispositions, for although the latter may be explained plausibly in terms of the inspection of ordinary behavior by our ordinary senses, the former could not. But it is pointless to speculate further because Ryle never did reveal his hand in regard to his account of *Le Penseur's* introspection of his own ruminations.

5 Skinner and the "Problem of Privacy"

Burrhus Frederick Skinner, arguably the most famous behaviorist after Watson, reluctantly admitted the need to give something approaching a careful and comprehensive explanation of consciousness and introspection. On the other hand, the title of his first book, *The Behavior of Organisms: An Experimental Analysis*, summarizes his main concerns in psychology.[31] His work was almost entirely experimental and was notable for the fact that he moved away from conditioning in terms of the control of reflexes to operant conditioning or the conditioning of operant nonreflex behavior. For example, in operant conditioning, the psychologist does not seek to stimulate an existing reflex, such as the salivatory one, by controlling the external conditions, as did Pavlov; he waits for the animal under observation to emit operant (in nonbehaviorist terminology, purposive) behavior and then exercises gradual control over its emission and so turns the behavior into a reflex (in the sense of habit) by manipulating the environmental conditions. Thus if a dog happened to jump up on a chair, you, the experimenter, might give it a reward of some food. Gradually the dog would jump on the chair in order to get the food (though such teleological description is anathema to the behaviorist) and in response to some signal associated with its availability. In general, all behavior is a bit like that on Skinner's view, for his view might be characterized as behavioral Darwinism. The behavior that any organism engages in is that which best fits in with its environment. If an animal does certain things rather than others, it is because the former are "rewarded" in the sense that the environment enhances the chances of survival of the organism that behaves in that manner or at least satisfies better its immediate biological needs. As Skinner remarked in a fairly recent review, "Purpose in the origin of responses is to be found where Darwin found it in the origin of species, not in prior design or plan but in the selective action of consequences."[32] It might be worth recalling that Skinner was first trained as a biologist, for his account of behaviorism is probably closer to the biologist's account of evolution than to previous versions of behaviorism, though he shared and endorsed the original impetus behind behaviorism: the dissatisfaction with introspective psychology and the desire to align psychology with the natural and experimental sciences.

Although in his later work he felt compelled to give some account of what might be going on when we claim to introspect, he generally eschewed theorizing (except, presumably, about behaviorism itself) and conceptual models.[33] He believed that psychology was the science of behavior, which in turn was the gaining of knowledge of the relationship of external causes, or independent variables, to behavioral effects, or dependent variables, in order the better to control the latter. The science of psychology, like all other science, was aimed at order and control. There was no need for theories of human nature or even motivation; much less was there need for concepts of alleged inner causes such as intentions, desires, or thoughts. Insofar as he gave accounts of anything inner, it was to give reductive accounts of them in behavioral terms and chiefly in answer to the demands of his critics, for ultimately he suggested that "to spend much time on exact redefinitions of consciousness, will, wishes, sublimation, and so on would be as unwise as for physicists to do the same for ether, phlogiston, or *vis viva*."[34] Yet one cannot avoid feeling that Skinner was fascinated or even worried by the challenge to say something about what nonbehaviorists refer to as consciousness and introspection. In his masterwork, *Science and Human Behavior*, Skinner goes so far as to suggest that the behaviorist account of so-called inner mental events "is perhaps one of its most important achievements."[35]

In *Science and Human Behavior* Skinner also insists that his science of behavior is to be expressed in terms of "functional analyses," which he explains in the following terms:

The external variables of which behavior is a function provide for what may be called a causal or functional analysis. We undertake to predict and control the behavior of the individual organism. This is our "dependent variable"—the effect of which we are to find the cause. Our "independent variables"—the causes of behavior—are the external conditions of which behavior is a function. Relations between the two—the "cause-and-effect relationships" in behavior—are the laws of a science. A synthesis of these laws expressed in quantitative terms yields a comprehensive picture of the organism as a behaving system.[36]

At the beginning of section 3 of this book, which includes his account of "private events in a natural science" and the "self," Skinner reminds us that "proving the validity of a functional relation . . . is the heart of experimental science." The stage is set for Skinner's functional analyses of consciousness and introspection.

Skinner first points out that because some behavior is inner, it should not be thought of as possessing any special structure or nature on that account. Being inner implies nothing more than limited accessibility, limited most often solely to the person behaving. But then he startles readers by suggesting that, whatever these inner behavioral events might be, they can be observed by the possessor of them. He writes, " 'I was on the point of going home' may be regarded as the equivalent of 'I observed events in myself which characteristically precede or accompany my going home.' What these events are, such an explanation does not say."[37] Further on he also describes a statement such as "I said to myself . . ." as a report.[38]

It seems clear that Skinner will have to give answers to the question about what these inner events are, which are of limited accessibility "but not, so far as we know, [distinguished] by any special structure or nature" from ordinary events in the world, and to the question of how we gain knowledge of these inner events.[39] Clearly his answer to the second question, and its plausibility, will depend very much on his answer to the first question.

Understandably Skinner is concerned as much with giving a careful and nonmentalistic account of the allegedly inner mental events that introspectionists claim to introspect as with giving a subsequent account of what introspecting such alleged events will turn out to be. In some cases Skinner's account of the allegedly inner mental events will be in terms of ordinary overt behavior, at other times in terms of covert and reduced forms of the former, and at yet other times in terms of some amalgam of (or alternation between) the two. Skinner suggests that, depending on the case in question, inner events are to be given one of these three possible kinds of explanations, and in any particular instance what an alleged case of introspection will turn out to be will depend on which sort of explanation is appropriate.

6 Skinner's Substitution of Inference for Some Alleged Cases of Introspection

Skinner's first sort of explanation of inner events, and the explanation of the alleged introspection of them, is rather elusive (though in regard to the latter explanation there are similarities to Ryle's account of introspection as retrospection). In the case of someone not actually going home but merely being on the point of going home, he suggests that what is occurring is what is captured by "describing a history of variables which would enable an independent observer to describe the behavior in the same way if a knowledge of the variables were available to him."[40] "Variables" here presumably means "independent variables" or environmental causes, and what Skinner probably means is that to say I am on the point of going home is really to refer elliptically to the sorts of things that usually prompt me to go home, such that if someone else knew my causal history on this matter as well as I, he or she could equally well conclude that I was on the point of going home. 'I'm on the point of going home' is logically of the same structure as 'I shall probably go abroad next summer.' It is a prediction about my behavior in the next hour or so based on knowledge of my own behavior in the past. With such an explanation, the inner event is not so much explained as explained away. There are no inner events of being on the point of doing something. An explanation in terms of any sort of inner behavior is not appropriate here. The only events that have occurred are certain external environmental ones that prompt me to forecast that I am about to go home.

Although such an explanation may well fit such a first-person statement as 'I shall probably go abroad next summer,' it fits less easily on the shoulders of 'I'm on the point of going home,' for it implies that we can infer the latter only from environmental clues, which in turn are clues only insofar as they are collated and then correlated with my past history in regard to going home. It is beginning to look farfetched as an explanation, for who would or could claim to have gathered and retained and correctly tabulated and correlated such information as to what sorts of environmental things prompt one (cause one) to go home such that one could predict from environmental conditions alone what one was going to do? Besides, it would seem to follow from this account that few of us, and then only rarely, would be able to make the claim 'I am on the point of going home,' and that since others may be better at the complicated process of gathering, retaining, tabulating, and correlating the relevant information and then making correct deductions from it, they may be consistently better at knowing when I am on the point of going home than I am.

Skinner might reply that we do not positively and consciously engage in such gathering and tabulating and so on; we do so without realizing it, and because we are more often in our own company than others are, we do it better. When we make such inferences, we think we have introspected an intention when in fact we have engaged merely in collating, correlating, and deduction.

This reply hardly allays our doubts about the feasibility of ever gathering the information in question and so our doubts about the plausibility of an explanation based on the feasibility, indeed facility, of such a process. At this point, we might also mention that there is an unacknowledged Skinnerian substitute for introspection—gaining access to and then reporting on these covert processes of collating, correlating, and inferring—and this looks like if not an inner observation of an inner occurrence then at least a set of inner processes of some sort, though none of these processes needs to be conscious. Skinner has not analyzed away the need to refer to inner processes or occurrences when giving an account of how we come to gain the information we report as 'I am on the point of going home.'

To put this another way, on Skinner's account, something must have taken place internally, at least in our brain, if we have calculated that all the signs are that we are about to go home, and somehow we must have gained internal access to the results of such calculations. Would it not be fair to suggest that a strict behaviorist would want to attempt a behaviorist account of at least our access to such inner processes? Certainly Skinner has committed himself to giving a behaviorist account of introspection, and, in the case in question, this seems to come down to an account of how we gain access to the results of our inner calculations. Yet this is precisely what is missing from Skinner's account at this point.

There also remains the oddity entailed by Skinner's account of treating our knowledge of our own external behavior exactly on a par with our knowledge of someone else's, for there remains the fact that we do have a control over our own behavior that we do not have over another's and—this is the crucial point—we do seem to have a privileged knowledge of the exercise of that control. We do seem to have the last word about our own going home, and we seem to be the adjudicators of which "word" is the last. In other words, we do seem to engage in (internally engage in) decision procedures such that, when a decision emerges, we know what it is immediately, *ambulando*, without any process of inference, at least on many occasions, and others cannot easily, if at all, know of the decision on such occasions.

7 Skinner's Revival of the Classical Behaviorist Account of Introspection

Skinner's second sort of explanation is reminiscent of Watson's and Lashley's accounts of subvocal thought, for allegedly inner mental events will often turn out to be, Skinner suggests, "covert" or "reduced" or "unemitted" forms of overt behavior; "the private event is incipient or inchoate behavior," which in turn is to be explained as the internal muscular movements, which usually precede overt behavior but now occur in a truncated and impotent form. Further, these covert and reduced internal behavioral movements generate the usual proprioceptive stimulation—that is, the feelings that usually accompany the position and movement of the body in ordinary unreduced behavior but are present here in truncated and reduced form. By means of these we become aware of these inner events and so come to refer to them in our talk. As did many other behaviorists before and since, Skinner felt that this explanation was particularly appropriate for such cases of inner events as thinking in one's head, talking silently to oneself, or reading to oneself. Watson was more explicit, suggesting that the inner bodily movements in question were those of the neck—in particular the throat—and tongue. Such an account proved to be false. Not all cases of thinking in one's head or talking to oneself or reading to oneself are accompanied by such inner movements, or substitutes for them, much less by proprioceptive stimulation from these movements.

Another difficulty with this second explanation of Skinner is that it seems highly unlikely that we could ever get much information by means of our awareness of the reduced proprioceptive stimulation from the reduced inner forms of behavior. If, as Skinner admits, proprioceptive stimulation is so unsubtle that one can be unaware of ordinary unreduced overt behavior—for example, "one may be 'unaware' of a facial expression because of the inadequacy of the accompanying self-stimulation"—what chance have we of picking up and correctly interpreting the stimulation from behavior of an inchoate, reduced, unemitted, and impotent form?[41]

There is another, connected difficulty: if at least on some occasions introspection is to be explained in terms of the reception of and reporting on proprioceptive stimulation, why is it that on such occasions we do not give introspective reports of our inner life in terms of proprioceptive feelings? Why is it that we report in terms of soliloquizing or thinking or wanting or hoping or the like? Must a behaviorist also postulate a special, internal, compulsory stop "translation center" where proprioceptive data from internal truncated behavior are translated into ordinary introspective talk in terms of thinking, wanting, and so on? Leaving aside the uneasy feeling a behaviorist ought to get when caught multiplying internal entities or processes, the behaviorist is caught having to explain how the translation can take place. The behaviorist has to explain how we learn to correlate this lot of proprioceptive data with thinking, that lot with intending, and that other lot with hoping.

A more basic, more theoretical difficulty for Skinner's second account of introspection is that it is nonbehaviorist. To explain a process, such as introspection, in terms of self-stimulation is not to explain the process in terms of either overt or covert behavior, the two sorts of explanation favored by Skinner in all other areas. Self-stimulation remains mysterious in terms of behaviorism; indeed it looks dangerously like a Cartesian infiltrator, for self-stimulation would be interpreted by many as a momentary or more than momentary feel (a twinge, tickle, pang, stab, or what have you). Feels of this sort look very like raw Cartesian awareness. Of course, Skinner would not want to say they are that, but he is understandably noncommittal about what exactly they are.

Finally how can an account of introspection in terms of receiving proprioceptive data from internal unemitted and reduced behavior be part of a Skinnerian functional analysis? A functional analysis should be a description of a dependent variable (the behavior) as a function of the independent variable (events in the environment). Here it looks as if the dependent variable (the reception and reporting in the light of proprioceptive stimulation) is a function of an admittedly private series of independent variables (the inner, unemitted, reduced behavior). The only way out seems to be for Skinner to suggest—implausibly, it would seem—that inner, unemitted, reduced behavior always occurs in circumstances that would otherwise prompt overt, emitted, unreduced behavior. Skinner must hold that the proprioceptive stimulation and the reporting on the basis of it are really a function of external events that would (normally?) prompt ordinary unreduced behavior similar in kind to the reduced, unemitted behavior in question. This is a variation of the common behaviorist claim that our inner life is a repression or deliberate hiding of our external behavior, a trick or artifice that we learn as we mature from child to adult.

How plausible is it to say that I only think to myself when I would otherwise think out loud in speech or on paper or in some other public manner, and only because I have learned to suppress the latter? One obvious difficulty in this position is in coping with the fact that children and deaf and dumb people, who have only lately acquired language, can tell us about their prelinguistic thoughts and musings; they can tell us about thoughts that could not have been revealed at the time because they possessed no means for making such revelations. In such cases it seems implausible to maintain that the inner musings took place in circumstances when thinking out loud or in some public way would be the norm. Another difficulty is with the numerous cases where the inner life seems to be disengaged from the circumstances. One is not thinking about the environment or in the light of what is happening, but one is ruminating on some personal problem or idly daydreaming or just wondering about oneself or running over past events. These thoughts seem not merely to be unprompted in any way by the environment, but they also seem to be the sort of thing one would not typically reveal publicly.

8 Skinner and "Observing Oneself as One Executes Some Identifying Response"

The third sort of explanation that can be produced by a behaviorist to explain talk of inner mental events is that which is appropriate to claims to see or hear things (and this has some similarities to the Rylean account of perception as an investigational success).[42] When, for example, a speaker says, 'I hear so and so,' he or she has not introspected an inner event such as a sound or a hearing but has observed his own discriminative behavior. If we say, 'Did you hear the oboe?' when a full orchestra is playing, we can be certain that the reply 'Yes' is correct only if the person can back up this reply by, say, humming the notes produced by the oboe player. We grant that someone has heard or seen something only if they can perform suitably convincing discriminative tasks. We grant ourselves the accolade of having seen or heard in the same way. If we can perform the requisite discriminative tasks, we grant to ourselves that we have seen the bird in the tree (it was a male kestrel) and heard a shout from the house (it said 'Dinner's ready'). Of course, we often think we have performed suitable and adequate discriminatory tasks when we have not and say we have seen or heard things we have failed to see or hear. As Skinner puts it,

> A verbal repertoire which describes the discriminative behavior of the individual appears, then, to be established on external evidence that a discriminative response is taking place, rather than that stimuli are present or received. When the individual comes to describe his *own* discriminative behavior, presumably he does so, at least initially, on comparable evidence. He observes himself as he executes some identifying response.[43]

In brief Skinner's thesis here is that when we say 'I heard so and so' or 'I saw so and so,' we do so not on the basis of an introspection of internal states or events such as internal sense data but on the basis—whether adequate or inadequate—of having performed discriminative tasks that demonstrate, or we believe demonstrate, that we have indeed received through our organs of hearing or sight information of the sort we are claiming.

Skinner may well be right to say that someone else will believe that I have seen something only if I can prove it or at least adduce evidence that I probably did, but this is a very different matter from giving an account of what forms the basis for my saying, 'I heard someone say "Dinner's ready." ' In such a case I am not trying to prove anything to myself or bolster a belief I have about the reliability of a particular employment of a particular sense organ. My statement is more in the nature of describing what I think I have registered through a sense organ, for I am as likely to make the statement before I have engaged in any discriminative activity, which might or might not corroborate the statement, as after it. Saying 'I heard so and so' may not be a postscript to a process of introspection, but I find it an implausible alternative to say that it is a verdict on some sort of examination test for the senses set and sat by oneself. A child, for example, very early talks about seeing and hearing things without having any notion of checking on it in terms of noting his or her own discriminative behavior, much less any idea of how such a check might be engineered. It is possible that the child engages in such checks without realizing that it had learned to do so, but this suggestion cries out for supporting evidence if it is not to appear as a last stand in a forever hidden ditch.

Most important, Skinner's account of perception, sensation, and imagination and our knowledge in respect of them may not avoid reference to internal events of a nonbehavioral kind, though I find his account unclear on this point. His account sometimes seems to be that one engages in discriminative behavior, which in turn, when noted, is used as a corroborating check on what one alleges on the basis of, presumably, direct acquaintance with some sort of internal product of the activation of the sense organs. At other times he writes as if the discriminative performances, at least in certain circumstances such as imagining one sees, were the sole internal products of the sense organs—that is, they are the seeing or hearing or supposed seeing or hearing and not the evidence supporting it.[44] Presumably these performances must be inner and reduced and so truncated versions of overt, discriminative behavior. But this latter account, if it is Skinner's account, seems implausible on a number of counts. It cannot account for the immediacy of our reports following on, for example, imagining. If inner, reduced discriminative performances were the product of the reactivation of our sense organs in imagination (which Skinner seems to say), and if inner, reduced discriminative behavior takes more or less as long to run through as would outer, unreduced discriminative behavior, in the way that inner subvocal speech matches outer vocalized speech in that respect, then we would take a good while very often to report on what we think we have seen, heard, or imagined. To discriminate for ourselves in regard to the claim to have heard the oboe player's part in the last orchestral piece (even if we have only imagined hearing it) may involve something like a repetition of the oboe player's performance or some other involved and lengthy discriminative performance.

Is there not something fundamentally odd about the whole notion of an inner, reduced form of outer, discriminative checks? The discriminative force seems to be lost in the inward translation. How can the check on whether our senses really are "locked on" to, say, a yellowhammer in a tree be carried out inwardly if the outward check would be to go and take another look, while at the same time looking up the relevant section in the *Birds of Britain* or to take a photograph and do the research later, or to ask an ornithologist to take a look as well? Does one take inner, reduced looks and inner, reduced photographs? Of course not, but what could inner, reduced checks amount to?

All things being taken into account, one gets a strong impression that, for Skinner, the basic and most appropriate behaviorist explanation of any internal, supposedly mental, event will always be in terms of "covert" and "reduced" behavior. Because "covert" in this context means "inner" and so is an attribute acknowledged equally by his own account and by rival accounts, all the weight of his account (and, it is probably fair to add, behaviorist accounts in general) falls on the evidence for and plausibility of the claim concerning the existence of "reduced" forms of external behavior. If such "reduced" forms of behavior cannot be discovered in the muscular systems appropriate to unreduced ordinary behavior, there remains only the hope that they can be identified with other (as yet undetected) systems associated with unreduced ordinary behavior. Skinner himself admits as much when his last word on the matter in his chapter on private events in natural science, in *Science and Human Behavior*, is as follows:

> The line between public and private is not fixed. The boundary shifts with every discovery of a technique for making private events public. Behavior which is of such small magnitude that it is not ordinarily observed may be amplified. Covert verbal behavior may be detected in slight movements of the speech apparatus. . . . The problem of privacy may, therefore, eventually be solved by technical

advances. But we are still faced with events which occur at the private level and which are important to the organism without instrumental amplification. How the organism reacts to these events will remain an important question, even though the events may some day be made accessible to everyone.[45]

Given that the most plausible claimant for being a successful example of showing that an alleged mental event is nothing but reduced behavior—the proposal that thinking in one's head or talking to oneself is just subvocal speech—proved illusory, Skinner can only rest on the hope that science will yet come to the rescue of the behaviorist's theoretical accounts of inner processes and events. One must conclude that, at present, in regard to internal mental processes and especially introspection, the science of behavior has not produced the hoped-for important achievement of translating Cartesian mentalist accounts into behavioral ones.

The way was open for philosophers and psychologists to suggest that although the behaviorists were correct in refusing to give an account of consciousness and introspection in terms of inner Cartesian phenomena, they failed to show how one could explain or explain away introspection in terms of either overt or covert behavior. The solution, they suggested, lay in explaining consciousness and introspection in terms of items that were inner or covert but neither Cartesian nor behaviorist. Thus it was behaviorism's failure to cope with the "problem of privacy" in general, and introspection in particular, that led to current centralist (brain-centered) psychologies and philosophies. In recent years, center stage (at least in theoretical matters) has been taken by latter-day cognitivist psychologies (computational cum artificial intelligence accounts of what goes on between enviromental input and nonreflex behavioral output in the human organism) and, in philosophy, by first eliminative or reductive materialism (the elimination or reduction of the mental to brain states and processes) and now functional materialism (the interpretation of the mental in terms of the abstract, functional, or "program" properties of the brain). It is to these developments that we must turn in our search for an adequate account of introspection.

PART II
The Mechanization of Introspection

Chapter 3
The Brain Scanner

---

1 The New Materialism

The behaviorists, or at least the majority of them who were psychologists, appeared rather halfhearted in their efforts to give an account of introspection. Their natural inclination seemed to be to want to dismiss consciousness and introspection, if not as myths, at least as items that were not amenable to investigation by a scientific psychology. Insofar as they attempted to give an account of what, if anything, might be going on when people claimed to introspect, they did so more from a desire to curb the carping and complaining of the outraged introspectionists than from any real interest in such alleged states and processes. When they felt that they could decently turn away from such unprofitable and improbable topics to the real business of behavioral science, they did so without regret. More by default on the part of the psychologists than anything that could be construed as usurpation on the part of the philosophers, the problem of giving a post-Cartesian account of introspection devolved for the most part on to the philosophers.[1] At about the time that psychologists were turning away from a consideration of consciousness and introspection, philosophers, chiefly under the influence of the philosophical behaviorists Wittgenstein and Ryle, were turning away from Cartesianism and, in general, dualist accounts of the mind-body problem. After the comparatively short reign of behaviorism in modern philosophy, the dominant or at least the most vociferous viewpoint in philosophy of mind and philosophical psychology became that of the neomaterialists.[2]

Materialism is at least as old as the pre-Socratic Greeks of the fifth century B.C., but it is only the advocates of comparatively recent forms who have felt the need to attempt a detailed theory of introspection.[3] Even Hobbes, who may be considered to be the major source of the revival of materialism in philosophy[4] after the long, more or less uninterrupted, dominance of dualism from the Christian era to Descartes, seemed unconcerned about making introspection the chief method of investigation in psychology and, in general, the social sciences,[5] and he seemed oblivious to any particular problems that such advocacy of introspection might generate for a materialist. Just as in Hobbes's day it was in part the rapid increase in knowledge of human physiology— exemplified by Harvey's dramatic explanation of the circulation of the blood in terms of pumps, pressure, valves, and conduits—that provoked materialist views in opposition to the religion-based dualism of the day, so it may have been the sudden increase toward the end of the nineteenth century in our knowledge of the physiology of the brain— exemplified by Broca's discovery in 1861 of the area of motor or expressive speech and Wernicke's in 1874 of the area for understanding speech—that in part generated contemporary materialism with its compelling interest in giving explanations in terms of brain states and processes of what up to then had generally been held by dualists to be sui generis mental faculties and operations. Another influence on the revival of materialism is clearly the new modes of explanation suggested by the programming and mechanisms of computers and the systems of artificial intelligence modeled in terms of them. What were previously described as occurrent mental events, and which had proved resistant to the behaviorists' analyses in terms of dispositions to exhibit certain patterns of behavior—states such as those of pain or operations such as those of doing mental arithmetic—could now be explained, it was hoped, in terms of occurrent brain processes, which were roughly equivalent to the sort of electrophysical operations by means of which a computer is made to solve problems, store or recall information, and describe or amend its own operations. About twenty years ago, for example, Hilary Putnam drew a fairly detailed analogy between the logical states of a "Turing machine" (the concept of a simple automatic computing machine described by A. M. Turing) in relation to the structural states of the same machine and the mental states of a human being in relation to the physical states (brain states) of the same person.[6] This latter relation, however, was described by Putnam in a quite different way from that employed by the philosophers I will be discussing here. They argued that inner mental states and activities were to be seen for what they are: brain states and activities, or at least states and activities of the central nervous system, to which, because of the unfortunate legacy of our Cartesian past, we still refer in mental language.

Arguably the first shot fired off by the modern philosophical materialists of the twentieth century was that fired by the logical positivist Rudolph Carnap: "Now it is proposed that psychology, which has hitherto been robed in majesty as the theory of spiritual events, be degraded to the status of a part of physics."[7] But regarding introspection and much else, Carnap's view was still broadly that of the behaviorists.[8] Regarding introspection in particular, Carnap's account is that we learn to apply psychological terms to ourselves—such as those we are prompted to apply to ourselves as the result of alleged introspections in exactly the same way as we learn to apply psychological terms to others—that is, on the basis of observation or ordinary inspection of a person's behavior. I pronounce, 'I now am excited,' not as a result of introspecting inner states but by observing, say, that my hands are trembling, hearing that my voice is quavering, and so on.[9]

Such an account is hardly plausible for cases of alleged introspection when no external behavior is going on. Here a behaviorist has to search for inner covert behavior that is somehow observed by the alleged introspector (but then, for some reason, possibly confusion and ignorance, expressed as mental observation of conscious states). But the question remained, What and where exactly is this inner behavior? Given the discrediting of the usual response of the classical behaviorists in terms of inner "reduced" muscular activity, the need for a better answer was becoming urgent. What was becoming clear was that

> the fate of the doctrine [of central state physicalism] seems to hang on its ability to deal adequately with the peculiarities of introspective knowledge and to clarify the identification of mental with neural states and on the continuing success of physiologists in their efforts to discover neural changes corresponding to every change in consciousness.[10]

Thus giving an account of introspection in concepts compatible with the physical sciences became the central task for any self-respecting physicalist (the name by which the neomaterialists generally liked to be known). In one of the classics of modern physicalism, Ullin Place's "Is Consciousness a Brain Process?" we meet this urgency to advance and confidence in the ability to advance beyond behaviorist accounts if one is to produce acceptable nondualist accounts of mental items:

> In the case of cognitive concepts like "knowing", "believing", "understanding", "remembering", and volitional concepts like "wanting" and "intending", there can be little doubt, I think, that an analysis in terms of dispositions to behave is fundamentally sound. [Here Place refers the reader to Wittgenstein's *Philosophical Investigations* and Ryle's *The Concept of Mind*.] On the other hand, there would seem to be an intractable residue of concepts clustering around the notions of consciousness, experience, sensation, and mental imagery, where some sort of inner process story is unavoidable. It is possible, of course, that a satisfactory behaviouristic account of this conceptual residuum will ultimately be found. For our present purposes, however, I shall assume that this cannot be

done and that statements about pains and twinges, about how things look, sound, and feel, about things dreamed of or pictures in the mind's eye, are statements referring to events and processes which are in some sense private or internal to the individual of whom they are predicated. . . . I shall argue that an acceptance of inner processes does not entail dualism and that the thesis that consciousness is a process in the brain cannot be dismissed on logical grounds.[11]

Place's account of introspection is very brief and somewhat ambiguous, and a great deal of it is taken up with the negative task of demolishing what he calls the "phenomenological fallacy," which he explains as the error of believing that "when the subject describes his experience, when he describes how things look, sound, smell, taste, or feel to him, he is describing the literal properties of objects and events on a peculiar sort of internal cinema or television screen, usually referred to in the modern psychological literature as the 'phenomenal field.' "[12] To put this another way, when a human experiences something as green, it is a mistake for him then to suppose that there must have occurred inside himself a phenomenal patch of green and an event called "seeing," phenomenally, that patch of green. Building on this negative demolition work, Place suggests that if we can dismiss as pure invention all reference to phenomenal operations, objects, events, and fields, then introspection can be given a plausible physicalist account.

Introspection is that process in the brain of a human organism whereby a person is able to describe his or her experience of an external object or event. We are tempted into the phenomenal fallacy on those occasions, in particular, when the subject's experience of events in the world is at variance with those events, and he or she knows it. At such times the subject uses words such as "it appears," "seems," "looks," "feels," which easily seduce the person into talking of awareness and so in turn into phenomenalism. What the subject should say in such cases, if he or she wishes to make clear what is happening, is that such and such an object in the world is experienced as if in fact it were a so and so object. For example, a stationary light might cause the sort of experience normally caused by a moving light source. On such occasions we might say, 'The light seems to be moving'; more accurately we should say, 'My experience was like the experience I would have if my eyes were directed at a moving light source.'

This account of introspection became the account of introspection for a physicalist—at least for a good while—for, although it was elaborated, clarified, made more explicit, and in general discussed at length over many years, it remained in all its essentials unchanged. J. J. C.

Smart in particular made it clear that on this account of introspection, introspective claims are reports.[13] They are reports of brain processes because, though we do not have direct knowledge of the neuro-physiological details, we could report similarities or dissimilarities between experiences (which are brain processes) in terms of what external event typically causes such an experience. Thus we can know and so say things that are literally true of our brain processes, even now. For various reasons, some good and some bad, we do not report on our experiences in this metaphysically neutral or topic-neutral causal way but in the Cartesian language of our culture, that is, in the language of sensations, after-images, feels, and so on. No claim is being made on behalf of such a physicalist account that sensation statements mean the same as, or can be translated into, statements about brain processes or even that the logic of sensation statements is the same as that of brain process statements, for, among other things, the latter are specialized, technical descriptions and the former are not. All that is claimed is that the referents of sensation terms will turn out to be brain processes, and so, as a contingent matter of fact, sensation terms will be discovered to have the same reference as technical brain process terms, just as the terms "morning star" and "evening star" were found to refer to one and the same star. In the former case, however, one set of terms, the brain process ones, is scientifically more accurate and useful than the other, the sensation terms. So, Smart argues, all objections that amount to saying such things as 'Sensations cannot be brain processes because a sensation might be red but a brain process cannot be' or 'We know about our own sensations but not about our brain processes, so they cannot be one and the same,' or ' "I have a red after-image" does not mean the same as "I have such and such a brain process," therefore an after-image cannot be a brain process,' miss the point.[14]

2 Armstrong's Causal Theory of Mind

David Armstrong's view of the mental is characterized by a caution that makes his account subtly different from that of the foregoing materialists, and in some respects his view is more akin to that of the functionalists.[15] As he is at pains to point out, his theory is a causal theory of mind and not a materialist theory as such, though he admits that additional considerations, based in particular on the recent conspicuous success of the natural sciences and their physicochemical view of the human, incline him toward—or to bet on if he were asked to wager—a materialist theory of the human. His account is a causal account because it describes mental processes—where "process" is a convenient umbrella term for state, event, or process—as factors that cause humans or higher animals (usually in conjunction with other factors such as environmental ones) to behave in a certain way. What these factors are, including whether they are physical, is an open question, to be solved in the future by science (probably the neurosciences). To decide now that mental (in the sense of nonphysical) states do not exist—to adopt, for example, some version of a disappearance theory of mind—is to give a premature answer. Besides, it is important to note that even if we do find out that mental processes are, say, nothing but brain processes of a certain sort (say, those intimately related in some way to behavior), nonetheless we may wish to separate off these particular physical processes from other physical processes by reserving the title "mental" for them. After all, a concept may change without the change necessitating a change of label. There may be all sorts of reasons, including those of linguistic consistency and convenience, for keeping the label "mental" in our vocabulary of words for describing humans.

On the other hand, Armstrong agrees that he has been drawn to his cautious adoption of materialism for much the same reasons as other philosophers have been drawn to it: the partial success but ultimate failure of behaviorism and the recognition of the startling amount of solid knowledge that has been accumulated in recent decades by science, including the natural sciences, that deal with humans. Behaviorism was right, he believes, to move away from Cartesian accounts of the mind as a ghost in the machine and to proffer an account of the mental in terms of behavior. Their failure was in not realizing that while some mental concepts might be elucidated in terms of behavioral output seen in the light of environmental input, others were best elucidated by means of a different sort of connection with behavior. It was behaviorism's failure to cope with the so-called problem of privacy that was most influential in subsequent theorizing about the mind, for it is now notorious that behaviorism cannot give an analysis of covert acts of, say, thinking or imagining except in terms of the discredited postulation of internal miniature behavior.

What a successful anti-Cartesian theory of the mental needs, Armstrong has consistently pointed out, is a fuller account of dispositions, one that makes clear that when we say this glass is brittle but that one is not, we are not merely saying that the former glass will shatter if struck even lightly with a hammer or let fall to the floor from even a moderate height, but we are also making reference at least implicitly to some nonhypothetical but real categorical structural feature in the glass (probably in this case a feature of its crystalline structure), which causally interacts with floor or hammer. With this explanation of dispositions, one could predict behavior or reactions, and so make dispositional attributions, even though no behavior has yet taken place and no reaction has been exhibited, for one could discover within someone or something a factor whose behavior-or-reaction-causing powers are known or discern the absence of a factor whose causal powers are known. Thus a doctor might predict that this baby is a hemophiliac because of the absence of a clotting agent in the baby's blood. Quite simply this fuller account of dispositions is a better account than previous accounts because it has more predictive power.

Armstrong suggests that mental processes are nothing but the internal causal factors that lead to the sort of behavior, verbal or otherwise, on the basis of which we normally make mental attributions to humans and higher animals. "A mental state is a state of the person apt for producing certain ranges of behavior."[16] If we are further inclined to suggest, as Armstrong is, that these internal factors are brain processes, then this can only be for additional reasons such as the impressive amount of knowledge about the brain's role in human behavior accumulated by the brain sciences. The causal theory of mind is neutral as to what is the categorical or structural basis of any particular mental dispositional attribution to humans.

3 Armstrong's Account of Introspection in Terms of a Brain Scanner

David Armstrong's views on introspection, spelled out at length in A Materialist Theory of the Mind, are more obviously in the same tradition as those of Carnap and his successors (in particular of Place and Smart) than some of his other views, and may be said to give the most detailed and explicit physicalist account of introspection.[17] He explains introspection as a "self-scanning process in the brain," though we should not speak of an organ of introspection. This scanning process can be in error just as perception or our scanning of the environment can: "We can very easily conceive that, in a future where far more is known than at present about the workings of the brain, it would be possible to be quite sure that certain introspections were illusory. I might appear to myself to be angry, but know myself to be afraid."[18] Both introspection and perception should be viewed as scanning devices that causally produce beliefs; they differ mainly in terms of the environment they happen to scan. Just as our organs of perception scan the environment in order to enable us better to cope with it and act purposively in it, so the internal scanner or brain hookup that is introspection enables us to organize in a purposive way our internal calculations and deliberations and so, in turn, our present and future behavior. One part of the brain, whose activated process is what we think of as a first-level mental state, say what is commonly called a "sensation," can cause another part of the brain, the introspective scanner, to generate a belief about the presence of that sensation, where belief in turn is to be interpreted as a state of the person (or the person's brain) apt for the bringing about of certain bodily behavior.

Armstrong suggests that the most startling conclusion resulting from the adoption of a physicalist theory that gives an account of introspection as just the scanning of one part of the brain by another is that introspective knowledge cannot be indubitable (that is, it cannot be the case that if a person believes something as a result of introspecting, then his or her belief must logically be true), nor can our states of mind be self-intimating (that is, it cannot be the case that, if there is a mental state or occurrence, then the person having it must ipso facto know about it), nor can anyone claim to have absolute privileged access to his or her own mental states (that is, it cannot be the case that, in principle, only the person "housing" the mental states has access to them). A physicalist theory of introspection makes room for error and for others besides the person with the mental states to gain knowledge of those mental states. Thus these others may also be in a position to correct beliefs about those states held by the possessor of those mental states. Armstrong is suggesting that introspection, being nothing but the employment of a scanning device in the brain, leaves room for the possibility that the device, the scanner, can go wrong and so miss out, misrepresent, or not work at all. Thus reports based on a defective scanner would most likely be false. Since what is introspected or scanned is a brain state or process that in principle is available for scrutiny by a neurophysiologist, then a report on such states or processes resulting from such scrutiny could be more reliable than an introspective report.[19]

Armstrong suggests that the doctrine of incorrigibility which might be used as the generic title for the congeries comprising the doctrines of indubitability, self-intimation, and privileged access, has resulted from philosophers' having a one-sided diet of cases:

> Philosophers have brooded upon statements like "I am in pain now" and have wondered how we could possibly be wrong about them. They have failed to brood upon statements like "I have a head now" which are really more difficult to deny than statements about our current mental state. But in each case there is the bare logical possibility of error.[20]

I do not find the claim that introspective reports are not incorrigible in the least startling. Rather I find startling the claim that they are incorrigible. After all, some philosophers have claimed that one of the alleged products of introspection was the knowledge that we have mental states in the Cartesian sense, that we perform volitions or acts of will, engage in acts of intellect, receive sense data, and produce the images of imagination. Yet all these claims have been questioned at one time or another by other philosophers or by psychologists. As we have seen in psychology, the reports from introspection, even though conducted in the most painstaking way and under the most stringent laboratory conditions, proved notoriously unreliable and unhelpful when used as the evidence for asserting the existence of anything. Introspection seemed to have much less reliability than ordinary perception in that respect. We are much less certain about the alleged existence of sense data and other mental items and their operations than we are about most sensible objects in the world. As Donald Broadbent suggested, the reason why psychologists gave up introspection as a method in psychology was that "they became impatient with the elaborate analysis of experience which had led to such doubtful conclusions."[21] If to cast doubt on a report or to reject it as unreliable on the basis of sound evidence is to correct the claim made by such a report, then psychologists have been correcting introspective claims for a long time.

4 *Some Problems for the Brain Scanner Model of Introspection*

My failure to be startled by the physicalists' doctrine about incorrigibility leads me to one of my main criticisms of their doctrine, at least when spelled out in the way that Armstrong has spelled it out. If this picture of introspection were an accurate blueprint of what goes on, then it is hard to see how introspection failed as the method in psychology. On their account introspection should be startlingly reliable and useful as an instrument for telling us of the existence of mental (brain) entities, operations, and events.[22] This point might be made clearer if we consider for a moment another sort of scanner, a radar scanner. Radar scanners, if regularly checked to see that they are in working order and regularly serviced, rarely break down, such that if the cathode ray tube indicator—or in general the receiver attached to the scanner—is also in working order and so correctly registering any interference to the pulsed beam of electromagnetic waves broadcast by the radar transmitter, then its display of received signals must be a true report in the language of blips of what is detected by such radio detection. Human operators may misinterpret it when they get around to giving a verbal report, but that is another matter. Armstrong frequently describes the physicalist position on introspection in terms of just such a scanning device in the brain and so, given that it does work in some such reasonably and relevantly similar way, it is hard to see how, on the physicalist account, introspective reports could be so unreliable if introspectors were given a neurological bill of health before they went to work in Wundt's or Titchener's laboratories—particularly so when one also bears in mind that the equivalent in the case of introspection to the radar interpreter in the case of radar would be another part of the brain neurologically hooked up to report linguistically on information received by the introspective scanner and so would fall under the general neurological bill of health already posted. To put all this in another way, if this physicalist account of introspection were true, the behaviorists and other nonintrospectionist psychologists would be ruled out of a job before they had even applied. They would be literally redundant.

I am not saying that introspective reports are unreliable in all respects, only that they are unreliable as a method of finding out about the number, variety, and nature of mental (or brain) entities, operations, and events. At one level, a person's introspective account clearly furnishes us with something that only that person can give, and maybe it does so reliably in some sense of that term.

Physicalists may object that introspective reports are unreliable only because of the inadequacies of contemporary neuroscience. When neuroscience advances, the physicalist account of introspection will be seen to be sound. Just as radar scanners need to be calibrated in order to be usable, so would our internal linguistic reporting device need to be calibrated, using the introspective scanner, with the brain states or processes being scanned and reported. So that a radar receiver can interpret incoming signals, the designer must have worked out correlations between what is seen in terms of the language of blips on the cathode ray tube and independently describable objects (such as echo beacons at known points or with known trajectory in a given airspace). Similarly with an internal introspective scanner-cum-receiver-plus-linguistic-reporter, in order to be able to interpret incoming signals, we will have to work out correlations between what is reported in mental language by means of the speech center(s) in our brains and the scanned brain states or processes independently describable by neuroscience.

There are two worries about this reply. The first is that it would follow that, at present and during all the other centuries in which people have been making introspective reports, we must be said to be in possession of an uncalibrated and thus useless introspective scanner-plus-reporter. Evolution has left us with a promissory note about possible future fitness, not with something that can function usefully now. Worse, we have been misled into thinking that we are being provided with useful information when we are not. We are piling up useless, uninterpretable output from our internal system for gaining information about our internal deliberations, decisions, and plans. Nature has not merely failed to deliver the goods; it has misled us with counterfeit goods.

The second worry arises whenever a philosophical defense is couched in terms of "future advances in science." Future science can go either way: it may show that what we consider to be data from an inner scanning are no such things or reveal that there are no hoped-for correlations at all.

5 Scanners, Scramblers, and Shredders

A more fundamental difficulty for physicalist accounts of introspection is that there is a basic implausibility in saying that when people give what appear to be immediate and noninferential introspective reports of phenomenal experiences, they are really reporting on something else—a brain process or state, for, according to the physicalist position being discussed here, phenomenal moments of feeling, seeing, smelling, or tasting probably do not exist as such. Described in phenomenal terms, they are Cartesian ghosts whose fictional existence obscures our recognition that what exists (really exists) is merely the brain and its processes and operations.

Behaviorists and materialists of a behaviorist inclination tend to try to avoid the implausibility of such a claim by rejecting the suggestion that what appears to be immediate and noninferential—that is, not the product of a process of inferring the existence of states of the brain from something else such as external behavior—is in fact so. They claim that, all appearances to the contrary, introspective reports are inferential reports, the result of inferences on the basis of behavior (reports about internal states in the light of input and output), albeit immediate reports made without deliberation. The implausibility of introspection being analyzed as noninferential reports of brain states is avoided. But we saw that, in part, modern physicalism grew up as a result of dissatisfaction with just this sort of reply in regard to introspecting one's present thinking or imagining. Often such happenings are disengaged from the environment and unaccompanied by behavior, purposive or otherwise, or by any significant and related physiological changes that show externally and so are unaccompanied by anything that could serve as the basis for an inference.

Most physicalists will hold fast to the view that introspective reports are immediate and noninferential. They try to defuse the current of intuitive implausibility running through such a response by suggesting that it does not follow from the fact that one is introspecting brain states that one *knows* that one is so doing. They suggest that the true picture is that we are wired up to report the information gained by our brain scanner, which is monitoring our first-level brain states (information about our thinkings, imaginings, and so on), but we do not know, except we make reference to a hypothesis such as physicalism, that what we are reporting is information about certain aspects of first-level brain states. We report in language that is literally misleading (or is likely to be if not handled by the "expert"), in that it leads us to posit mental entities in a guise in which they do not exist and is opaque to the true facts. We report in Cartesian phenomenal language and, unknown to us in any direct way, what we are reporting on are in fact certain aspects of our brain processes and states.

One philosopher who has defended this move in some detail and in uncompromising fashion is Richard Rorty:[23]

> And why should it not be the case that the circumstances in which we make non-inferential reports about brain processes are just those circumstances in which we make non-inferential reports about sensations? For this will in fact be the case if, when we were trained to say, e.g., "I'm in pain" we were in fact being trained to respond to the occurrence within ourselves of a stimulation of C-fibers. If this is the case, the situation will be perfectly parallel to the case of demons and hallucinations [parallel to the case whereby in reporting that he sees a demon, a witch-doctor is in fact accurately reporting the occurrence of an hallucination]. We *will*, indeed, have been making non-inferential reports about brain processes all our lives *sans le savoir*.[24]

This is an intriguing solution, but it throws up a host of new questions. For a start, why have humans adopted phenomenal talk if it is illusory? The physicalist would reply, presumably, that it was adopted under the influence of a false theory, the Cartesian one, and for the moment we are stuck with it. But one might object that there must be more than that, for if we were wired up so that we could directly monitor brain states, how is it that no one in any culture ever reports in a way that could be construed as direct reference to brain states? The physicalist might reply that it must be the case that we are not so wired up. If we do have a brain scanner that monitors or scans first-level brain processes and states, information from this scanner must be passed through a scrambler, which causes humans to receive reports in such a way that they cannot unscramble the information and, unless neurophysiology advances much further and faster than it has done so far, may never be able to do so. At present, in order to report, we have to invent a hypothesis about what is going on inside our head and invent one that will be useful in organizing our purposive behavior and in explaining ourselves to others or to ourselves. But the explanation cannot yet be in terms of brain states.

This is an extraordinary picture and returns us to the basic problem of calibration. It seems that nature must again be said to have gone badly wrong in scrambling such vital information as our direct access to information about our own current cognitions, computations, deliberations, decisions, motor sets, plans, and so on. Nature has not supplied the necessary calibration that will enable introspective reports to be interpreted. Of course, it might be the case that it is better to have access to such vital information only by means of a scrambler, though why this should be so remains a mystery. Scramblers are usually employed for the purposes of secrecy, but such a use is clearly without point in this case. Besides, if this were the case or part of the physicalist hypothesis, then why should the physicalist (or some physicalist) declare that the language of sensations and, in general, mentalist phenomenalist talk is misleading or illusory or part of a myth or a category mistake? Scrambled or encoded reports, given the accuracy of the scrambling and encoding, are as factual or otherwise as what they scramble or encode. President Reagan's scrambled telephone conversation is as sensible as his conversation ever is. Scrambling and encoding, like translating, do not or should not lose the accuracy of accurate reports in the process of scrambling and encoding.

If we cannot report directly in terms of brain states, how do we know that the substitute "encoded" talk, in terms of which we must couch our reports, has any truth-bearing relation to the brain setup? What are the grounds for claiming that, in reporting so-and-so sensation, I am really reporting accurately on at least some aspects of my brain states and processes? For example, are the brain states underlying sensations and thoughts, or which are those sensations and thoughts, really distinct sorts of brain states or processes, as is suggested by our scrambled Cartesian reports of them? When we speak of two distinct sensations, are there two distinct brain states or processes? Clearly we cannot answer such questions now and may never be able to. This being so, how is it that, on the physicalist account, it is now claimed that 'I have a pink after-image' is a report? Given the physicalist picture of introspection, it seems to be in the nature of a pious hope to describe avowals as 'I have a pink after-image' or 'I am in pain' as reports. It could be that the relation between our mentalist talk and brain states is either nonexistent or at least completely other than the former being a report, albeit scrambled or encoded in some sense or other, of the latter. Indeed it might be argued that the claim that the relation is one of reporting seems the least plausible.

It is even conceivable if the physicalist account is correct that nature has blundered in a more radical way by providing us with a scrambler for which there can be no key—that is, that it has provided us with a random scrambler that is more like a shredder. If so, the full picture of our physiology now includes a very anomalous item, one completely at odds with the rest of the items in the organism. Although it is arguable that a complete picture of our physiology should include items that if they ever had a function, now appear to be useless (such as the appendix and the pineal gland) and items whose function we have yet to discover, it must be said that so far there have been no grounds for the inclusion of any item (such as the random scrambler or shredder would be) that has only a disruptive function or function that acts directly counter to the rest of the system. I do not think that physicalists or anyone else would want to retreat into that corner.

I do not think that the physicalist can avoid the difficulties connected with his account of introspection in terms of a brain-scanner-plus-linguistic-reporter by suggesting that introspective reports will not give any clues to the neurophysiological nature of the brain because these reports are about different aspects of what a neurophysiologist will report on in neurophysiological language; to expect introspection to give information about our neurophysiology is like expecting our eyes to give us information about the nature of light waves. Armstrong said explicitly that he is not positing a special organ of introspection that would produce sui generis information (information couched in terms appropriate to a special sense modality). Quite clearly there is no evidence at all that there is any such special organ that gives information of a unique type or in a unique mode.

Leaving aside the lack of empirical evidence for a special organ of introspection or special mode of gaining information about brain states and proceses, to posit such an organ or mode could at most only push back the real difficulties to another stage. The physicalist must still explain how the introspective reports, couched in special modality terms, could be correlated or calibrated with what is going on at the scientifically accurate neurophysiological level in the brain and what use they might have in uncalibrated form. Thus all the problems to do with the scrambler simply recur at a different point or points.

6 Neurophysiology and Introspection as Brain Scanning

The most worrying difficulty for this sort of physicalist account is that not merely is there lack of empirical support for the details of this claim but what evidence is available seems to suggest a different picture. Admittedly it is hard for an outsider to get a clear picture of the state of the art of neurophysiology. The only thing that seems certain is that there is no clear picture at present; however, it seems reasonably clear that there is an increase in the number of those who would question the "localization" view of brain function. Data now available from the brain sciences, as the functionalists have pointed out, seem to suggest that it is naive to look for direct correspondence in terms of tissue difference or different location in the brain for either the number or type of items we report on in mental terminology.

As far as the brain sciences are concerned, the nearest to a consensus is that, although there is evidence for some sort of localization, there are not precise and different locations or even different sorts of brain tissue corresponding, say, to different thoughts or feels or even to different types of thoughts or feels. Thought is most probably the activation of a system in the brain—that is, an interconnected complex of different sorts of cells located in a number of different parts of the brain and activated by a variety of transmitter chemicals. To take a parallel case drawn from large-scale human physiology, the human organism can transport oxygen to the alveoli of the lungs and then absorb oxygen into the bloodstream by the activation of the respiratory system, but this system may use different physiological units and thus different body cells and different interconnections and different transmitters to do this task from one occasion to the next. If the diaphragm and intercostal muscles are damaged and inoperative, the muscles of the larynx are called into action, and the person swiftly gulps or swallows air to maintain the flow of oxygen to the lungs by a different route. What remains constant is the successful functioning of the system, at least while a significant proportion of it is working in a reasonably healthy manner. Now consider the case of something that is less reflex and so more demanding in regard to higher brain activity. Apraxia, the inability to manipulate objects in certain ways, was thought in classical nineteenth- and early twentieth-century neurology to be the result of a lesion to a very localized part of the brain, the inferior parietal region. But it has been discovered recently that apraxia is the breakdown of a complex system; the breakdown can result from a lesion in any one of a number of areas in the brain, for these areas are interconnected to form a complex whole. One can identify the kinesthetic aspect of the manipulation of objects—say, wielding a paintbrush—that is, the necessity to have a feel for one's own muscle tone if one is to move one's limbs properly. Then there is the visuo-spatial aspect, for to wield a paintbrush or anything else requires that one be able to place one's hand correctly in space in order to make an effective brush stroke. Then there is the kinetic organization for any ordinary manipulative movement. For this a subsystem in the brain sees that the parts of what seems to be a single human movement come together as a single seamless whole. Finally there is the goal-directed aspect of such manipulative movements, which requires another subsystem, just one of the parts of the complex system whose breakdown is termed "apraxia."[25]

The same is almost certainly true of the thoughts, feelings, sense perceptions, and other alleged objects of introspective scrutiny. Insofar as they can be said to be located in the brain, they will turn out to be not simple localized brain areas or excitations but highly complex systems encompassing various parts of the brain and other organs. As Aleksandr Luria observed in his book *The Working Brain*,

> Although this "systemic" structure is characteristic of relatively simple behavioural acts, it is immeasurably more characteristic of more complex forms of mental activity. Naturally all mental processes such as perception and memorizing, gnosis and praxis, speech and thinking, writing, reading and arithmetic, cannot be regarded as isolated or even indivisible "faculties", which can be presumed to be the direct "function" of limited cell groups or to be "localized" in particular areas of the brain.[26]

The upshot is that there is little or no basis in fact for any interpretation of introspection as a literal reporting, no matter in how roundabout a way, on discrete brain states or processes. Our mental terminology, as employed in ordinary introspective reporting, at most probably bears only a very indirect relationship to what happens at the level of brain systems. At least, it might be suggested, one could always claim that to report introspectively on, say, a thought about Pythagoras's theorem is to report, in a way that is indirect and as yet unknown, on the activation of some system. To think of Pythagoras's theorem must involve the brain, so why cannot we say that to report in terms of the phrase "thinking of Pythagoras's theorem" must be to report on the activation in a particular way of a certain system in the brain? Even this claim, however, is more modest than it might appear. It cannot be a report about which cells in the brain were active because the same report will be true even when quite different cells are active. The same is true about the interconnections among the cells and of the transmitters by means of which the interconnections are made electrochemically live. The same thought can be a function of different cells and different interconnections on different occasions. A brain system is fluid in regard to particular cells, particular interconnections, and particular transmitters and thus fluid in regard to particular places and pieces of the brain up to a point.[27]

What is left of the original suggestion that one could always claim that to report introspectively on, say, a thought about Pythagoras's theorem is to report on the activation in a particular way of a particular system? This much might appear to be saved: we can say confidently that an identifiable system, though built on water, has been activated in an identifiable way. The claim is something like the claim that I know Liverpool scored a goal but not who scored it or how it was scored.

Even this modest claim is more in the nature of a pious hope than a fact. It may well turn out that on one occasion to think about Pythagoras's theorem is to activate brain system S_{12}, but on another occasion to entertain what, at the level of our ordinary mental description, is the self-same thought is to activate a quite different system of the brain, say, S_{298}. The brain might well be capable of "entertaining" Pythagoras's theorem by means of a number of different systems. It is known that musical hearing and speech hearing, for example, involve quite different brain systems.[28] This being so, it would follow that if a person reported that she had been thinking of the concert she heard last night or, more precisely, of the last verse of the *lied* sung by Janet Baker, she would be reporting what at the brain level could be the activation or reactivation of either of these two systems or of neither. She could be pondering on the words as speech or as song or pondering on some other aspect of the total performance, or just recalling the musical qualities or speech qualities or some admixture of the two. Yet to all these possibilities we might give the ordinary mental language tag of 'thinking.'

It should be noted also that to talk of various brain systems being activated is likely to be misleading. The brain is always active to some degree. Even sleep appears to be a system that, paradoxically, is active and, even more paradoxically, is active even when we are not asleep, though the way it is active in the latter case is different from the way it is active in the former. One can induce sleep by electrical stimulation of various parts of the brain, and drowsiness, inattention, and sleep itself have long been associated with a variety of electrical rhythms in the brain, including the sigma rhythm bursts and high-voltage "active sleep" waves.[29] What occurs, then, are different levels of activation in different systems. Mental activity of a given type probably occurs when an appropriate system—from a set of possible systems—or complex of systems coordinated at some higher level reaches an optimal level of excitation or activation.[30] It is by no means clear that to say I was thinking of Pythagoras's theorem is, at the brain level, even as informative as saying that I know Liverpool scored a goal but not who scored it or how it was scored. The most we might be able to say is that I know Liverpool did something or other from a range of possibilities, all of which are generally referred to as "scoring a goal," because we have not the capacity at present, and may never have it, to distinguish the range of possibilities and then to isolate the particular system that was operative.

In the light of all this, there seems to be little comfort in any thesis that claims that our introspective utterances, couched in mental terminology, are in any literal and direct sense to be considered as reports of brain states or processes. It has been claimed that, in regard to materialist accounts of introspection, "the most promising materialist suggestion is that the intrinsic qualities of sensations are in reality purely schematic and enable us only to distinguish one sensation from another. The sameness or difference of inner states but not their nature is given introspectively."[31] I have suggested reasons for believing that introspection does not even provide information about the sameness or difference of inner states, that is, about what type of brain function is going on by reference to the type of mental act one believes one is introspecting, though one may wish to hope that we will discover a key by which we can read off types of brain function by reference to types of introspected mental item.

7 Shift toward a New Way of Looking at Introspection

Donald Davidson expressed a related dissatisfaction with this sort of physicalism when he put forward an account of the mental and the physical as "anomalous monism, monism because it holds that psychological events are physical events; anomalous, because it insists that events do not fall under strict laws when described in psychological terms."[32] He was moved to take this position not because of being struck by the lack of fit between the structure and function of the brain according to existing knowledge and our ordinary description of our mind and its acts but because of his belief that in general our talk of such things as beliefs, motives, and intentions is really a deliberately simplified and clarified model constructed out of our general knowledge of human behavior, our own and others, and subjected to artificial "conditions of coherence, rationality, and consistency. These conditions have no echo in physical theory, which is why we can look for no more than rough correlations between psychological and physical phenomena."[33] To transpose this to the context of introspection, Davidson's view would seem to imply that we should not expect anything but a rough probabilistic fit between the type and number of entities and events as revealed by introspection and the type and number of entities and events as revealed by the brain sciences. We could not expect anything more because one set of pieces that we try to make fit is invented, or partly so, by ourselves as we try to make sense of our own and others' behavior and so not strictly discovered, while the other set of pieces is laid bare piece by piece—or so it is hoped—by observation, instrumentation, and experiment. Indeed this sort of thinking led to a new phase in thinking about the mind in relation to the brain and to a new model of introspection; the phase has become known as functionalism.[34]

Chapter 4
The Computer Printout

1 Putnam and the Computer Analogy

Recent essays on functionalist accounts of the mental, at least on the part of philosophers, have often been a result of dissatisfaction with the reductionist accounts of the mental championed by such physicalists as Place and Smart. In particular this new account gained momentum from the growing belief that our map of the mental, at least in regard to the higher cognitive functions, does not seem at the same time to be a map of the brain and its processes. The more we find out about the working brain, the less we are able to cling to the belief that our talk about beliefs, evaluations, intentions, desires, and motives gives us information about the structures or processes of our brains. The relation between the mental and the physical (if to talk of such a relation is not to misconstrue the nature of things) must be much more subtle and indirect than a correlation or identity of the mental and the physical or reduction of the mental to the physical. William James's positivist hope of making psychology into a science by using our privileged knowledge of events in our stream of consciousness as the means to identify the functioning of the underlying structures in the brain has been fulfilled in some respects but not in most. Wilder Penfield and others were successful in using introspective reports as a guide to discovering the function of some areas in the brain, but it has since become clear that at most what was discovered was only part, though in some cases arguably a crucial part, of the functioning of the brain on such occasions.[1] Further, in general the higher (evolutionally speaking) is the mental act or operation, the greater is the complexity and the more widespread is the system in the brain that is to be associated with that act or operation. The more the act becomes clearly cognitive, the vaguer becomes our understanding of the role of any relevant brain states or processes because our picture of such cognitive activities, often gained allegedly from introspection, seems to give few or no guidelines to discovering the relevant brain states or systems and their operations.

The result in empirical and philosophical psychology was a move away from reductionism to a functionalist account of the mental. It is neither easy nor particularly important to try to locate the exact beginning—if such exactness is possible in regard to what, most likely, traces its origin to a blurred transitional period—of what has since been called the functionalist account of the mental.[2] What is not in dispute is that Hilary Putnam's papers have been of seminal importance in generating contemporary discussion about functionalist accounts of the mind.[3] The baldest statement of Putnam's functionalist account of mental states is in the introduction to volume 2 of his philosophical papers, *Mind, Language and Reality*.

> The theory for which I argue is a form of functionalism—not functionalism as a doctrine about the meanings of psychological words, but functionalism as a synthetic hypothesis about the nature of mental states.
>
> According to functionalism, the behaviour of, say, a computing machine is not explained by the physics and chemistry of the computing machine. It is explained by the machine's *program*. Of course, that program is realized in a particular physics and chemistry, and could, perhaps, be deduced from that physics and chemistry. But that does not make the program a physical or chemical property of the machine: it is an abstract property of the machine. Similarly, I believe that the psychological properties of human beings are not physical and chemical properties of human beings, although they may be realized by physical and chemical properties of human beings. Although any behaviour of a computing machine that can be explained by the program of that computing machine can, in principle, be predicted on the basis of the physics and chemistry of the machine; the latter prediction may be highly unexplanatory. Understanding why the machine, say, computes the decimal expansion of π, may require reference to the abstract or functional properties of the machine, to the machine's program and not to its physical and chemical make up.[4]

Sketching in an even larger picture, Putnam suggests that the whole mind-body problem has been bedeviled by the question, Are we made of matter or soul stuff or some combination of the two? This question is the wrong one, he maintains, for all the usual answers to it must miss the essential nature of the mental. Although we are not made of soul stuff in whole or part, this does not mean that the mental, if not reducible to the physical, is nonreal. It is "a real and autonomous feature of our world."[5] To answer the question, Are we made of soul stuff? negatively does not rule out the reality of our mental life and does not brand it as mythical. It merely leads us to regard the question as largely unimportant and irrelevant. As Putnam puts it in "Philosophy and Our Mental Life,"

> Now, imagine two possible universes, perhaps "parallel worlds," in the science fiction sense, in one of which people have good old fashioned souls, operating through pineal glands, perhaps, and in the other of which they have complicated brains. And suppose that the souls in the soul world are functionally isomorphic to the brains in the brain world. Is there any more sense attaching importance to this difference than to the difference between copper wires and some other wires in the computer? Does it matter that the soul people have, so to speak, immaterial brains, and that the brain people have material souls? What matters is the common structure, the theory T of which we are, alas, in deep ignorance, and not the hardware, be it ever so ethereal.[6]

For Putnam, then, the relation of the mental to the physical is analogous to that of the functional description—or "machine table"[7]—of a simple computer or Turing machine to the physical description of its realization in any particular way.[8] That is, one can describe a computer in terms of the various operations it can perform, and the ordering of operations for complex performances or computations, without mentioning (and while being indifferent to) whether the computer is made of plastic or wood or even of people in an office organized into a smooth working unit. The "machine table" can be fully described in terms of the relations among the various current states, plus inputs and outputs, and these relations in turn can be described entirely in logico-linguistic terms. Thus the computer has properties describable only in terms of its "machine table" and properties describable only in terms of its physical structure. Similarly humans have "abstract properties" describable only in terms of their psychological functioning and concrete properties describable only in terms of their physiology.[9] Two computers, or two humans, can be functionally isomorphic but quite different in physical constitution.[10] Indeed in the future a computer or robot might be made functionally isomorphic with a human, but this functioning might be realized in the robot in a physical way quite different from human physiology. The mental life of humans is their "machine table," so to speak.

We do not as yet know a human's "machine table" because we do not yet have a good, much less a complete, psychological theory of humans. We do not yet have a comprehensive "program" for the brain. Part of the reason is that to talk thus about a human's "machine table" is to talk in terms of an inexact analogue for human psychology. Humans are not a simple closed programmed system such that one can speak literally of a "machine table" or "program" for them. Humans are a hotchpotch of many overlapping or discrete, interlocking or clashing or simply unconnected systems. If a human is at one and the same time angry, intending to have dinner, hoping for rain, and a pessimist, it is unlikely that one could ever refer to a single program as explanation for what the human is likely to do at that time.[11] Moreover, whatever might turn out to be the best functional model of humans' higher cognitive activities, such a model may be indifferent to any particular realization in terms of brain function because it is so formalized and idealized that it bears little or no relation to what actually goes on in the brain. A functional psychological model is something that enables us to plot and make sense of human activity. Its restrictions and limits are determined by whether it makes good sense and is a good explanation, not by the neurophysiology of the brain. In that sense, as Putnam puts it, "We have what we always wanted—an autonomous mental life. And we need no mysteries, no ghostly agents, no *élan vital* to have it."[12] That is more or less where Putnam's speculations end. He does not proffer many details about how particular mental acts or processes are to be explained under this model. In particular he gives no more than a few passing hints as to how introspection might be treated and never directly addresses that problem.[13]

2 Dennett and "Intentional System" Functionalism

Daniel Dennett, on the other hand, in one of the other classical sources for a functionalist view of mind, *Content and Consciousness*, directs special attention to consciousness and introspection precisely because they are connected with "the feature of the mind that is most resistant to absorption into the mechanistic picture of science"[14]—intentionality, or the fact that mental activities possess some end or other activity as their content—and he too looks to computers as the most useful analogue for what he wants to explain.

Dennett explains that to try to correlate mental talk with brain events is to mistake the nature and origin of mental talk. To illustrate his view, consider the case when one describes a zebra as having realized it is in danger. The use of the word "realized"—a mental, intentional term— is on the basis of our knowledge of the context or environmental conditions at the time plus our knowledge of how the animal reacted to them. We say that the zebra realized that it was in danger because there was in its line of vision and upwind from it a large lioness and because the zebra raised its head, sniffed the air, made certain noises, and then took to its heels in the opposite direction. The response was appropriate to the dangerous situation, and it was cognitively correct, so we can use the appropriate mental phrase "realized it was in danger" of the zebra: "*What the animal was doing* . . . can only be told in intentional terms, but it is not a story about features of the world *in addition to* the features of the extensional story, it just describes what happens in a different way."[15] So it should be clear that to consider mental talk as oblique or even inexact and prescientific reference to brain activity is to be ignorant of how and why we attribute mental acts. Mental or intentional attribution is made on the basis of the large view of what some behaving organism is up to, which in turn can be made sense of only by considering the context, the organism, and the resulting behavior. Further, this behavior must be understood in the light of its usual successful outcome (again in the long term and in general) if one is to give some substance to the words "appropriate" and "correct" in the phrases "appropriate behavior" and "cognitively correct." Mental talk is not poor-quality talk about brains or even poor-quality guessing about what goes on inside some animal's brain; it is talk about the animal in the large context of usual appropriate responses to noted stimuli. In our mental talk we may occasionally say that realizing, as well as believing and hoping and guessing, "go on inside our head" or even that they are the content of our brain states, but such ascriptions are "essentially a heuristic overlay on the extensional theory rather than intervening variables of the theory."[16] Mental talk is making sense of what goes on in our head in the light of input and output. To imagine that our mental talk can lead us to make predictions about what animals or people will do, which could not be made on the basis of the empirical (or extensional as opposed to intentional) knowledge we have of those animals or people, is to put the cart before the horse. Just as the cart must (almost) always follow the horse (at least causally speaking), so must intentional explanations or mental talk be parasitic on our knowledge of the environment and an organism's appropriate response to it.

Before I examine Dennett's accounts of introspection, it should be pointed out that in the introduction to *Brainstorms*, he is at pains to distinguish his brand of functionalism ("intentional system" functionalism) from what he calls earlier "Turing machine functionalism."[17] According to this earlier form of functionalism, mental predicates are to be identified with functional predicates. If two people share the same belief, their shared mental state will be characterizable by the same functional description, which in turn can be couched in terms of a shared program. Thus to be in the same mental state is to be at the same point in the working through of a shared program.

Dennett suggests that one reason why Turing machine functionalism is implausible is because it interprets functionalism too narrowly and literally in terms of a program. It is implausible because it is based on the assumption that, although we do not yet know its details and may never do so, nevertheless we all share the same program in terms of which we organize information and behavior. This assumption ignores the vast differences in the nature and nurture of individual humans. Think of the difference in the upbringing of a native of the Fly River area in Papua New Guinea and of an inhabitant of Manhattan in New York. How could it be envisaged that these two share the same program?

On this point (though not on others) I am inclined to think that Dennett is exaggerating the difference between his own form of functionalism and Turing machine functionalism, and, in so doing, distorting the views of those, like Putnam, who first made the analogy between the mental and the computer's "machine table." Putnam at least, as we have seen, was at pains to point out that there probably is not, and could not be, a single program for humans and that the original analogy must not be carried too far.

It might be suggested, however, that there is a much more important worry about the mind-program analogy: that a computer does not function intentionally (that is, it does not function by grasping object, target, or content either by means of understanding some representation or description of it or by some other similar means). It merely processes information and carries out instructions without understanding or believing or planning or being in any intentional states; it manipulates formal symbols without understanding the interpretation of the symbols. The programmer understands the interpretation, as does the person who interprets the output, but the computer does not. Thus, it might be argued, it is misleading to view the mental as merely the brain's computational program.

John Searle has produced a powerful argument to underline this worry.[18] Searle proposed the following thought experiment (I will give it in slightly adapted form). An English-speaking person who does not understand Chinese is placed in a room in which there is stored a complete set of Chinese characters plus a set of instructions in English; according to the set of instructions certain written characters are pushed out under the door of the room whenever a particular combination of characters is fed in under the door. Clearly an observer outside the room who did not know who or what was inside the room would most likely be fooled into thinking that the room contained someone who understood Chinese (or else that the "room" did). Equally clearly the person in the room does not understand a single character but merely follows faithfully the instructions about how to manipulate output in the light of input.

But does Searle's argument really cast doubt on the mind-program analogy and so on functional interpretations of the mental? Although our intuitions balk at suggesting that the person in the room understands Chinese, should we refuse to admit that the complex of prepared instructions, person in the room, and store of characters lacks understanding? Our intuitions—used to attributing understanding to persons—might indeed balk, but should they stop us from attributing understanding to such a system? It might be suggested that they should not, because after all the instructions had to be written by someone who does understand Chinese (otherwise the whole thing would have to be put down to magic), and so the instructions are generated by and incorporate understanding. Thus the complex—the set of instructions, plus the person in the room carrying them out, plus the store of Chinese characters—does have or "embody" or "contain" understanding of Chinese.

Some might be prepared to grant (though probably not Searle) that while the complex has understanding, it should also be clear that, by himself, the person in the room who carries out the instructions—who engages merely in "formal symbol manipulation"—does not have understanding. Further, and this is Searle's main point, to characterize a person's mental operations in a purely functional way is like characterizing that person's mind as if it were an inner room in which a computer merely carried out instructions about output in the light of input—that is, followed a program. (Waggishly, Searly has remarked that if mere processing of output in the light of input is the criterion, then our stomachs are cognitive systems.)

This argument of Searle's, it seems to me, may count against Turing machine or computer functionalism but not against unreduced "intentional system" functionalism, for this latter version describes our cognitive functions in terms of intentional items—that is, states like believing, knowing, and understanding that already incorporate understanding as part of their characterization. Where Turing machine or computer functionalism will give an account of a mental term such as "believing" in terms of a particular point on a human's "program," "intentional system" functionalism on the other hand will give an account of belief in terms of a particular point in an intentional system. Thus "intentional system" functionalism explains a mental or intentional item, such as belief, either in terms of a web of beliefs (a belief system) or in terms of a system of more basic intentional items or explains that the term is better discarded altogether. Thus, with "intentional system" functionalism, our current intentional terms might be retained, reduced to more basic intentional terms, or simply discarded as unemployable.

To remain at the level of unreduced "intentional systems," however, would be to do so at great cost. It would entail giving up the goal—which Dennett shares—of absorbing the mental wholly into "the mechanistic picture of science," for to remain at the level of unreduced "intentional systems" is to fail to produce a purely functional account. To say so-and-so has a belief, or a certain item in a belief system, is not merely to connect input to output by way of a followed instruction to do something. A belief, besides involving (always?) a "motor set"— or readiness to behave in a certain way in suitable circumstances— involves understanding a content (usually expressible in propositional form), and this in turn is usually characterized as some form of endorsement (itself an intentional concept) of that content as true or as the best available hypothesis or something cognate.

The wholehearted acceptance of the considerations underlined by Searle's thought experiment would lead to a permanent dilution of hardline computer functionalism in the the direction of "intentional system" functionalism. The acceptance of Searle's argument in effect would present a functionalist with a dilemma: to stick at the "intentional system" level is to fail to mesh the mental with the mechanistic physical sciences and to run the risk of giving comfort to Cartesian psychologies; to move from the "intentional system" stance back into the reductionist stance of pure computer functionalism is to be confronted with Searle-like arguments and in general to leave oneself open to the charge of having given an unconvincing portrayal of the mental. Dennett was clearly alert to these tensions and could be interpreted as attempting to keep a foot planted in both positions, believing that he could do so without permanent philosophical injury because he was not attempting to keep his feet in both positions at the same time. He believed that, initially, to preserve intentionality in our functional characterization of the mental, one must take up the "intentional system" stance or the "intentional stance" and describe mental functions in terms of such ordinary "folk psychological" intentional terms as beliefs, hopes, and desires. Eventually as our understanding of these operations became deeper, we could replace the intentional characterization of each one with an account of (probably of a series of) nonintentional subroutines or processes. It would be a little like gradually replacing the neuronal circuits of our brains with microchips but at the same time preserving what, at the top or macrolevel, we describe as our ability to believe, hope, desire, understand, and so on. Insofar as this possibility of replacing the intentional with a complex of nonintentional subroutines remains plausible, the functionalist has an answer to Searle. The

"Chinese room" will eventually embody intentionality when the instructions to carry out the routines involving Chinese characters become complex enough to mirror the myriad subroutines that a functionalist believes can incorporate the essence of understanding Chinese. (I shall discuss this crucial aspect of functionalism again when I consider Dennett's model of introspection in detail.)

Dennett maintains that the original Turing machine or computer analogy was and still is illuminating, important, and basically right. The best way, the correct way, of characterizing the mental is in functional terms. But it must be remembered that this account of the mental is much more open and messier than Turing machine functionalism seems to suggest. Mental states cannot be identified or picked out against a background of a clear and agreed and shared program for humans because there is no such shared computational program. At most we can say that we all have (what at present must be characterized as) a roughly similar intentional system but not the exact same one. An intentional system is a first-stage functional characterization of the mental and is made up of intentional items (such as beliefs, wishes, hopes, desires), some of which will be lifted more or less untouched from "folk psychology" and bear our current mental terms, and some of which will not. Further, some of our current mental terms will not feature in any description of the system at all but must be eliminated as too ghostly and Cartesian for honorable mention at any stage. The (at least initially) acceptable items—let us for the moment allow that belief and desire are such items—are to be grouped together as a system because it is possible in terms of the functioning of these items and the (rationally conceived) interrelations among them to predict the behavior of something to which such items are correctly attributed.[19] We cannot attribute, then, a specific program to all organisms or things of a certain kind—to all humans, for example—we can only attribute to a specific human whatever beliefs and desires, for instance, it seems sensible to attribute to him given that he is human, given our knowledge of his history (his culture, education, and so on), and given reasonably accurate knowledge of the sort of information he must be taken to possess and the spectrum of goals he can be supposed to have. We can only predict what he will do if he can then be supposed to act rationally in respect of his beliefs, desires, and goals. We take up the "intentional stance" in regard to a person and attribute to him or her an "intentional system." There is no grand "intentional system" or program that a person must be said to have and so no grand view of the spectrum of mental events. Thus Dennett asserts, "The details of my view [of the mental] must for this reason be built up piecemeal, by case studies and individual defences that are not intended to generalise to all mental entities and all mental states."[20]

3 Dennett's Computer Model of Introspection

Dennett's first elaborated account of introspection occurs in *Content and Consciousness*, and this account becomes the foundation for his subsequent construction of a functionalist model of consciousness.[21] For Dennett, according to this first account, the essential feature of introspection is that it delivers error-free reports of functionally characterized inner states. Indeed the key to understanding introspection lies in the correct account of how and why such reports are infallible.

Dennett suggests that the human person is like a perceiving machine that registers whatever impinges on its perceptual apparatus or organs. Such a machine does not depict the outside world on some screen in an inner cinema—who would view it?—but by an analyzer produces intentionally analyzed and edited verbally expressible accounts of the outside world. The machine can be tricked into generating false descriptions, say, by placing a cardboard cutout soldier next to a real one amid some undergrowth a hundred yards from the perceiver. The perceptual apparatus, with its analyzer, will most likely generate a description of two soldiers deployed in undergrowth. Once that descriptive account is generated without malfunction by the analyzer and given that no extraneous content is fed into the speech center along with the contents of the analyzer—no hunches, guesses, prejudices, or presuppositions—then the only other possible error that can occur, when the machine gives an "introspective" account of what it has seen, is verbal error. Strictly speaking, only the latter sort of error directly pertains to introspection, for to introspect is not to report on the contents of the analyzer, with the attendant possibility of misreporting, but it is, after the analyzer is hooked up to the speech center and its contents fed into the speech center, merely to print out those contents. There is no further processing after the contents of the analyzer (or any other contents) are fed into the speech center. All that occurs in introspection is that the speech center's contents are printed out in "introspective reports." This printing-out facility can malfunction—make a verbal slip, so to speak—but it cannot mis-see, misinspect, misretrospect, misreport, or misidentify because there are no such mysterious ghostly processes going on. Thus, barring verbal slips, introspection must be error free.

This account of introspection is the basis of Dennett's account of consciousness or awareness. There are, he alleges, two levels and so two concepts of awareness, and the blurring of these in ordinary speech generates the paradoxes in our ordinary conception of consciousness. One is aware$_2$ (or conscious at the lower level) of something if one has input from that thing (object or event) into the "perceptual analyzer" and so can organize and control one's behavior in terms of it, but the ensuing analyzed content may not be passed on into the "speech center." One is aware$_1$ (or conscious at the higher level) of that thing if and when input from it is passed on into the "speech center" and so becomes accessible to introspection (can be "printed out" in our introspective talk). Insects and birds, and most animals, are aware$_2$ but not aware$_1$ because they do not have a speech center and so cannot introspect.[22] Humans, on the other hand, have both levels of consciousness; however, even with humans the introspective printout of internal computations, such as reasoning in general or mental arithmetic in particular, is an intentionally analyzed and edited version of what the brain does, which has been fed into the speech center. We can say that we first multiplied seven by four, then added two, and so on, but we do not know how we multiplied seven by four. Did we print out serially four lots of seven units and then add them up, or did we refer to a line in an embedded version of the seven times tables?

In *Brainstorms*, first published nearly ten years after *Content and Consciousness*, Dennett has given up the very ground on which he had built his first functionalist account of introspection—that it delivers error-free "reports" of functionally characterized inner states—and so elaborated a significantly different functionalist model of introspection. In the light of the history of psychology, it is very difficult, indeed highly implausible, to maintain that introspection delivers error-free reports (or "reports"), and so I believe that Dennett was right to rebuild his model of introspection so as to accommodate its unreliability. As he put it in *Brainstorms*, there is a world of difference between "our feelings of special authority in offering introspection reports"—which stem from the fact that we have the ability to report accurately on what is available (in the speech center) to us to report—and the ability to report accurately on our internal data, computations, and decisions.[23]

In *Content and Consciousness* Dennett had limited the introspective process to the process of printing out what was in the speech center, or "out" tray. In a sense, he was driven to do this by having first committed himself to the proposition that introspection was free from error. As he realized that all sorts of editing, censoring, glossing, and interpreting could go on before the material got to the "out" tray— that the resulting manuscript was more likely to be palimpsest than original codex—this meant (unless he were to give up the error-free thesis) that introspection must refer only to the more of less uninterruptible and automatic process of posting what was in the "out" tray (or publishing what was in the speech center). Freedom from error was gained at considerable cost. Introspection was no longer reporting of any sort but just a process of publishing. There was no searching, discovering, collecting, inspecting, retrospecting, or anything else of that sort in the process to which the label "introspection" properly applied. To preserve the freedom from error of introspection, Dennett realized, one had to emasculate the process.

By giving up the error-free criterion in *Brainstorms*, the way was now open for a more potent and convincing account of introspection.[24] As one has come to expect in regard to functionalist theories, the new model of introspection is expounded in the language of computer software:

> Suppose Control [a higher executive component in the brain] "decides" for various reasons to "introspect":
>
> (1) it goes into its introspection subroutine, in which
> (2) it directs a question to M [short-term or buffer memory];
> (3) when an answer comes back (and none may) it assesses the answer: it may
>   (a) censor the answer
>   (b) "interpret" the answer in the light of other information
>   (c) "draw inferences" from the answer, or
>   (d) relay the answer as retrieved direct to PR [a "public relations" or printout component].
> (4) The outcome of any of (a–d) can be a speech command to PR. The point of the buffer memory M is that getting some item of information in M is a necessary but not a sufficient condition for getting it accessed by PR in the form of the *content* of some speech act command.[25]

This theory clearly makes room for and allows for some explanation of the unreliability of introspection. Introspective reports can fail to mention internal information received or processes performed, or they can give edited "bitty" versions of them, or they can give interpreted, biased, loaded versions of them. Introspective reports can mention information or processes that have not taken place, for Control can mistake a hunch or hope or expectation of an event for its occurrence and place such material in PR in such a way that it is then indistinguishable from factual material and so is issued as fact. On this model, introspection is the series of processes whereby Control, the higher executive component in the brain, directs questions to memory, sifts and edits the answers if necessary, and passes on the material to the speech center, which, if so commanded, publishes it. Introspection is now genuinely a process of reporting on what has been stored in memory regarding events perceived, and internal computations, plans, and decisions made, albeit with the proviso that between these internal states and Control, and between Control and lip, there may be many a slip.

Another important aspect of Dennett's model is that it entails that we do not have direct and immediate introspective access to mental processes as they happen but only to some version of them stored in memory. That is why the processes of introspection are best represented, he seems to be suggesting, not as a direct scanning or monitoring of first-order processes but as asking questions and receiving answers. Introspection may deliver a series of consecutive answers related to the same process or series of processes, and this may look like direct and immediate access to the process itself, just as a series of light flashes in linear sequence can look like a single traveling light source. Because of introspective evidence, we may think that we are directly registering internal mental processes and so all too easily fall prey to talking about "perceiving" with the "inner eye." In fact, it does not follow that if we do not have direct and immediate access to first-order mental processes, as Dennett claims, the result must be that our information about such processes can amount to no more than discrete snapshots of what is really a process already completed, for memory might plausibly be construed, at least in regard to introspection, as more like an instant replay facility whose answers to questions comprise (continuous) replays of the original processes.

Dennett went on to suggest that "that of which we are conscious is that of which we can tell, introspectively or retrospectively," that is, he tied awareness or consciousness—consciousness at the higher level—to introspection once again.[26] Thus creatures who cannot tell (i.e., have no language) are not conscious in the full or higher sense of the term because they cannot introspectively report.

This may seem to be an unnecessary hostage to fortune. Since, on this account, the more important processes of introspection are Control's getting and sifting answers from Memory, why did Dennett not define ordinary consciousness as the ability to get and sift such answers so that one could be conscious in the full sense of something inner but not be able to tell? The answer, I suspect, is that we do not ordinarily claim to be aware of such complex processing—of actually retrieving material from storage, of asking questions, or, in general, of engaging in the subroutines we engage in—but we do claim awareness of the end-product of this processing, that is of what we are about to tell, of what is in the speech center (though not as being in the speech center). For the purposes of consciousness or awareness, the emphasis must be placed on what is in the speech center or on the tip of one's tongue, ready to be told more or less immediately. Dennett's position is the reverse of William James's, who held that introspection was parasitic on consciousness because the proper account of introspection was in terms of a stream of contents of consciousness of which we are aware. Introspection was access to that stream of consciousness, albeit at one remove when it was frozen in memory. Dennett's position is that consciousness is parasitic on introspection, which in turn is explained as a routine by means of which a person gains access to and reports on the contents of his or her buffer memory, albeit at times in censored, biased, or tampered form.

4 Functionalism versus Eliminative Materialism

While the functionalist approach to the mental is undeniably attractive, it is time now to look carefully at the model of introspection that has resulted from this approach. Inevitably this examination will also yield comments about the functionalist approach in general, and I shall begin with a problem that does just that. I shall point up some of the conflicts that appear in Dennett's account of introspection in the light of his overall strategy of explanation of the mental in terms of "intentional systems."

If to characterize mental states and processes functionally, according to Dennett, is to locate them as part of an "intentional system," which in turn is to give an explanation in terms of a complex constructed out of beliefs, hopes, desires, and the other rough-and-ready items of our ordinary quotidian "folk psychology," how is his explanation of introspection (in terms of control sending questions to memory and sifting and analyzing and censoring and editing) a genuine Dennettian functionalist account? It might be objected that such an account is supposed to be a stiffened-up part of "folk psychology," that is, a systematized version of some more or less common intentional explanation that has been used over the centuries as a means to understanding the behavior of ourselves and others. But there is nothing at all in the "folk psychological" account of introspection about (or even equivalent to) Control, buffer memory, editing, censoring, interpreting, printing out, and so on.

The answer lies in the fact that Dennett also envisages an eventual reduction of explanations in terms of higher-level intentional systems to explanations in terms of lower-level, nonintentional, mechanistic, science-compatible systems. So as merely a downward stage on this program presumably, Dennett has reverted in part to the analogy between computers and humans; he has conceived of introspection for the time being in terms of a model such as those working in artificial intelligence might produce. Although he makes no specific claims about how Control, Memory, speech center, printout, and so on might be incarnated in the brain, it would follow from his general program—and here he departs from the aims of many of those working in artificial intelligence—that he is putting this account forward (at least when the reductive program is complete) as a correct, functional account of human introspection. Ultimately he will be putting forward what he believes is not merely a reduced (to the nonintentional) functional explanation of introspection but what he believes is also a correct description of the moves our brain makes—that is, of its design—though how it makes them—how in neurophysiological detail the brain works—is another matter, a matter for neurophysiology.

To put this another way, Dennett seems to want to inject an eliminative materialist strand into his intentional systematizing because he intends his account to be assimilable to and so his work to be relevant to the brain sciences. Ultimately he wants his models to be "subpersonal" and scientific; he wants to explain personal behavior "by analysing a person into an organisation of subsystems (organs, routines, nerves, faculties, components—even atoms)," which are not the subjects of ordinary personal experience, but he also wants these subsystems to portray accurately how the brain works.[27] Thus, in explaining the details of his model of introspection, Dennett refers to "feature detectors" and points out that brain scientists have discovered these to be part of the structures by means of which we perceive the external world. When explaining the function of Control, he draws on evidence from experimental psychology for the existence of an executive component in the brain that controls the flow of information in the brain and directs its analysis.[28]

This program of ultimately reducing explanations in terms of "intentional" systems to nonintentional descriptions of brain design, however—and this is the point of broaching these more general considerations—can be seen as a necessary move to allay a worry in regard to explanations in terms of "intentional systems" proper: whether there are sufficient limitations on what can count as an acceptable explanation for any such explanation to be said genuinely to explain. But in soothing away this worry, he creates another one.

The worry in regard to his use of "intentional systems" proper (or pure "intentional systems" explanations) arises in the following way. We should recall that for Dennett, an "intentional system" explanation is not so much an inference to the correct explanation (in the sense of *the* explanation of how the human mind works) as an inference to the most coherent explanation in functional intentional terms of why that behavioral output followed that environmental input. The resulting explanation will be in terms of "putative events, states, achievements, processes," which are "idealized fictions in an action-predicting, action-explaining calculus."[29] But in giving such explanations, he now has the problem of finding a good reason why anyone should accept his "idealized fiction" in regard to what goes on when we introspect rather than your one, or the version the grocer at the corner might produce when in a reflective mood. Explanations in terms of "intentional systems" proper, according to Dennett, are anomalous and autonomous. Such explanations not only repudiate psychophysical correlations of a lawlike sort but seem to demand that there be no constraints at all to be acknowledged from the direction of the brain. A pure "intentional system" is the product of a free-floating explanation, which is indifferent to possible physical realizations. It is an "idealized fiction" upon which is placed only the constraints that it be rational and coherent and explain output in terms of input. Dennett realized that from this, we could reasonably ask why we should endorse his account of introspection (and "endorse" seems the best word here rather than, say, "deem correct," which might suggest that there was a sense in which one could check an "intentional system" explanation for accuracy).

Why should we endorse Dennett's account of introspection in terms of Control, buffer memory, putting questions, receiving answers, censoring, interpreting, drawing inferences from, and publishing rather than one like Armstrong's in terms of some scanning device, with scrambler or encoder added, perhaps an interpreter as well, and then reporter?[30] A suggestion that his explanation in terms of Control, buffer memory, and so on is a priori more rational and coherent than other rival explanations that are equally comprehensive and explanatory of output in the light of input is not easy to maintain. A priori there must be little to choose in terms of "rationality and coherence" between his explanation, Armstrong's, and a dozen other possibilities. For example, without loss of rationality or coherence, one could immediately substitute for Control a well-organized Committee where one member does the questioning, another the editing, and so on. Or one could do away with Control or Committee and postulate that the various processes previously under the thumb of Control or Committee now proceed automatically according to "wired-in" procedures.

In regard to introspection, the limitations imposed by having to make one's explanation explanatory of behavioral output in the light of environmental input seem particularly minimal. Because introspection is not a process that seems to be aimed directly at generating appropriate output and is very often such a self-contained internal process, it causes difficulties for functionalism. One can introspect quite independently of what is going on in the environment and without producing any "motor set." One can close one's eyes and think of England and then introspect one's thinking. Or one might run over some scene witnessed last week, wondering why it has stuck in the memory. Of course, introspection can be useful for planning behavior, but it can also be disengaged from circumstance in a way that, say, most deliberating, decision making, evaluation, and emotion are not. Introspection is often the mind in purely reflective mode. An introspective person is often an introverted person.

The temptation for a functionalist to allay this worry about the "free-floating" nature of functionalist explanations by looking for further constraints on one's model is very strong in the case of introspection, and the obvious place to seek such constraints is from the direction of the brain. Ultimately the temptation to be an eliminative materialist cum brain scientist must be all but overwhelming when one has succeeded in making the move from giving an explanation at the personal intentional level to one at the subpersonal level in terms of components, routines, and printouts. When one deintentionalizes "intentional system" accounts, one cannot replace the intentional processes with just any series of nonintentional mechanistic processes that would produce the same output from the same input. If one replaced the intentional processes merely with some rational and coherent series of subroutines, this series may only imitate or simulate a human intentional act functionally rather than reproduce it. It may act only as a good substitute for what the human intentional act does. But the brain may work in a quite different way—perhaps in a much messier, less coherent, noneconomic, less rational way. To simulate the part played by human intentionality by means of simplified and smoothed-over nonintentional mechanistic processes would not show that this is what humans do when they engage in intentional activity. For this reason the temptation for a functionalist to be a brain scientist must be quite strong, for his account or model of something such as introspection becomes useful and important—rather than just a clever simulation—only insofar as it sheds light on how humans, human brains, in fact engage in intentional activities. The functionalist in philosophical psychology should try to produce not a simulation but a duplication, which is explanatory and revealing of psychological reality.

I would not want to deny that there may be (perhaps ought to be) intermediate stages between functionalist explanations and brain science. For example, it may be useful (and a lot of cognitive scientists believe it is) to reduce functionalist explanations to "information processing" accounts. Thus, for example, it may be useful to reduce talk of knowing something and deciding on the basis of it to accounts in terms of information held, information added, aggregation of the two, possible deductions to be drawn in the light of targets set, and so on. But it is hard to see how one is advancing knowledge of human psychology unless ultimately one attempts to see how the brain encodes and manipulates such information. At that stage, one must ask the fundamental question, Is the "information-processing approach" the correct picture of how the brain works? It might turn out to be wildly inappropriate. The brain may not encode at all. It may work in a quite different way. However—and here is a new worry Dennett has generated in the process of stilling the old one—to yield to the temptation to be a brain scientist is to land back in the orthodox physicalist (or reductive cum eliminative materialist) camp whose problems functionalism was designed to avoid. If in order to be aligned with explanations in the hard sciences, "intentional system" accounts must be reduced ultimately to mechanistic accounts and if such accounts will be of real interest only if they duplicate how the brain works, then Dennettian functionalism collapses into eliminative materialism. In effect Dennettian functionalism is committed to reducing our "folk psychological" account of the mental, by means of a more sophisticated "intentional system" account, and perhaps an "information-processing" account, to an account in terms of brain states and processes. To the "true blue" functionalist, this is philosophical recidivism.

5 Some Further Reflections on Dennett's Account of Introspection

I want to look now at some of the finer details of Dennett's functionalist case study of introspection. First I want to bring forward again a matter I have already referred to as an unnecessary hostage to fortune on Dennett's part: his insistence that introspection does not and cannot take place unless one can get the information from perception or subsequent deliberation into the speech center and publish it verbally and that consciousness in the full sense (consciousness$_1$) is parasitic on this account of introspection. Intuitively this seems odd and close to a reductio ad absurdum of this model of introspection and consciousness, as Dennett seems to realize when he coyly admits that he will be taken to be the "Village Verificationist." Given his view of consciousness in the full sense (consciousness$_1$), Dennett seems to believe that it entails that children, some deaf-mutes, and dogs, being without the ability to employ language, cannot publish verbally the contents of perception or internal computation and so cannot be conscious (conscious$_1$). This is odd because it seems fair to say that we take it as one of the facts that an adequate account of introspection and consciousness must cope with, that children and deaf-mutes are fully conscious and able to introspect.

I believe that Dennett has no need to play the "Village Verificationist"; why this is so will become clear from a closer look at his own views, together with a consideration of a passage in *The Principles of Psychology*.[31] In this passage James refers to the now-famous childhood experiences of a deaf and dumb man, Mr. Ballard, who, when he had learned sign language, related that, before he could convey thoughts and feelings to his parents and brothers other than "by natural signs and pantomime," he had a rich inner life woven out of his tactile and visual experiences. This inner life included metaphysical speculations about the origin of life and the world itself, which he was unable to communicate by means of natural signs and pantomime.[32] While Mr. Ballard does not mention specifically that he introspected his thoughts as well, nevertheless since he clearly enjoyed reflective thinking of a most abstract kind, there is no obvious reason to believe that he was incapable of introspection or that he was not fully conscious.

Dennett, however—and I think this can come about without much or even any real adjustment to his account—could accommodate the Ballard case and the case of children who have yet to learn a language. As Mr. Ballard was able later to report on his prelanguage metaphysical speculations and introspections, it could be argued that he must have stored the contents of these speculations and introspections in his speech center or at least stored them in some language-compatible way. Thus, if Mr. Ballard was conscious and could introspect before he learned sign language, Dennett could say that it was because he could put his thoughts into linguistic form in an etiolated sense; that is, he could put them in storage in a form such that later they could be published in language of some sort.

In effect, then, a more circumspect account of Dennett's view would make it clear that someone is occurrently conscious$_1$ if he or she can put the contents of current thoughts into the speech center (or into language-compatible storage) irrespective of whether now he or she has the ability to speak or, in general, to publish the contents of the speech center. To put this another way—in terms of Dennett's own account of introspection—it should be clear that the Control in a child's or deaf-mute's brain should be able to relay information from M in terms of a speech command to PR irrespective of whether PR is functioning properly. Unless Dennett stipulates that children and deaf-mutes who have yet to learn language do not yet have a speech center, which would be very odd, he can clearly accommodate the case of prelanguage children and deaf-mutes. (The case of dogs is more difficult unless he allows them some form of language or at least publication of what they think and perceive. Could he not allow that canine behavior of certain sorts is revelatory in a sufficiently controlled and directed manner of dog thoughts, or "thoughts," and perceptions?)

There is another more important puzzle in the details of Dennett's account of introspection as a subpersonal routine. In describing Control as assessing, directing questions, censoring, inferring, and interpreting—albeit in quotation marks—he has underlined the confusion about the nature of his explanation, for he is clearly mixing the subpersonal with the personal. While Control—an "executive component" in the brain, recall—and its activities are unknown to us in our personal life, he describes the activities of Control in everyday terms. It seems odd, having imported into his account the subpersonal mechanistic item Control, that he should then describe its functions in personal, intentional terms. Control turns out to be a homunculus with intentional attitudes in disguise—not a higher executive component in the brain but a miniscule executive sitting at his desk in the brain. To claim to explain how introspectively we find out about the contents of our conscious thoughts, desires, and intentions by claiming that we have within our heads a subpersonal component that asks questions and receives answers, assesses and interprets or censors them, and so on, is odd indeed.[33]

Most likely Dennett's response to this sort of complaint would be that the intentionality still remaining at the first stage of analysis, or at any other intervening stages, will be eliminated once such items are reduced to the rock-bottom level of analytic explanation. The underlying claim is that an intentional item differs from a nonintentional one only in terms of complexity, so that when the complexity of an intentional item is fully displayed, ipso facto it will be seen to have been reduced to a series of mechanistic nonintentional subroutines. Intentionality will turn out to be merely part of the surface-level or macrodescription, which we now give to what in the future we may be able to describe, and will be more accurately and scientifically described, as a complex organized subsystem or series of subroutines of a mechanistic sort. Intentionality is not an emergent property of the complex subsystem by merely a higher-level way of describing it (which is ultimately misleading).

The complexity, however, will be complex. It will not be just a matter of an apparently unitary process being broken down into a multiplicity of smaller processes. These multiple processes may be arranged vertically in a series of levels—or at least sets or series of them might be—in which higher-level processes, while being constituted by lower-level ones, may nevertheless have a reflex effect on the lower-level ones. Also processes at one level may loop back on to themselves, and so on. In short, how intentionality is constituted at these lower levels may be very complicated indeed, and there is no denying that from the viewpoint of the present, it remains a genuine mystery.

6 "Top-Down" Strategy and Psychological Explanation

Dennett has described this strategy of analyzing the psychological or intentional levels of explanation into bottom-level, probably biological, explanations as a "top-down" strategy—that is, a "strategy that begins with a more abstract decomposition of the highest levels of psychological organisation, and hopes to analyse these into more and more detailed smaller systems or processes until finally one arrives at elements familiar to the biologists."[34] The functional physicalist who employs this top-down strategy aims to reduce the top-layer intentional description to a bottom-level description of purely mechanistic processes, for only at this bottom level can the psychological be absorbed into the explanations proffered by the traditional natural sciences.

Besides admitting that this is a strategy that cannot be carried out now, Dennett also recognizes that the chief difficulty in such a program is in analyzing away the first-level reference to mental representation—and its companion ghost, the homunculus who understands or interprets the representation—which seems deeply embedded in our intentional descriptions. As Dennett puts it, "Psychology *without* homunculi is impossible. But psychology *with* homunculi is doomed to circularity or infinite regress, so psychology is impossible."[35] That is, prima facie it seems impossible to give an account of mental states such as knowing, believing, and imagining without at least implicitly incorporating into the account the need for some system of mental representation. For example, to believe that it will rain tomorrow is to take up a certain attitude (of believing to be true, or of holding that it is most likely to be brought about or some such) to a content (rain tomorrow), and so the content must somehow be represented now in the mind for the attitude in question to govern it or operate over it. If there is a representation (image, picture, code, icon, symbol) of something, then there must be a homunculus in the brain to understand (see, interpret, decipher) it. But if you posit a homunculus in the brain as part of the explanation of how we believe, know, desire, understand, then you will have to posit another smaller homunculus within the brain of the first homunculus as part of the explanation of how the first homunculus understands, interprets, or deciphers the internal representation, and so on ad infinitum.

The way out, says Dennett, is to posit "representations that understand themselves." The best way to achieve this is to replace the homunculi, first with a committee of *"relatively* ignorant, narrow-minded, blind homunculi" and then to replace these committees with subcommittees of "homunculi so stupid (all they have to do is remember whether to say yes or no when asked) that they can be, as one says, 'replaced by a machine.' " In general, then, says Dennett, "one *discharges* fancy homunculi from one's scheme by organising armies of such idiots to do the work."[36] This program, he suggests, can be said to have been begun already by those working in artificial intelligence.[37]

Dennett, however, immediately grants that "one never quite gets *completely* self-understanding representations" and that there is a danger in concluding from the success of current modest exercises in simulating, for example, human dialogue, that there is no reason to believe that in the future one cannot duplicate human understanding in the mechanistic subroutines of a machine.

This belief that the future will teach us how the mental can be reduced to a series of complex mechanistic processes that loop and swirl, interlock and overlap, may turn out to be merely a pious hope. Philosophers have a distinct fondness for the concept "future science" but, given the present paucity of genuine signposts, the present confidence in the future direction of the cognitive cum brain sciences—confidence that the future will show that the journey along the path of reductive analyses will be fruitful—may be misplaced.

Leaving aside the fact that functionalism that seeks such reductions contains a large element of promises rather than settlements, there is a far more fundamental worry about Dennett's particular program of reducing the homunculi to zombies, for this program runs counter to one of his own basic sources of inspiration. In major part the point of putting forward an account of the mental in terms of intentional systems is that it avoids the orthodox physicalist's (or reductive cum eliminative materialist's) difficulties in having to cope with the ever-increasing likelihood that nothing in the brain corresponds to what in ordinary "folk psychology" are called beliefs, desires, and intuitions. To attempt to reduce "folk psychological" items—whether by means of intervening stages of homunculi or not— to the mechanistic acts of zombies is to fall back into the very eliminative materialist's difficulties that the whole functionalist approach was designed to avoid.[38]

If Dennett were to suggest that the subroutines, to which the higher-level homuncular or intentional acts are to be reduced, are not meant to be or to mirror in any way biological processes or routines—though he says quite clearly in a number of places that this is what they are—then one is hard put to see the point of the exercise of reducing higher-level, fictional, computationally convenient routines to lower-level ones. The point may be only to simulate in the machines of artificial intelligence what goes on in a human's head before he or she acts, but this

can have merely tangential usefulness as part of the program—
psychology's program—of explaining the nature of human mentality.
The psychologist, when considering human mentality, wants to know
what it is for a human to believe, desire, and introspect, not how to
build a machine that simulates the intervening stages between input
and output in believing, desiring, and introspecting humans. To find
out about the latter may be instructive about some aspects of the former;
for example, it might inform us whether a particular elaborated model
for human mentality would produce something like human behavior.
It can be used as a test bed for certain aspects of theories of human
mentality.

Even if there was a successful artificial intelligence reduction of abstract intentional states to abstract but nonintentional subroutines, this
would show that there was no a priori barrier to an elimination of the
intentional, but it would not show how to reduce human intentionality
to brain processes or even whether this could be done. So even if it
sees itself as allied to the "artificial intelligence" stance, the "intentional
system" stance is still moving a long way from psychological explanation
(or, for that matter, from traditional philosophy of mind).

*7 Grounds for a Shift from Functionalism in the Explanation of
Introspection*

In general, then, Dennett's "case study" of introspection is revealing
of the difficulties in functionalism in psychological explanation, whether
it is free-standing functionalism (which might usefully be called "artificial intelligence functionalism") or functionalism that seeks reductions
from the intentional to subpersonal, biological, mechanistic subroutines.
In its most abstract, free-standing form, functionalism could be said to
have split off the psychological from the physical. The psychological
or mental "world" would be an invented world more or less wholly
indifferent to the physical world.[39] The pure functionalists would have
invented psychophysical lack of parallelism. In its reductive form, functionalism could be said to have reduced itself to eliminative materialism.
Regarding the functionalist view of introspection, it seems that what
we are presented with will most likely turn out to be not an account
of what humans are doing when they claim to be introspecting but an
account of a mechanistic routine suggesting how a perceiving machine
might monitor its own perceptual and cognitive information.

The worry I have underlined is that a functionalist account of introspection might accord well with what we know of the relevant
human environmental input and behavioral output but give a completely
distorted picture of what is going on when humans introspect. The

dilemma for a functionalist becomes either to allow one's functionalist accounts of mental or "mental" processes such as introspection to be "free-floating" inventions of a plausible cognitive-cum-computational story of what might be happening between input and output but run the risk of their being just that, pure inventions, or to seek to substantiate these inventions by enlisting the help of neurophysiology but thereby to run the risk of their failing to be substantiated in just the way that the reductive cum eliminative materialist accounts failed. Put even more bluntly, it is not clear what, if any, information about the real nature of introspection we are being given in these functionalist accounts, and it is not surprising that the extant versions look surprisingly like reiterations of orthodox but discredited accounts in cognitive cum computational dress. For example, to substitute introspection as "inner data retrieval and then publication" for introspection as "inner inspecting or scanning or recording and then reporting" is to leave the basic, orthodox, core account intact—that in introspection we have direct, immediate, and reportable knowledge of inner states and processes and their information content.

PART III

The Disappearance of Introspection

Chapter 5
The Elusive Nature of Introspection

1 Toward a New Account of Introspection

The points made in this chapter will be ones that I believe should lead us away from thinking of introspection as any sort of second-level process of monitoring, inspecting, registering, or immediate retrieval of data in regard to first-level perceptual or cognitive-appetitive processes. In a sense the most powerful argument to this end is the continual failure of the attempts to construe introspection in this way. It was this that I documented in great detail in the first four chapters. In this chapter I will bring forward considerations that have not been tabled already. Then in the following chapters I will outline the details of what I believe is the correct account of what humans are doing when they claim to be introspecting.

A little more about my general approach may make clearer what I am trying to do in part III. My strategy is not that of most earlier theorists who put forward accounts of introspection chiefly from the motive of showing that some overall position in the mind-body problem or some theory about the correct methodology in psychology could cope with the difficult case of introspective knowledge. The introspectionists certainly made introspection central to the enterprise of psychology; introspection was the method peculiar to psychology because it was thought to be the only one that provided direct access to mental events. There were always keen discussions about the nature of introspection on the part of the introspectionists, though it might be argued that their discussions came to a head only toward the end of the era of introspectionism and by way of defense against the skeptical incursions of the behaviorists. The behaviorists were for dismissing introspection as the method in psychology or even as a very useful method and for dismissing it from the list of appropriate subjects for study by psychologists. They discussed introspection as a defense against the backlash of the outraged introspectionists or to still the nagging suggestion that they should be able to give some explanation, even if it was ultimately an explaining away, of what was going on when ordinary people or at least other psychologists and philosophers claimed to be engaging in a process called "introspection." The reductive and eliminative materialists seemed to be interested in introspection chiefly as an admittedly difficult test case for theories that sought to reduce the mental to physical brain states and processes. Introspection became a chapter in materialist theories of the mind; otherwise it played little part in the discussions of mainstream theoretical psychology and philosophy after behaviorism. Functionalist accounts of the mental treated introspection in much the same way as had the more brutal reductive and eliminative materialists. Introspection was just a useful case for testing the adequacy of the new formulations of the mental. Admittedly an interest in introspection was sometimes a by-product of the growing interest in computer models of mental processes. Some of those engaged in this enterprise realized that sooner or later they would have to build into any adequate model of the mind something that played the role of what is normally labeled "introspection."

Why I think introspection deserves better treatment than it has generally received so far at the hands of philosophers and psychologists may be made clearer by means of a simile. The traditional way of viewing introspection is from the vantage point of a preestablished general methodology or general theory about the nature of the mental. This is a bit like someone first committing herself to conservatism or socialism and then attempting to solve a series of social problems with the at least implicit proviso that the solutions must be consonant with the adopted doctrine. A possible and even likely result of such a policy will be that an acceptable "solution" may bring little benefit to those whose ills are at the center of the problem and should be cause for concern.

Also, although I do not deny that it may be both interesting and useful to construct artificial abstract solutions to the problem of how in an artificial intelligence machine introspection might be accommodated, I am primarily interested in what in fact we humans are doing when we claim to introspect and why. A good model of introspection may be built into an artificial intelligence machine, but this may not at all resemble what is occurring in humans when they claim to be introspecting. This could occur in at least two ways. The first obvious way is that the machine modeling of introspection may be in terms of a current but what turns out subsequently to be a mistaken view of what introspection is. The second is that although the machine model may produce the same introspective output as does an introspecting human and in the light of the same input, and in that sense functionally resemble human introspection, it may go about the intervening tasks in a completely different way from humans. After all, one can go about the same job of distributing an equal number of examination papers to examiners in more than one way. You might pick up the pile and, looking at the scripts in serial order, sort them into pigeon holes set out in alphabetical order, then resort alphabetically (according to the second letter of each surname) each pile appearing in each lettered pigeon hole, then reconstitute the whole pile, and then finally distribute by internal post ten to each marker by apportioning ten to the first marker counting from the paper that comes first in alphabetical order, and so on. Another person, psychologically different, might leave the whole heap where she found them, in the secretaries' office, and tell each examiner to call and take ten papers, counting from the top.

For a variety of reasons I want to proceed on the basis of the available ground-level data—admittedly very thin on the ground—about introspection. I want to start from the ground up and, insofar as this is possible, ignore the mind-body problem and questions of methodology in psychology. As was the case in my critique of past and current theories of introspection, I shall attempt to build up a theory or model of the nature and functioning of what we normally label "introspection" by paying as much attention to data about introspection from normal and abnormal psychology, anthropology, and the brain sciences as to the discussions of philosophers and those engaged in artificial intelligence. The solution I seek to the problem about what we are really doing when we claim to be introspecting will be at the psychological level (at the level of talk about perception, beliefs, memory, imagination), not at the neurophysiological level. Even if I were capable of seeking a solution at the latter level (which I am not) it seems far too early to look for one—and anyway it may be the wrong place to look.

Ideally I would like to approach the subject without any preconceptions so that the nature of introspection will emerge from consideration of all that we know about this curious enterprise. But I suspect that such neutrality is impossible and that the diligent will be able no doubt to discern my unspoken and unnoticed allegiances far better than I can.

2 A Phenomenological Point

The assumptions that have lasted through all the major theories of introspection, and could be said to be more or less an immutable part of our model of the mental, cluster around the claim that to introspect is to look in on inner events, such as perceptions, thoughts, feelings, wishes and wants, imaginings and rememberings, deliberations, and decisions, whether these inner events are construed ultimately as events in the stream of consciousness, internal abbreviated movements in the mechanisms of speech, raw brain processes, or subroutines in the brain described functionally. Introspection has invariably been accepted as being a real act of internal inspection, though currently the looking is more often considered to be a metaphor for some mechanical process of obtaining access to information located internally or to the processing of it, and any reference to the "mind's eye" is always written in quotation marks. Allied to this apparently immutable standpoint is the position that the utterances resulting from introspection are reports in the sense of running commentaries on the internal perceptual and cognitive-cum-appetitive events that are occurring or have just occurred in the brain or mind or both.

If to introspect were in any literal sense to employ an inner sense,[1] then it would have its own phenomenology.[2] Just as the phenomenal experience of tasting is different from the phenomenal experience of touching and, linguistically, this difference provides different sets of unique predicates, so we should expect that if to introspect were to employ an inner sense, then introspecting would involve a sui generis experience with its own phenomenal qualities and would generate its own unique set of predicates when we came to describe these qualities in words. But when we come to describe our alleged introspectings, we do so in terms of what we introspect, not in terms of what it is like to introspect. Any experiential qualities in introspecting seem to be borrowed from the content of introspection. Any experiential qualities in introspecting a patch of blue seem to be borrowed from the first-level experience, which is perceiving the patch of blue.

Even when we introspect with our eyes closed, the result still seems to be much the same phenomenologically. We "see" introspectively our childhood nursery or "hear" grandmother's voice again. When we introspect our thoughts, it is in terms of a language and words. Insofar as they are words, they are words seen or heard, not words introspected. In the next chapter, when I give the positive side of my account of what it is we are really doing when we claim to be introspecting, I shall argue that "introspecting" is intimately tied and in unrecognized ways to perception.

Phenomenologically it seems impossible to detect our introspections. If we cannot do so, who could? At this point it is salutary to remind ourselves that although the failure to discover something is not a demonstration of its nonexistence, no observer of the brain has ever found and few today would want to suggest that there is any special organ of introspection or even any special "introspection center" in the brain.

3 A Hint from Developmental Psychology

Work in developmental psychology about how and when children develop any conception of their having an ability to introspect is not in great abundance. On the other hand, the available research is very suggestive of what introspection is not and of what it might be.

Not merely is it arguable that children are not born with anything that could be construed as a specific physiological basis for any special faculty or sense for internal scanning or monitoring or inspecting, children take a long time to develop any conception at all of introspection. This is in sharp contrast to their swift development of their conception of the ordinary outer senses and their function.

There seems to be a reasonable measure of agreement among developmental psychologists that a child acquires the ability, and some recognition of the ability, to do what goes under the label "introspect"—generally construed in this context as the "awareness and verbalization of one's own thought processes"[3]—somewhere around the age of eight years old.[4] Moreover some seem to conclude from this sort of inquiry that "such work does illustrate the fact that we are not born with some sort of inward eye that informs us about our own mental processes. We learn about these gradually just as we gradually attain a better knowledge of the behavior of things outside us."[5] That is, there is the explicit claim that research in this area should incline us to the view that the learning that takes place in regard to introspection is not in terms of fully developing and maturing a physiological mechanism by means of which we are enabled to look inwardly at mental events or gain access to brain processes. The maturation that occurs is in terms of the child's learning to use already existing abilities in more sophisticated ways. The child learns to analyze its own overt actions and to " 'reconstruct' them on the plane of thought."[6]

The age of "introspection" should not be construed like the age of puberty and the appearance of "introspection" like the appearance of facial hair and deep voice in the male adolescent. The ability to introspect develops in a child in much the same way as does the ability to see and make jokes. The ability to "introspect" is connected with the gradual growth of understanding and is enhanced by the putting of that understanding to work verbally, though I would not want to equate the beginning of the alleged ability to introspect with the beginnings of the ability to talk about what one "introspects," though one gets the impression that this conflation does occur at times in the literature of developmental psychology.[7]

4 A Warning Note from Anthropology

There is some reason to think that we not merely find what we expect to find regarding "introspection" but that we claim the ability to introspect occurrent mental or brain events because it is embedded in our culture that we have the ability to do this. The word "our" should be emphasized. Although it is arguable that the ancient Greeks of fourth and fifth century B.C. Athens did not make such a claim,[8] it seems clear enough that more or less since the time of Augustine[9] Western culture has enshrined the belief that we are able to introspect more or less in the way described by the traditional core or proto-model; we are able to look in on, monitor, or gain access to mental or brain events and then publish the resulting information. There is no such tradition in some other cultures, however. Although it is notoriously difficult for a European to translate and fully comprehend terms in languages that are not based on any of the languages or proto-languages of Europe and although it is acknowledged to be a very slippery inference from what are terms in a language to what are the conceptions in the thinking of those that use the language, and from what is conceived in thought to what exists, it is clear that some cultures have no words that readily translate into our word "introspection" or employ descriptions that could be taken to refer to or circumscribe in any way what we traditionally understand by the process labeled "introspection."

The Balinese, for example, or at least those still untouched by Western culture, seem to have no terminology for a private self with an inner private mental life and so no terminology for introspecting the events of that inner life. In Bali "it is *dramatis personae*, not actors, that endure; indeed, it is *dramatis personae*, not actors, that in the proper sense really exist," though possibly this should be interpreted as not that the Balinese do not introspect but that they try to suppress that side of life in favor of an ideal, stylized life where a person lives out a role assigned by birth and circumstances and that can be sustained only when the sort of individuality nourished by introversion is deliberately squashed.[10] But even so, what was long ago a deliberate act, once it is anchored to what has become a basic attitude in the culture as a whole and become a fixed disposition over many centuries, can become such that the agent could not do otherwise. The Balinese may well be blind to any inner self. There are also grounds for thinking that if they have any conception of introspection at all, the Maori and the Ifaluk of the Pacific regions have at most a very wizened one in comparison with the Western notion.[11] In regard to the Maori, Johansen writes:

> Psychology did not interest the Maori very much. The main clas-
> sification is made according to kind and degree of bodily percep-

tions, through which things are united which to us are quite different, and the word which covers our word "mind" best, viz. *ngakau,* is just expressing a whole ["a total picture of man in a situation"] which is not analysed. . . . Conflicts in the mind, unconscious motives, or the like are never mentioned.[12]

Nicholas Humphrey's claim that "there is, so far as I know, no language in the world which does not have what is deemed to be an appropriate vocabulary for talking about the objects of reflexive consciousness, and there are no people in the world who do not quickly learn to make free use of this vocabulary," is unsupported by what we do know of some non-European cultures.[13] This assertion will probably not lead to many doubts if I add that Humphrey believes that the "gist" of "a remarkable convergence in the accounts which people of all races and all cultures give of what reflexive consciousness reveals to them" is that "in association with my body there exists a spirit, conscious of its own existence and its continuity in time. This is the spirit (mind, soul . . .) which I call 'I.' "[14]

Even if a majority of people in our culture said that they had a strong conviction that they had an ability to introspect in an immediate and noninferential way occurrent mental or brain events, it may only be the case that—and this is a truism—people in Western culture have accepted uncritically their culture's belief that every adult human normally has the ability to introspect according to the traditional protomodel of introspection. I would guess, however, that any poll of the whole population, or of a judiciously selected sample of it, would not reveal a wholesale commitment to a belief in introspection as described traditionally, partly, I suspect, because most people would not even know what was meant by the word "introspection" in the pollster's questions. Generally "introspection" is a term reserved for the debates and theories of philosophers and psychologists. As Ryle put it,

> "Introspection" is a term of art and one for which little use is found in the self-description of untheoretical people. More use is found for the adjective "introspective," which is ordinarily used in an innocuous sense to signify that someone pays more heed than usual to theoretical and practical problems about his own character, abilities, deficiencies and oddities; there is often the extra suggestion that the person is abnormally anxious about these matters.[15]

As Ryle pointed out, it does not follow from the fact that ordinary people do not employ the term "introspection" that they have no alternative "ordinary expressions" or any conception of something that corresponds to the references of this term in technical discourse or any belief in its reality. Equally it does not follow that they hold anything approaching the traditional doctrine as found in philosophy and psychology, for even if ordinary people speak about inner mental events and knowledge of occurrent ones, most likely they have no clear picture at all of what such knowledge consists or of how it has been gained. The existence of the term "introspection" in the academic reaches of our culture, in other words, does not guarantee much.

It is also worth reminding ourselves that psychologists and philosophers came to have a reasonably precise and formal account of what exactly is going on when we claim to be introspecting only when it became important to do so—that is, when it became important, particularly to psychologists, to explain and defend the claim that introspection was the unique method whereby investigators seeking facts about our mental life could gain direct access to mental entities and events. Up to the time of Brentano and Wundt, there existed only a rather amorphous concept of self-reflection. It was when psychology became separate from philosophy and, aspiring to align itself rapidly alongside the traditional natural sciences, set up laboratories and started discussing experimental methods that the details of introspection as we now talk about it came into being.

5 Some Unsettling Suggestions from Experimental Psychology

Although contemporary psychologists, philosophers, brain scientists, and those working in artificial intelligence refer to the "data of introspection" from time to time, a growing body of work in psychology should be unsettling to anyone who still maintains a belief that "introspection" is some kind of direct private access to occurrent mental or brain states or events, which in turn bestows special status, if not unique reliability, on "introspective evidence."

There is, for example, plenty of evidence to show that we report on incoming sensory information and, via "introspection," its use in ensuing deliberations and decisions with unfounded certainty in the reliability of that sort of immediate reporting. Because our ability to attend to what is pouring into our sensory receivers is severely limited, we can concentrate only on very little of it. Often we fail to or are simply unable in principle to concentrate on the salient features, the features that turn out to be the ones influencing our subsequent beliefs and behavior. For example, the following sort of experiment has been performed many times and with many variations.[16] An ambiguous sentence, such as 'The bank was destroyed,' is fed through an earphone at a reasonably loud level into one ear. Another sentence that makes clear which sense of the word "bank" is being referred to—say, a sentence like 'Because the river was in spate'—is fed through an earphone into the other ear at a level of five or ten decibels less. Because of the limitations of attention, one can attend to only the louder, more insistent sentence, 'The bank was destroyed'—that is, attend in the sense of being able subsequently to repeat the sentence. The other sentence, the disambiguating sentence, is unattended in this sense. The subject in the experiment cannot say what is coming in through the so-called unattending ear; the subject cannot even be sure in what language the information was couched or whether it was information. Yet when asked for the meaning of a sentence like 'The bank was destroyed,' subjects invariably interpret it in terms of the information coming through the unattending ear.

The general point is that this experiment is a precise illustration of what happens all the time. We can readily report on what took up our attention when it was on the way in to our head but not on the wealth of unattended information, though this latter may have formed the basis for the cognitive states and acts governing subsequent action. What was attended to may have been only the most insistent as regards attention, not the most important in causal terms. A more homely example would be someone's apparently giving an account of why he did something—say, giving an account of his alleged deliberations, which led to the choice of this toothpaste rather than that one. What made him and most of those others asked choose this toothpaste rather than the other ones on the market researcher's tray might have been because this one was placed on the right. Because English speakers read from left to right and so tend to scan from left to right, whatever is on the far right is seen last and so has a preeminent status in regard to choice. Yet he tells the market researcher that he chose it because its taste had something special to it.[17]

It might turn out that we are remarkably unreliable whenever we give "introspective reports"—no matter how immediate and on the spot—on deliberations that precede choice or action. We come up with the choice or engage in the behavior, and we produce a convincing account or rationale for why we did so, but the superimposed conviction that we have privileged access to the cognitive moves that produced the choice or behavior seems to lack evidence, for the regularities of choice and behavior seem better explained in other ways.

The same may be the case very often with accounts of how we came to remember something. Often we can remember but are at a loss to say why. The sorting, sifting, or shuffling that preceded the recollection seems to be hidden from us.

> If a person is asked, "What is your mother's maiden name?", the
> answer appears swiftly in consciousness. Then if the person is
> asked "How did you come up with that?" he [or she] is usually
> reduced to the inarticulate answer, "I don't know, it just came to
> me".[18]

He cannot say whether he referred to a stored file of family names,
which included an entry for his mother's maiden name, or replayed
in memory an occasion when he saw his mother's maiden name written
on her school diploma, or whether he asked himself the name of his
maternal grandfather. If asked how he recalled his mother's maiden
name, he might well reply in terms of one of these maneuvers. Indeed
some philosophers and psychologists have been so impressed by what
we do not know about our cognitive processes that they have adopted
the startling dictum, "No activity of mind is ever conscious."[19]

When we claim to introspect, the deliberations that precede our
choices and actions, and in general make claims to be privy to our own
cognitive processes, what we seem to be doing is more like adopting
a likely rationale for a person exercising a choice in such a situation
or deciding to act in such circumstances rather than engaging in any
process of observation of internal cognitive events or retrieval of information. It is more like producing a machine simulation of some
cognitive process of Smith's without knowing, or being able to know,
whether it resembles in any way what Smith in fact did in cognitive
terms. Nevertheless clearly such an agreed simulation or shared rationale
is useful if it supports useful predictions. A shared rationale, if it is not
completely arbitrary and if it is based on some sort of evidence, even
if not on direct evidence of internal processes, would enable us and
others to make sense of our behavior and predict its future occurrence
with an accuracy on the positive side of the point where random guessing
would be placed.

Thus when subjects are asked to give an account of the considerations
they tossed about in their mind and influenced them to take the course
of action they in fact took, and when the requests are made within
seconds of their occurrence, they not only give an account, which can
be shown to be at variance with what in fact must have been the
cognitive-appetitive processes behind their behavior but they also give
a remarkably stereotyped account.[20] To take another example, it can
be shown that the likelihood of persons going to the aid of another
person in distress varies more or less inversely according to the number
of other people there are about and in a position to see anything the
persons might do. Yet when such persons are asked for an account of
what went on in their minds before their action or inaction, they make

no mention of the influence of bystanders. The account they give is in terms of the plight of the victim and their own power to lend aid and comfort—that is, in terms of what we would all like to think would be our cognitive (and appetitive) processes on such occasions: processes that make sympathy and altruistic action the prime considerations. The true account of our cognitive processes would probably be in terms of items from the following list: shyness, hesitancy, worry about what others would think, hopes that someone else would make the first move, wonderings if others would see through any attempt to pretend that one did not see or hear the victim or that one had a broken arm, and so on. All in all it is hard to resist the conclusion that frequently we delude ourselves when we purport to give introspective reports on the cognitive processes that precede choice and action and that what we are doing very often is much more like making reference to a stereotype or conventional model of someone's cognitive processes in such situations.

It is also hard to resist seeing the whole unhappy history of intro-spectionism in psychology as pointing toward this conclusion as well. Introspectionism fashioned its own disrepute not only by so multiplying the conditions under which "introspective experiments" could be con-sidered valid and by making them so intricate that the whole routine became bizarre but also because even trained "introspectors" from the same culture could not agree on any results from these "introspective experiments." What agreement there was seemed to go along with previous theoretical agreement or allegiance to some school of intro-spectionist psychology. Wundtians agreed among themselves, as did the followers of Ach and Bühler and the disciples of Titchener, but there was little or no agreement on particular issues that could be sustained across all schools.[21]

6 The Elusive Nature of Introspection

None of these points I have made are knockdown arguments in regard to what I have been calling the orthodox core account or proto-account of introspection that has lasted to the present time. Rather they were brought forward as considerations, based nonetheless on a variety of facts, which may make us conscious of the fragility of our conviction that we have immediate introspective access to the contents and work-ings of our own mind. I doubt whether there is ever a *quod erat dem-onstrandum* or anything of that sort in philosophy of mind or theoretical psychology. What is more likely to happen is a gradual shift in our theoretical picture or model, but even this can have profound and far-reaching effects.

In these considerations, I have alleged that there are hints that introspection, when explained as any form of monitoring, inspecting, scanning, or immediate retrieval of data with respect to cognitive processes, is a myth of our culture, an invention of our "folk psychology." The alleged introspection of perception is another sort of myth, by and large a concoction of psychologists and, especially, philosophers.

Chapter 6
On the Alleged Introspection of Perception

1 Introduction

This chapter is a short, bridging one, though it is not an interlude. Although the case I make in this chapter is one that in the main others have made before, there is a good reason for giving it a brief airing here. The case against introspection in regard to perception needs at least a brief mention so readers will not be distracted by the thought that I have overlooked it. It will allow me to clear the way for my account of what is going on when we claim to be introspecting our cognitive and appetitive acts, for the claim that we can introspect these acts is the core of the orthodox account. In brief the contention of this chapter is that we do not need to postulate introspective apparatus or access in order to make sense of our immediate or more reflective reports on our perceptions. In this context the postulation of introspection is a superfluous fabrication.

2 On the Supposed Introspection of the Products of Perception

It might be argued that there is one sort of mental state or event to which we clearly have introspective access and that nothing I have said so far should or could lead us to be skeptical about this claim. At least, it might be thought, when we report on our feelings, on what we see and taste and smell, especially if we do so after being urged to concentrate our attention, then we are introspectively reporting on the products of an act of perception. We can attend to, focus on, or isolate twinges, patches of blue, tastes of saltiness, and then report what we find when we are so attending to, focusing on, or isolating them.

The theoretical source of this conviction is the view that there are phenomenal sense data that are the immediate products of the exercise of sense perception of any kind. At least from the time of Descartes, some philosophers have suggested that when we employ our senses, the information or data are in the form of an idea, impression, representation, presentation, percept, or sense datum in the mind (or at least our head) to which we have immediate, reportable, privileged access. Indeed we could not know what we are seeing, hearing, or tasting unless we could report on the qualities of these mental artifacts called sense data, for an object thus "interposes its appearance, like a sheet of glass, between itself and the observer."[1] This view has seemed to be particularly compelling when one has, say, visual experiences such as hallucinations, for in such cases one has the sense data without any external object seen; one sees only the sheet of glass. The sense experience is in the mind when one sees a mirage or drug-induced phantasms, and there is no temptation to a naive realism whereby the sensory qualities are held to be in some external object.

A. J. Ayer has suggested that one can quite sensibly hold a sense datum theory without being committed to a further theory that to report on sense data one must "observe" them in any sense. There is no need to argue from 'it now seems to me that I see x' (where x might be, say, shimmering water or a kaleidoscope of flashing lights) to 'there is a seeming-x which I now see' (where the seeming-x is a sense datum). If one does so argue, then one is landed in the absurdity, as Ryle put it, of saying that one sees the look of things or eats nibbles of biscuits.[2] A sense datum theorist need not commit what Ryle called this "logical howler" because he or she can hold that sense data are knowable and so reportable without holding that the knowing and reporting must be in terms of introspection or some other mode of observation of mental items. It could be the case, for example, that our brain is so constructed that when our eyes are focused on a tomato or when we have a hallucination of seeing a tomato that we are moved to believe and able to assert that we are seeing a red patch shaped like a tomato. There need be no question of any internal process of observation of sense data going on; the theory needs only to commit itself to the claim that one is able to report about sense data obtained from the senses.[3] When I say I see a red tomato or an amorphous patch of red, even if this is after a particularly concentrated effort, there is no need to suggest that this report is the result of introspecting some mental state or event characterized as a mental picture or image. The effort of concentration will be in terms of attempting to attend more carefully or to interpret more carefully or else simply to banish distractions.

I doubt if people who are unacquainted with the sense datum theory or cognate theories are tempted to suggest any such thing as that we perceive sense data. After all, we see the red tomato as outside of us, projected in front of our noses, at the point of our twin-eyed focus. We report what we see. The information seems to come from the exercise of the sensory systems plus some interpretation, not from any alleged additional system for inner observation of the products of the first-level sensory systems. This is reflected in ordinary usage, and especially so in the language of seeing and touching. As Ayer puts it,

> And when we come to the most important senses, those of sight and touch, we find that ordinary usage does not provide them with accusatives on the analogy of sound and hearing. One may speak indifferently of hearing a clock or of hearing its tick, but one does not speak of touching the feel of a clock or of seeing its look.[4]

Admittedly feelings in our limbs, rather than feels of objects, seem inner by comparison with sights and sounds, smells and tastes, but they seem inner not in relation to our mental life but in having a location inside our epidermis. On the other hand, we are not even naively tempted to place them in the same "arena" as cognitive and appetitive processes like thoughts, desires, and decisions. They are part of the three-dimensional life of our limbs, head, and torso. I do not think that those untouched by sense datum theories are tempted, say, to talk in terms of introspecting even headaches and a fortiori pains in the leg. It needs an accomplished philosophical askesis or set of spiritual exercises brought about by considerable devotion to the sense datum theory to isolate the pain from a pain in the leg and to contemplate it in the mental arena in our head.

3 On the Supposed Introspection of Perceptual and Cognate Processes

It might be objected that one clear case of introspection—at least in accordance with the traditional proto-model and one that I cannot explain away—is that of attending to one's perceptual processes. To perceive and then attend to one's perceiving are clearly two processes, it might be argued; in general this goes for attending to one's remembering, imagining, thinking, and so on. Furthermore the second meta-process seems to fit the traditional profile of introspecting.

My response is to deny that to attend to a process-as-experienced is a meta-process parasitic on a first-level process or activity. Attention is an adverbial modification of some first-level experience or activity. In short, I would make a Rylean move against such an objection, saying that to perceive a beaker in front of oneself, on the table, and then to attend to one's perceiving of it is not to engage in two processes or activities but to modify one's approach to the one and only activity: that of perceiving. One can perceive the beaker, and then one can do it attentively—that is, with care, banishing distractions, with alertness, concentration, and so on. The same will be true of imagining. One cannot imagine a beaker full of water and then focus on the imagining.

One can focus better only on the beaker, or, more accurately, for there is no internal beaker that one can move around or focus on, one can produce or try to produce a clearer version of seeing a beaker in imagination by, say, producing or trying to produce imagined seeings of the beaker from several angles, and in isolation from any background, and in long focus as well as by magnified details, just as one might do when carefully and attentively inspecting a real beaker.

It might be claimed, however, that I have merely sidestepped the real objection: that even if I perceive a beaker on the table or imagine a beaker on a table, and do so attentively, I can still stand above that activity, so to speak, and be a "spectator" of it. That is, when one has modified the first-level activity, such that one can now say it is done with attention to what one is doing, one can still stand off and attend to this attentive performance.

First, regarding this remolded version of the objection, it must be said that the whole scenario invites considerable doubt as it begins to look as if it will fall into the old introspectionist pitfall in respect of the division of attention. If one is perceiving something attentively and if what can be attended to is severely limited, then it is doubtful that one could engage in any second-order process of attending to it.[5] What one can do is, say, be looking at something and then, only later, realize one is doing so. But realization is not the product of some introspective process but, as the adverbial phrase "only later" suggests, a dawning of knowledge. I might have been staring vacantly at the man's disfigured face and then suddenly know that I am so doing and consider the possible impoliteness and hurtfulness of this. My attention has caught up with the operation of my sensory apparatus. The subliminal becomes conscious. My attention may have been inward, on the recalling of something or with my musings, and then suddenly it shifts outward again. When one is doing something like looking, hearing, or tasting in a conscious or attentive fashion, then ipso facto one has knowledge of so doing, for part of the analysis of such attention, consciousness, or awareness will be that one knows what one is doing and is able to describe it if one has sufficient linguistic competence. To know that one is perceiving, one does not have to engage in some second-order process of inspecting the perceiving.

Another sense of realization is that which applies to such cases as perceiving something—say, a shape moving in the undergrowth dead ahead—and then the sudden conviction that it is a kangaroo. Suddenly one is able to categorize the incoming sensory information in a way that fits with previous knowledge. Perhaps one must first go through some sort of process or processes of sorting, sifting, and testing, and then there is the sudden dawning, the sudden illumination, so that one can produce a label and probably a description of what is going on. One knows.[6]

4 On Being Misled by the Interpretative Nature of Perception

Everything coming into our heads is interpreted in ways that serve our aims where the word "our" has to be interpreted further in terms of our culture. Even what we call perceptual information is far from being the raw sense data the empiricists led us to believe it was. When we report on what we see, for example, we have been led far beyond what is immediately received through our organs of vision. When we see a road as slippery, being slippery is not visual information. The received perceptual information is something like a black, shiny surface. From previous knowledge we "infer" (though not consciously) that shine of that sort, on what we know already from knowledge of perspective and other such theorizing is a road, indicates either water or ice or both, which we know from experience will often make a vehicle traveling on it slip.[7] We cannot but interpret such data because by the time we as persons are able to make use of and talk about them, the data have gone through many stages of filtering, editing, and interpreting. One good reason why this happens is that, if it were not so, we could not cope with all the information coming through our senses. Our eyes are continually gaining information that neither reaches consciousness, nor is ever made use of or even stored, for our eyes pick up peripheral information even when they are focused on something quite definite, like the page in front of me and the words on it. Besides receiving information at both the center and periphery of attention, our eyes continually saccade over objects or pan across the visual field, producing myriad microscopic data about the environment. The brain silently and swiftly sorts and sifts and puts a residue together and—this is important for our present purposes (most often our present or future actions)— "a composite based on information accumulated over a period of time" will usually reach our brains in its deliberations about what to make of what is happening around us and what to do about it now or later.[8] On the other hand most incoming signals will be treated as irrelevant "noise" and be filtered out.

Perceptual signals, as received immediately by the organs of sense, are radically underdetermined. The same signals can often be interpreted in two or more ways. The well-known optical illusions make this fact explicit. For example, the Necker cube (a cube drawn in outline only, on paper—that is, in two dimensions) can always be seen in two ways, where the bottom edge and the square on it are seen as the leading external face of a three-dimensional cube or where the bottom edge and the square on it are seen as the rear internal wall. Then there is the illusion popular in children's books where a drawing of a vase can be seen as two identical profiles facing each other if you look "hard" enough (for many years, what appeared to be Mussolini's profile was a favorite, perhaps because it made an interesting vase).[9]

The conditional clause, 'If you look hard enough,' is not a warning that you need to use the eyes more strenuously but a suggestion that you interpret the raw signals differently.[10] At both the moment when you "see" the picture as twin Mussolinis facing one another in profile and at the moment just before when you "saw" it as a vase, the pattern on the retina caused by light entering the lenses of the eyes and the ensuing electrochemical patterns in the visual cortex are exactly the same.[11] To put this another way, if one could put something like a photographic plate at both the retina and the visual cortex and these plates could be developed after they had received the incoming light signals, then the set of photographs from inside the head of a person who saw a dalmatian dog against a dappled background of trees and pavement would be identical with the set from a person who saw only a meaningless (uninterpretable) dappled pattern, though in fact perceptual information is more like discriminative information than photographic information.

The conditional clause, 'If you look hard enough,' is equally not an invitation to introspect. Even if we did have an introspective apparatus, it would not help us to decide whether we were seeing an abstract dappled pattern, a dalmatian, Mussolini, or a vase. Introspection would be only another meta-look at our first look. An extra "scope," even if it is some sort of microscope or telescope, is not the way to decide on these matters. Once the eyes have done their job, "seeing what is there" is a matter of interpretation, and we are not even aware, most often, of the process of interpreting. We are certainly not aware of the brain's putting bits of information together to form a coherent "picture" of something.

This ability to interpret useful facts from extremely little information is very useful. That it is a hidden process is not a reflection on its importance or usefulness. We estimate distance by means of acquired rules of perspective, for people who have lived all their lives in confined areas, such as dense forests, have no conception of perspective. When taken out for the first time into open country, they wrongly interpret distant human figures as very small people.[12]

My point is that the fact that our alleged introspective reports are highly interpreted versions of incoming sensory signals shows that they cannot be immediate reports on those signals. They are reports at many removes and of a highly interpretive sort. If there was any question of immediate access, it would be to the cognitive processes of editing, sifting, collating, inferring, and in general interpreting. This—the alleged introspection of cognitive processes—will be the matter of the next chapter.

Chapter 7

"Introspection" as the Replay of Perception

---

1 What "Introspection" Is

In parts I and II of this book I cast doubt on the traditional conception of introspection, which underlies both ancient and recent accounts of introspection. In chapter 5 I drew upon a wide variety of data from the behavioral and social sciences in order to point us in a completely different direction. On the other hand I have yet to spell out in detail what I believe humans are doing when they claim to be introspecting. I propose to do so in this chapter. If I wanted an epigraph for this chapter, it could well be the following passage from *Philosophical Investigations*:

> It makes sense to ask: "Do I really love her, or am I only pretending to myself?" and the process of introspection is the calling up of memories; of imagined possible situations, and of the feelings one would have if. . . .[1]

Although I would not want to be so rash as to say how Wittgenstein himself would have interpreted this passage, on one interpretation this passage illustrates what I want to say about introspection: when we "introspect" in order to discover things about our cognitive, appetitive, and affective lives, we engage in a process of perceptual "replay." We "replay" or recreate—at least with "edited highlights" or in "dramatized form"—what we think we said, or would have liked to have said, or did or felt. For example, if we "introspect" in order to discover whether we love someone, we "replay" how we look or reacted and what we said or did (or how we thought we looked or reacted, and what we believed we said or did, or might have or were going to or had it in mind to) when he or she, the beloved, was present or the topic of conversation or when the beloved was noticeably absent. "Introspection" is not a special and privileged executive monitoring process over and above the more plebeian processes of perception, memory, and imagination; it is those processes put to a certain use.

In certain circumstances we may be led into thinking that we are introspecting when we are simply perceiving. When we look at a red tomato or a yellow daffodil and if we are influenced by certain philosophical theories of sense data, we may report our perceptions in terms of seeing round red patches and bell-shaped yellow presentations. But, as we have already seen, this way of talking is misleading or even erroneous.

Leaving this sort of case aside, my central contention is that "introspection" is our employment of perceptual memory and imagination to find out about our motives, thoughts, hopes, desires, and the like by finding out about our published, revealed-in-speech-gesture-expression-and-behavior motives, thoughts, hopes, desires, and so on, for these are all we have conscious access to. From our point of view, what we can experience and directly know about and so use to build up our picture of "mind" is the world-as-perceived and the world-as-processed by the perception-based processes of memory, imagination (and dreaming, daydreaming, hallucination), the rest lies hidden in the brain.

I am suggesting that "to introspect" our cognitive processes is

(1)   to employ perceptual memory and imagination;

(2)   to produce models, which are substitutes for our ignorance of our brain's cognitive life,

(3)   and which take the form of edited, interpreted, or imaginatively reconstructed "replays" of experienced or perceived overt public intelligent performances,

(4)   especially overt intelligent performances employing language, codes or calculi, or significant gesture or expression;

(5)   that is, in particular the "replay" of our own or others' recalled or imagined talk or written performances or communicative expressions,

(6)   which in turn are formed and understood inevitably against the background of a shared, stereotyped, orthodox, culture-based, "folk psychological," intentional account of human mental life,

(7)   such that any creativity or novelty in our "introspective" performances is only so within and against that "folk psychological" background.

2 Copy Theory versus Replay Theory of Imagination

Given this overall picture of what it is that humans are really doing when they claim "to introspect" and given that unmistakably the central part is played by imagination and perceptual memory, it is essential for me to give a clear account of what I mean by imagination and perceptual memory.

It might seem that in attempting to escape the traditional proto-account of introspection and the various versions embodying it, I cannot escape falling back into another Cartesian pitfall: that of depicting the "picturing" of imagination and the "replay" of perceptual memory as a process of "picturing" or "imaging," which in some literal sense produces film that can be played back. Ryle, as one might expect, was scathing about this part of the Cartesian myth:

> If a person says that he is picturing his nursery, we are tempted to construe his remark to mean that he is somehow contemplating, not his nursery, but another visible object, namely a picture of his nursery, only not a photograph or an oil painting, but some counterpart to a photograph, one made of a different sort of stuff. Moreover, this paperless picture . . . [is] in a gallery which only he can visit. And then we are inclined to say that the picture . . . must be in his mind, and that the "eyes" with which he contemplates it are . . . his mind's eyes.[2]

Ryle depicts the Cartesian view of imagination as a copy theory of imagination. Thus to fancy or imagine one sees one's nursery is to see a real mental image copy or attempted copy of one's nursery. To see a unicorn is to see a mental image labeled 'unicorn,' which happens not to copy anything in the world. As Ryle points out, the copy theory quickly lands itself in a mess. While it may seem sensible to describe visual imaging as if it were a process of looking at a likeness or copy of what one sees in perception, it is nonsense to give an account of smelling an acrid, smokey smell in imagination in terms of an inner smelling of a copy of a smell of burning, for a copy of a smell or a copy smelling can be only another smell or smelling. We can make sense of visual copies of things—that is, the reduction of three-dimensional views to, say, a two-dimensional representation of those views, but how could one have a copy of a real smell in different dimensions or whatever category is appropriate to smells? One could not distinguish between smelling and "smelling" smoke in imagination if the copy theory were true. The same, Ryle avers, is true of "a taste and a likeness of a taste, a tickle and a dummy-tickle."[3]

I do not want to support a Cartesian theory of imagination or visual (or in general perceptual) memory, nor would I want to endorse any version of a copy theory of either (though I do not think that the copy theory is quite as weak and forlorn as Ryle makes out).[4] The theory I would advocate might best be called a reactivation or replay theory.[5] This theory holds that neither imagination nor memory is involved in producing internal copies of reality but is involved in producing a reactivation or replay of sorts of something that occurred in ordinary perception. There will be times when one will mistake the reactivation in imagination or perceptual memory for the real thing; that is, one will confuse the causal sequences, believing that, say, a smell of burning in one's imagination or dream is caused by a real fire in the house. According to a replay or reactivation theory my smelling a slipper burning by the fire in imagination involves a replay or part replay of the experience of smelling a real burning slipper in front of a real fire with one's own nose except that the causal sequence is different. There is in fact no burning slipper and no fire, and one probably does not need to use one's nose. Whatever are the brain processes that are the end product of receiving signals through the olfactory nerve endings in the nasal cavities from a burning slipper and are the basis of the experience of smelling a burning slipper, in imagination or perceptual memory they are reactivated by some purely internal causal sequence. The original experience left some trace or residue, which was stored in some form and is now reactivated to produce a replay. The replay is not a copy of the original experience; it is having the original experience again, at least in its essentials or else in a form edited to suit one's present purposes. A copy is often just a simulacrum in different materials and in dimensions different from the original. A replay or reactivation, on the other hand, is the regeneration of what went before, albeit in edited or interpreted form at times (perhaps most times). One does not visually imagine or recall in two dimensions what one might have seen or has seen in three dimensions in perception. One imagines in just the same terms as one sees.

One of Ryle's former pupils, Daniel Dennett, has put forward another argument against the mental image theory or in general an image account of dreaming and imagination:

> Consider the Tiger and his Stripes. I can dream, imagine or see a striped tiger, but must the tiger I experience have a particular number of stripes? If seeing or imagining is having a mental image, then the image of the tiger *must*—obeying the rules of images in general—reveal a definite number of stripes showing and one should be able to pin this down with such questions as "more than ten?", "less than twenty?". . . . Of course in the case of actually seeing a tiger, it will often be possible to corner the tiger and count

his stripes, but then one is counting real tiger stripes, not stripes on a mental image.[6]

The implication is that one cannot count the stipes on an imagined tiger, so imagination and dreaming cannot involve images.

The usual reply to this argument of Dennett is that one cannot count the stripes on an imagined tiger not because an imagined tiger is not really an image but because it is a poor, indistinct image. Alastair Hannay, for example, suggests that counting stripes is impossible because an imagined tiger is "fluttering, febrile, vanishing," "evanescent," "vague," and "fleeting."[7] J. A. Fodor argues for the same conclusion because an imagined tiger is "labile," "blurred," and there are "many visual properties which would not be pictured."[8]

If one is a reactivation or replay theorist in regard to imagination (and perceptual memory and dreaming), however, there is a much more convincing reply to Dennett. It would follow from a reactivation or replay theory that one cannot be more sophisticated in imagination than one can be in perception. Thus visual imagining will follow in the footsteps of visual perception just as in general imagination is parasitic on perception. If one realizes this, then one can count stripes on imagined tigers, and there is no need to take refuge in some alleged inability owing to the blurred nature of the "images" of imagination.

The reactivation or replay theory need only say that whatever are the visual qualities of ordinary perception, then these are—in some way as yet unknown—shared by visual imagination. If we look at how we count stripes on real tigers, we will realize how it must be done in imagination. When we have steadied the tiger with an anaesthetizing dart or with a hefty meal and decided on a procedure for individuating stripes, we can set about counting the stripes. Let us suppose that the tiger has 273 stripes. We cannot see, much less count, 273 stripes or 273 anything else in one go. We cannot focus on the 273 stripes as stripes all in one go. The result would be a blurred blob of stripiness before the eyes. What one does is scan slowly up the hind legs, focusing on individual stripes as we go, then along the sides, and so on. Perhaps the bravest among us might stick out a finger to help the process.

In ordinary perception, counting stripes will involve a large number of focused perceptions—273 if we take each stripe singly (fewer if we feel we can take them in twos, threes, and so on). In imagination we can expect no better than what is possible in perception, for it is sensible to suppose that whatever the pictorial or imagelike nature of imagination, it is pictorial or imagelike insofar as it is based in some way on ordinary perception. To count stripes in imagination will involve a series of images of single stripes (perhaps with our finger pictured as picking out the stripes), repeated 273 times. That is how to count stripes in imagination because that is the only way we can count them in ordinary perception.

To demand of imagination that the one imagining be able to hold steady the "picture," which is an imagined tiger, and then run a finger along the body of the pictured tiger, and thereby count the stripes, is to misunderstand not merely the nature of imagination (and dreaming and perceptual memory) and the nature of perception but also the intimate relation between them.[9]

3 Experimental Psychology and the Replay Theory of Imagination

A wealth of more specialized data from experimental psychology seems to lend considerable positive support to a reactivation or replay theory of imagination. Early in this century C. W. Perky, whose work remains relevant, conducted experiments in which his subjects were asked to sit down facing a wall made of ground glass and to visualize various objects, such as a tomato, a book, and a leaf.[10] Then, unknown to the subjects, Perky projected an image of the visualized object on to the ground-glass wall. His subjects were not aware of the projected images on the glass wall (unless the projector wobbled) and believed that these images were the images of their own imagination. When questioned about the precise color or shape of the object in his or her imagination, a subject invariably answered in terms of the images Perky had projected. Perky's subjects clearly mistook real images for the "images" of imagination, and so equally clearly there are grounds for believing that there is an intimate relation between the two.

More recently Roger Shepard found that to accomplish a task such as finding the number of rooms in one's house, subjects progressed slowly from room to room in imagination in some sort of replay of touring the inside of their house, or else they journeyed in imagination (strictly speaking there should also be a reference here to visual memory) around the outside of the house.[11] Then there are the by now well-known "mental rotation" experiments. The task given the subjects is to try to decide whether illustrations, each depicting a similar three-dimensional object but from a different angle, are of exactly the same object. "Subjects claimed that to make the required comparison they first had to imagine one object as rotated into the same orientation as the other and that they could carry out this 'mental rotation' at no greater than a certain limiting rate."[12] That is, the "mental rotation" takes time (and the time taken varies directly with the amount of angular rotation to be performed), and you cannot go too fast, which is what happens in the actual manipulation of three-dimensional objects when you try to see if they match up.

Some of the most suggestive experiments in this area are those devised by Alfred Binet, the inventor of intelligence testing.[13] The experiments concern what is called a letter square, such as, for example, a card containing the following letters:

m   t   s   n

g   e   x   o

d   c   r   h

l   a   f   y

Subjects in the experiment look at and memorize the letters; then the card is removed or covered. They are then asked to visualize the card and read off as many letters as they can. A subject invariably does so by reading from left to right along each line and line by line from top to bottom. If a subject is asked to visualize the whole letter square and then read off the right-hand column from top to bottom, usually he or she cannot do so unless each line is first rehearsed from left to right, the last letter in each line memorized, and then the remembered last letters recalled in descending order. It is even more difficult to read off the diagonal series of letters, say, from lower right to top left.

The suggestion is that in visual memory or imagination, one does not form anything like a static picture; rather one rehearses, reactivates, or replays the moves one made with one's eyes (and head and perhaps whole body at times) when one first saw and tried to record the letter square. Visual memory and imagination are the replay of perception. We can do in visual memory and imagination only what we have done (at least in some partial way) in perception.

A much simpler illustration of this point can be produced by asking someone to imagine the word "Watergate" and then asking him or her to use the "image" to spell the word backward. This task is not easy and is certainly not a matter of just reading the letters in reverse order as if they were written on some inner mental blackboard. The difficulty is increased, and the point made more vividly, if a relatively long word like "depredations" or a relatively unfamiliar word like "charivari" is used. To take the example of "depradations," if one is to spell it backward using only imagination and visual memory, then one has to engage in special maneuvers. One way is to break the word up into syllables and visualize the last syllable (or segment of two syllables) in such a way that it can be "seen" whole and then read off in reverse; then one takes a penultimate syllable (or segment) and does the same, and so on.

Chess is another favorite area for experiments of this sort because it is claimed that part of the armory of a good chess player, and that which enables him or her to play blindfold chess while an average player cannot, includes the ability to visualize the path of a chess piece in order to "see" what lies in the path and to store a wealth of complicated patterns of moves in memory in visual form. It is suggested that in chess, reflection on past or future strategy is done in great measure (though not entirely) in terms of visual images.[14]

From the point of view of the reactivation or replay theory of imagination, dreaming, and perceptual memory, a more interesting development is a series of experiments relating to dreams. Using rapid eye movements as the indicator of the time when the subjects were dreaming, the experimenters kept waking up subjects in the middle of dreams and getting them to relate their dreams on the spot while they were still fresh. Then the experimenters matched recordings of the eye movements with the dream reports to see if there was any relation between the two.

> Of course this was not possible in every case. (Indeed, we can be fairly sure that many of the eye movements of sleep have no visual significance; similar motions occur in the sleep of newborn babies, decorticated cats and congenitally blind adults.) Nevertheless, there was appreciably more correspondence between the two kinds of record than could be attributed to chance. The parallel between the eye movements of the dreamer and the content of the dream was sometimes striking. In one case five distinct upward deflections of the eyes were recorded just before the subject awoke and reported a dream of climbing five steps.[15]

None of this demonstrates that there are mental images of a Cartesian sort, but the accumulating evidence points to the fact that whatever is the nature of the visual imagery of imagination, dreaming, and perceptual memory, it is intimately connected with seeing, for it is derived from visual perception in the sense that it uses some of the same mechanisms, draws on visual experience for its content, and shares at least some of the essential "pictorial" and "dimensional" qualities of seeing and dealing with real objects and events in the world.[16]

4 Neo-Hobbesean Nature of This Replay Theory of Imagination

I do not think it is too farfetched to label this replay or reactivation account of imagination "neo-Hobbesean." It is certainly quite remarkable, at least with hindsight, to see the extent to which Hobbes anticipated this account of imagination. Leaving aside his understandable seventeenth-century commitment to a mechanistic view of the working of the brain (he believed that the brain worked entirely by means of pressures and counterpressures generated mainly in the sensory systems and terminating in the nerves and fluids of the brain itself), Hobbes construed imagination as clearly parasitic on sensation. As he put it so vividly and stylishly,

> And as wee see in the water, though the wind cease, the waves give not over rowling for a long time after; so also it happeneth in that motion, which is made in the internall parts of a man, then, when he sees, Dreams &c. For after the object is removed, or the eye shut, wee still retain an image of the thing seen, though more obscure than when we see it. And this is it, the Latines call *Imagination*, from the image made in seeing; and apply the same, though improperly, to all the other senses. But the Greeks call it *Fancy*; which signifies *apparence*, and is as proper to one sense, as to another. IMAGINATION therefore is nothing but *decaying sense*; and is found in men, and many other living Creatures, as well sleeping, as waking.[17]

Hobbes went on to explain dreaming as just a version of imagination that occurs while we are sleeping, caused by the agitation of some "inward parts of a man's body."[18] Memory is just a case of imagination when the imagining is compared with the sensations from which the imaginative experience originated in such a way that one can date and give a location to the imagining in terms of when and where the original sensation occurred.[19]

5 Memory and "Introspection"

When discussing memory in connection with introspection, I may have given the impression that all remembering is of this perceptual sort. In fact my point is that some experiences that have been interpreted as cases of "introspection"—cases such as "introspecting" one's childhood nursery, or "introspecting" in order to count the number of rooms or windows in one's house, or "introspecting" how one did a subtraction sum—are more plausibly and simply explained in terms of perceptual memory plus imagination. I would not want to say that all memory is of a perceptual kind, for we have memories that may have little or nothing to do with perception and so are not candidates for what we might be doing when we claim to be "introspecting." For example, our memory for skills and bodily movements may not involve anything of a perceptual nature, though the matter is not as simple as it might first appear. Remembering how to ride a bike, drive a car, or stand on one's head after many years of not performing these feats does not seem to be a matter of perceptual memory, at least prima facie. The matter is complicated by the possibility that these feats or skills are recalled, at least in part, by a memory for patterns of, in general, kinesthetic sensations and, in particular, proprioceptive stimulation. But it could be that all that occurs is the reactivation of some embedded disposition to balance oneself in certain ways, engage in certain manipulative performances, or in general engage in certain subconscious routines. The trick in recalling might be in somehow triggering or reactivating these routines, and that is all. Once the routine is begun, it continues along well-worn tracks.

In fact a less contested example of nonperceptual memory might be a case where the triggering of a routine or disposition to engage in some performance seems to be the most obvious candidate for what is going on in such cases. Certainly cases of people remembering a poem from schooldays may be more associated with getting going some embedded rhythm for the reason that if they try to think about it or stop midway, they are unable to continue. But even with this sort of case, it could turn out that the rhythm is maintained in some way as yet unknown in terms of heard rhythms and so is connected somehow with having heard oneself learn the poem by recitation out loud when a child. Perhaps the best sorts of examples of nonperceptual memory are cases like those of remembering the answer to a question. Remembering the capital of Argentina may be more like an instantaneous reflex response to an appropriate cue rather than any response involving any sort of replay of the seen or heard words "Buenos Aires," though even here it is hard to be sure.

Finally the memory in regard to introspection is most likely to be long-term or "storage" memory rather than short-term or "buffer" memory, for the latter seems to have a life span of only seconds. In the literature on this topic, the most common example of short-term memory is the following. When we look up an unfamiliar number in the telephone book, we retain it for the period it takes to dial the whole number; if the line is engaged or we get cut off, we have to look up the number again in order to redial. To store for a long period something as complex as a series of random numbers in correct sequence, we need to rehearse the number a few times by scanning it with our eyes or by saying it over to ourselves.[20]

Another point to remember in connection with memory, and in particular perceptual memory, is that it will deliver interpreted, reconstructed, or edited versions of original perceptions. For example, if you set yourself to recall your having a bath last night, you might recall this in terms of a replay of yourself sitting in the bath reading *Farewell,*

My Lovely. The "image" you have might be of a person seen from either the back or the front, sitting chest deep in water in a pink bath, and holding the Penguin edition of the book. But in fact we never see ourselves like this unless we have a large, suitably positioned mirror or set of mirrors in the bathroom. What we do most likely is something more like superimposing a "picture" of our faces on to general "snapshots" of persons sitting and reading in the bath.

6 Perceptual Memory and Imagination in the Service of "Introspection"

As we have seen when critically examining the transformation in the accounts or models of "introspection" from the psychological introspectionists to the philosophical functional physicalists, theorizing about what we call "introspection" can lead to bizarre solutions. "Introspecting" one's memory of one's nursery, one's motives, or one's engaging in mental arithmetic has been variously interpreted as observing an internal stream of consciousness, as making inferences from the ordinary observation of ordinary overt behavior or receiving stimulation from inner miniature behavior, as brain scanning, and as engaging in a software routine whereby one gains information from the brain's short-term data banks. In a way they are all fantastic and incredible suggestions brought about by assuming that "introspection" is a metaprocess that monitors first-level occurrences of perception, memory, imagination, thinking, and so on. It has been assumed that it looks down on to and reports about these first-level occurrences, so that in turn it must itself be an occurrence, a mental or brain operation, which is separate from these first-level occurrences. But if the assumption that "introspection" is at a different level from all these other activities is rejected and also the assumption that "introspection" involves some sort of process of monitoring, scanning, or immediate retrieval of data, then the possibility of a quite different and altogether less fantastic solution is available and one that does not stray outside the uncontentious levels of the perceptual and cognitive.

I am suggesting that if we were to make a survey of human perceptual and cognitive processes, we should consider the first level to be perception—that is, all the various avenues for gaining perceptual information and, when they occur, perceptual experiences. We should not forget that a lot of perceptual data never reach the level of attention and so never become experiences; maybe even the majority of them never do. Then, more or less at the same level, there are the processes parasitic on perception—perceptual memory and imagination—which are experiential in character.

But arguably at least as important from the point of view of the life of the human organism are what in "folk psychology" are called the cognitive processes (for convenience I will use this term to cover the cognate appetitive processes as well) of deliberating, desiring, choosing, planning, intending, and so on. The actual processes underlying our "folk psychological" talk of cognitive processes (or for that matter our more sophisticated functional or "information processing" talk of the same), however, lie hidden from our experience permanently and take place unmolested in the labyrinth of the brain. Unless the brain sciences enlighten us, they remain a mystery to us.

Regarding the relation between perceptual and cognitive processes, the analogy is less that of the tip and body of an iceberg than of a tuberous plant where the stem and leaves are visible above the ground and gather the light and air while the real business of feeding and growth takes place underground in the tuber and root system. But in the plant, some processing does take place in the stem and leaves, part of the important process of photosynthesis and other cognate processes. The equivalents to these processes in the human organism are, I suggest, perceptual memory and imagination. Like the cognitive processes, they are dependent on perception and in that sense second level, but unlike the cognitive processes they are at least partly "above ground" or experiential and in that sense on a par with perceptual experiences. Moreover they are perceptual in character when and insofar as they are experiential.

The solution I am putting forward is that perception is the first and most important level in the account of "introspection" (though not necessarily most important from the point of view of the human organism). Part of that level are the processes symbiotic with perception—perceptual memory and imagination—which involve editing, interpreting, elaborating, filtering, constructing, reconstructing, concocting, and then storing "artifacts" made out of perceptual material. "Introspection" is to be found at this level. Leaving aside the alleged cases of introspecting our perceptions or sensations, which have already been dealt with, "introspection" is to be explained in terms of operations by perceptual memory and imagination when their operations are at the level of conscious attention. To "introspect" our cognitive processes is to model—by means of perceptual memory and imagination or, in general, perceptual "replay" in edited and interpreted and elaborated form—the hidden cognitive life of our brain in terms of our nonhidden overt intelligent acts. To "introspect" is to use the first level in its experiential mode to model the second level, which never reaches experience.

The traditional proto-model of introspection that has lasted through the ages is dual leveled in that it posits a special act of inner perception, scanning, or retrieval in regard to a first level of inner processes in the brain or mind or consciousness. This new model is dual in a very different way. It describes the perceptual level (albeit as perceptual memory and imagination) as the model maker in respect of the hidden second level. The first level does not monitor in any way the second level, for it has no access to it; instead, in its acknowledged ignorance, it substitutes a working model or dynamic picture for what it cannot know first hand. We might think that we are catching ourselves monitoring, inspecting, scanning our acts of thinking, hoping, deciding, loving, or needing when in fact all that we are doing is replaying internally to ourselves or imaginatively constructing for ourselves a model version made out of overt behavior, gesture, and expression that we describe in our "folk psychology" as thinking, hoping, deciding, loving, and needing.

7 "Introspection" and "Folk Psychology"

Many cases of "introspection" will be relatively straightforward "replays" of "static" perceptions or of perceived performances, operations, or episodes. When we "introspect" what we remember of our nursery, the "replay" is likely to be simple and clear-cut. We simply "replay" an edited or, if necessary, an elaborated version of what we believe we saw in our childhood.

Even the "introspection" of certain cognitive processes or episodes will be relatively straightforward. When we "introspect" our doing of mental arithmetic, what we are doing is to "replay" a tidied-up, reconstructed, or more likely creatively constructed, "edited highlights" version of some of our or others' overt arithmetical performances in speech, in writing, on a blackboard, or printed in a book. It is a reconstruction of what we or someone else has done, or an invention of what we believe or surmise we or someone else would do if asked, and so on.

But the matter is more complicated. Most often mental arithmetic itself is such a "replay." It is doing arithmetic in a quick, neat, and "edited" way through perceptual memory and imagination. That is what the teacher was trying to teach us, to do the sums "in our head" (in our imagination) using the methods she teaches out loud or on the blackboard (that is, with the help of perceptual memory). "Introspecting" our doing of mental arithmetic will be a case of "play it again, Sam" or a "replay" of a "replay."

On the other hand, the "introspection" of other cognitive processes will be far from straightforward. The "introspectively discovered" versions of cognitive acts such as those of deliberating, finding out one's motive, producing an intention, coming to a decision, weighing up reasons, discovering needs, wants, or wishes, planning action, ordering our lives, and so on will often be highly elaborated. They also will be highly stereotyped because "deliberation," "motivation," "intention," "decision," "reason," "desire," and "action" are highly intentional "folk psychological" terms; they are far removed from being just labels for relatively simply perceivable scenarios, behavioral episodes, or events in the way that one's "pictures" of one's nursery or one's doing of arithmetic in one's head are. To impute a reason or intention to someone is to interpret the perceivable according to a quite elaborate "folk psychology." Intentions, decisions, plans, wants, and so on are at the highly interpreted and abstracted level of talk about behavior not at the simple level of description of perceived or perceivable episodes of behavior. "Folk psychology" is the web of intentional concepts—such as belief, desire, intention, decision, plan, deliberation—by means of which we explain our own or others' behavior. We "picture" our behavior in "folk psychology" as "launched" by "inner mental items" such as beliefs about our immediate environment, long- or short-term goals, perhaps values, which in turn generate behavior by the "propulsions" of wants, desires, needs, or wishes. This is the merest outline. The scene is also peopled by reasons, proposals, presumptions, fears, doubts, guesses, forecasts, hopes, insights, inspirations, and their kin.

As soon as our "introspecting," or anything else for that matter, involves this web of intentional concepts, it is also inevitably involved in a certain stereotyped culture-based outlook. Thus our "introspection" of our motives, desires, deliberations, plans, decisions, or intentions will be colored by and adapted from our own particular culture's "rough-and-ready" view of the mind and its operations. In that respect our "introspections" will employ "processes" and reveal "processes" borrowed from this general "folk psychological" viewpoint and not differ very much from everyone else's "introspections," for everyone else will borrow in much the same way from much the same source and with much the same expectations in regard to the "data of introspection." In a culture with a highly developed and centralized education system, common language, readily accessible store of knowledge and speculation, and constant widespread social intercourse, this "folk psychological" viewpoint will be continually buttressed by the fact that we learn much the same accounts, methods, procedures, and explanations in regard to anything of a cognitive sort.

There is an important caveat here. Although all of us, or most of us, produce much the same sort of "introspective" accounts in the sense described, I doubt whether there is good reason to claim that we all subscribe in any literal sense to a Grand Meta-Model of Our Cognitive Life. Certainly when they engage in professional analyses, philosophers and psychologists can extract from a scrutiny of our "introspective" claims and, in general, our cognitive accounts and explanations something they call "folk psychology." But I doubt whether ordinary folk produce such a synthesis. Why should they want to do so? To put this another way, the concept of "folk psychology" is itself a useful invention. It is useful in theorizing about the status of our ordinary accounts of our cognitive life. In particular it is a useful way of stressing that in Western culture (and probably in other cultures) there is a more or less shared view of the nature of mind and mental operations, and this view is stereotyped and by and large an orthodox, conservative concoction that does not easily change. Further this meta-view of the nature of "folk psychology" escapes our notice for the most part. Nevertheless, in a way and to a degree that is largely unrealized, "folk psychology" dictates our accounts of our cognitive life, including the "data of introspection."

There is another important caveat to be tabled here. I am not suggesting that all our thoughts, desires, motives, deliberations, decisions, intentions, and so on are stereotyped. They are not; otherwise nothing novel would ever be produced. There could be no science or poetry or philosophy worth the having. What I am suggesting is that when we claim to introspect the steps, moves, processes, methods, and means by which we produce the novel theory or poem or conclusion, by and large we give a stereotyped "folk psychological" account of how we produced the theory, poem, or conclusion. How could it be otherwise, for we do not know how our brain did the job. We have merely learned how to produce the "folk psychological" account or some more rigorous, amended, academic version of it.

This is still not the whole story. Within the confines of our "folk psychological" or cognate account of the workings of our mind, there is still room for novelty of explanation, model, theory, or thesis. Presumably that is what most "insights" in philosophy of mind and psychology are. Yet in a real sense, even when a novel explanation or theory about the workings of mind is produced, it is novel only when seen against the background of the existing orthodox, stereotyped, culture-based, "hand-me-down" account, whether couched in naive or sophisticated terms. Further it is built on the existing orthodox model or models. It is novel against that background and in that connected-to-the-background sense. It is novel insofar as someone conversant with the culture's view of the mental has then gone on to produce an original account of some aspect of the mind within that broad cultural viewpoint.

I should make it clear that I am not advocating some sort of epiphenomenal account whereby our "introspective" and "folk psychological" rationalizations are produced in perceptual memory and imagination in such a way that they have and can have no influence whatsoever on our behavior. Certainly I do want to suggest that often our "introspective" reports are concocted post factum and so could not have had any influence on the actions of which they are rationalizations. Moreover if the causal antecedents of the actions in question were entirely at the level of hidden brain processing, then the invented "folk psychological" and "introspected" account of these causal antecedents must be pure invention, albeit useful for our "folk psychological" understanding and explanation of action.

At other times, however, our "introspections" (our "replays" in perceptual memory and imagination) will be the direct cause of behavior. For if we allow that perception can lead to behavior, and if (as I have argued) "introspections" are just the employment of perceptual memory and imagination in various ways, and if (as I have also argued) perceptual memory and imagination are intimately linked with perception, then we should allow that our "introspections" can lead to behavior.

To take a simple example first—where the "replay" in question is straightforward and has little or no connection with the elaborations of "folk psychology"—our doing of mental arithmetic by employing perceptual memory and imagination may lead (causally lead) to our producing the verbal behavior "The answer is so and so." In parallel fashion, our "introspected" view of ourselves—that is, our elaborated "folk psychological" model of ourselves—will lead very often to behavior, verbal and otherwise. If I view myself as liberal, high-minded, and just, I might go around saying so either directly or in roundabout ways, or I might give money to various liberal causes, or give opinions which I think of as liberal, high-minded, and just, on a variety of public issues.

8 "Introspective Reports"

The old and not-so-old orthodox accounts of introspection hold that to report on what we have introspected is to give an "eyewitness" account of items floating by in the stream of consciousness, or to make available the results of some inner mechanism that scans the brain or registers patterns of proprioceptive stimulation in regard to the muscles of speech, or to print out what is in the "out" tray of some device for gaining immediate access to information about inner perceptual and cognitive processes, or merely to report about our own behavior in the mistaken belief that we are reporting on inner events. According to my theory, "introspective reports" are inner, and they are reports, but they are not reports that result from internal acts of scrutiny of any sort. The matter is much more complicated than that, for in certain respects the account will vary according to what is being "introspected."

I have already argued that there is no need to posit any process over and above our perceiving when giving an account of "introspecting" our sensations or perceptions. "Introspecting" them is just perceiving attentively and realizing the nature of what we are perceiving. There is no need to posit anything in the nature of a positive sense datum that has to be separately "introspected" on each occasion. In this case, reporting on one's "introspections" will simply be reporting on what one is seeing, hearing, tasting, touching, or feeling or of how one feels (how one's body feels to oneself).

The second sort of "introspective report" is not quite so simple. I refer to "introspective reports" on, for example, one's "introspecting" what one's childhood nursery was like or one's doing of mental arithmetic. Since I explained both of these cases of "introspection" as comparatively simple "replays" of overt public episodes, then the reporting of those perceptual "replays" will be as straightforward as the reporting of the perceptions of which they are "replays." I believe that this is one of the strengths of this "replay" theory of "introspection": it rides on the back of perception. If I can immediately report on what I see and hear and so on and if there is no need to posit second-level monitoring, scanning, or scrutinizing processes in order to achieve this, why should we not grant that I can immediately, without use or need of second-level devices, report on the perceptual "replays" of perceptual memory and imagination? The point of my giving such a lengthy account of perceptual memory and imagination was to establish how intimately connected with perception they are. It was to establish that they are really just perception in another mode. Why should we suddenly be led into thinking that imagining our nursery or engaging in mental arithmetic will need to be separately scrutinized by a special internal scanner or scope before we can "introspectively" say anything about it?

If it is agreed that we can report immediately—without special intervening mind or brain apparatus—on our seeings, hearings, and so on, then it would seem to follow that we can immediately report, again without intervening apparatus, on its "blood relations" our perceptual recallings and imaginings. I do not want to deny that there might be a mystery about how we report on what is in front of our eyes or nose—I await the details from neurophysiology as eagerly as the next person—I am just saying that, however we do it, the achievement will be much the same in respect of our reporting on our perceptual recallings and imaginings. On the other hand, I want to deny that in either case there is theoretical pressure or need to believe in that Loch Ness Monster of Philosophy of Mind, a faculty or facility or mechanism or device for introspecting.

This "package deal" can be carried further to the case of "introspecting" what in our "folk psychology" we call the cognitive acts of our mind, such as our deliberating, planning, reasoning, intending, deciding, inferring, composing, wishing, hoping, wanting, and so on. Insofar as we "introspect" these, we have engaged in producing internally a "folk psychological" model of these acts that is in the form of perceptual "replays." These "replays," as we have seen, are highly elaborated or edited, faithfully recorded or wholly invented, versions of our public perceived versions of cognitive acts. What will have been perceived and will be the perceptual basis for the modeling will be spoken or written "folk psychological" comment on matters mental or episodes of intelligent behavior, gesture, or expression, or some complex amalgam of some or all of these. But abstracting from the immense complexity of these individual pieces and how they come to play their part, the fact remains (at least according to my theory) that at the heart of this form of "introspecting" is once again perceptual "replay." Once again reporting in the sense of giving a "running commentary" on this "replay" will be direct and immediate and, more important, without need for postulating introspective apparatus.

This last account, however, has another level to it. When I "introspect" my so-called cognitive episodes—say, in order to find out whether I love someone, or what my motive was in telling such a lie, or whether I really believe in God, or why I feel that way about her—I may well engage in perceptual "replay" of a quite elaborate kind. I may do this in order to form a "picture" of my relationship with someone or my attitude to something. On the other hand I might report, to myself or someone else, in quite a summary way. I might say merely, "Yes, of course, I do love her" or "Well, I suppose I must have been jealous." Here I am making a final judgment by means of my "introspective replays," not giving a blow-for-blow account of them.

9 Corrigibility of "Introspective Reports"

While the reporting in "introspective reports" goes on in much the same way in most cases of "introspection," these reports will be corrigible in importantly different ways. If I "introspect" my imagining my childhood nursery, then what I do on my account is to "replay" edited, elaborated, or wholly concocted versions of what I think I recall of what I saw in my childhood. This being so, I could be wrong about my childhood nursery and be corrected on this matter by someone with a better memory than I or by reference to a photograph or contemporary record. On the other hand, no one could correct me about my "replay" of my childhood nursery, for only I have access to my memory, even if it is mistaken, and only I have access to my imaginings, even if they are entirely fanciful when I believe that they are not. So in regard to this sort of "introspection," we have privileged and incorrigible access of a certain sort.

It is a thin sort of privilege, however. It does not give us knowledge of any aspect of the nature of our cognitive life that is unavailable to others or any aspect of the nature of the "mind" that is unavailable to others, though it does give us knowledge of what is going on in my perceptual memory and imagination; that is what experience in perceptual memory and imagination I am having. In this sense it is akin to our knowledge of our own feelings.

In regard to our "introspection" of our doing of mental arithmetic, the matter will be more or less the same. I might be given a problem in mental arithmetic, or a brain teaser to be done "in my head," and then I might be asked the answer. Finally I might be asked to report on how I arrived at the answer (which, say, turned out to be right). It could turn out that the account I give of how I produced the right answer, if looked at carefully, could not possibly produce the right answer. My brain produced from my hand or lips the right answer, by luck or good management, but my "introspection" produced a "replay" that does not work and could not have produced the right answer. Here again my account of how I produced the right answer is corrigible by others. On the other hand, what is not corrigible is my report of what I "replayed" in "introspection," for no one else has access to my perceptual memory and imagination. Others can correct my account as an account (i.e., as an account that could produce the right answer) but not as my account. As before this sort of privilege is thin.

In regard to our "introspections" of our alleged cognitive-appetitive episodes, however, the matter is importantly different. Here one is— usually at any rate—not simply reporting on the "replay" of perceptual memory or imagination. One is not just giving a "running commentary." In one's "introspective" report on one's deliberations, motives, beliefs, hopes, and so on, one is giving a highly interpreted and theory-laden and model-based judgment about one's cognitive life. Certainly one is producing these judgments by means of the perceptual "replay" of perceptual memory and imagination, but when one reports, one does not simply give a "running commentary" on the "replay"; one sums it up or deduces from it a fairly crisp account or summary judgment.

Since the model on which the summary judgment is based is a "folk psychological" or cognate one, then additional levels of corrigibility occur. Hercule Poirot might be better at deducing motives than most of us, for he is an expert on the "folk psychology" of human motivation; that is why he is a famous detective. If I say that I committed the murder out of greed, he might be able to say, "Non, non, monsieur; it was jealousy"; then he will gently explain in the light of what I have been heard to say or seen to do how it all leads inevitably to the conclusion that my motive was jealousy.

In our "introspective" reports of our cognitive life, we can be wrong in our recall of what we said and did or mistaken in our fanciful constructions of what we would say or do in certain circumstances. Even if we do not go wrong at this level, we might err in our interpretations of our expressions, words, and deeds in the light of the "folk psychology" of our culture. Moreover, if our stereotyped orthodox "folk psychological" account can be corrected in the light of a more rigorous psychologist's account, then any "introspective" report based on the "folk psychological" account is similarly open to correction. The detective or psychologist might notice more details, or have a better memory for the details, or have a better grasp of what is relevant and significant, or make no mistakes of inference or analysis, or do all of these things better than I.

Put simply: if, for various reasons, someone else's account of my cognitive activities is based on a better model than mine or on a better interpretation of the modeling—which is not merely conceivable in respect of all of us but highly likely if I am a child or just poor at such perceptual model building and interpreting—then he or she is in a position to correct my report of my cognitive activity.

Of course, I retain a corner of incorrigibility. I can have privileged access to my version or my "replay," however mistaken, of what I believe are the significant episodes that reveal my motivation or belief or hopes or what have you. Also I have privileged access to my judgment (what I make of those "replayed" episodes) and could refrain from publishing it. But this sort of privilege is very thin in this context and does not bring with it any real epistemological privilege. One is not in a better position to give a correct "folk psychological" account of one's own cognitive states. All that one knows better than others is what one's stored and perhaps flawed account is.

It might be argued that I have overplayed the extent of the corrigibility of our "introspective" reports on our cognitive-appetitive life, for, it might be objected, I am in my own company more than others are in my company, and so I cannot help but notice more of my own doings and sayings, including the crucial significant episodes on which a correct "folk psychological" or cognate account of my cognitive life must be built. But this is balanced, unfortunately, by the fact that I can all too easily still miss things that others see. First, in the literal sense, they can see my expressions and gestures, which I usually cannot notice. In a nonliteral sense, they will often "see" more than I do. In regard to what both of us see, they might "read the signs better." Quite likely also, I will be biased in favor of myself when I come to interpret the public episodes in my life; they are much less likely to be.[21]

10 Some Links with Empiricism and Behaviorism

This account of "introspection" clearly has its roots in empiricism. I believe that the empiricists were right to suggest that the basic pieces out of which our mental life is fashioned are our perceptions, though I would not want to endorse the rest of the classical empiricist account. This classical account depicts humans as possessing a mind that receives from its senses raw sense data or impressions that in turn become transmuted into ideas and, combining with the ideas of memory, imagination, and reflection on the mind's own processes, then form a convoluted and complex choreography. When action is called for, this choreography becomes transmogrified into the diurnal dance of our limbs. On the other hand we can be basically sympathetic to empiricism and travel along a different theoretical path. We learn about mind by looking at mind-imbued behavior, not by trying to peer at some allegedly existing mental arena, stream, field, or forum. If we are constant witnesses of the behavior of ourselves or others but we are more or less totally ignorant of the workings of our brains, then it makes good sense to say that our knowledge of our mental life must be derived in some manner from what we are undeniably and directly acquainted with: our own and others' public behavior.

With regard to "introspection" it could also be argued that the behaviorists were even closer to the truth, for behaviorism held that "introspection" was derived from the analysis of perceived behavior. Where behaviorism went wrong was in concluding that since "introspection" was an inner covert process, it must involve the monitoring or recording of inner but real dwarf behavior, which was a surrogate for the outer, fully grown version—or else, as some of the philosophical behaviorists seemed to imply, that it was all a misunderstanding involving a misinterpretation of inferences we make from our perception of overt behavior. There was in this latter version nothing of the nature of an occurrent inner process at all.

I am not backsliding into a behaviorist position. The differences between my account of "introspection" and a behaviorist account may become clearer through a discussion of a suggestive passage in Ryle's *The Concept of Mind*:

> The combination of the two assumptions that theorising is the primary activity of minds and that theorising is intrinsically a private, silent and internal operation remains one of the main supports of the dogma of the ghost in the machine. People tend to identify their minds with the "place" where they conduct their secret thoughts. They even come to suggest that there is a special mystery about how we publish our thoughts instead of realising that we employ a special artifice to keep them to ourselves.[22]

When this passage is shorn of any behaviorist nuances of thinking being just internalized, stopped-short speech, I think that it points us in the right direction. It is true that children come slowly to form a concept of the mind and the mental. But this is true not because they have laboriously to learn the "trick" of reducing speech to inner stopped-short "speech" and then learn to monitor it and other forms of internalized behavior but because they learn quite late the ability to analyze their behavior and that of others in the light of "folk psychology." They have to learn the "trick," so to speak, of seeing the cognitive in what they do and say and how they react, and in what others do and say and how they react, understanding it to the extent of being able to build a series of "folk psychological" models or accounts of how they come to do and say such things. It is arguable that it is because young children do not have a large experience—if very young no experience at all—of behavioral and linguistic performances on which to draw for the production of the "replays" and because they also lack the ability to "filter" out the important features in the required way because they have yet to learn the "folk psychology" of their culture, that they engage in little or no "introspection."

Part of the "trick" or "artifice" the child learns is close to what Ryle and some of the behaviorists would want to say. Often the child, and the adult for that matter, will commit to memory and be able to replay on demand an account of a series of moves or techniques by which he or she was taught and has learned to do some task, for this account would constitute a model or constructed version of the cognitive strategy embedded in the task. Putting it in memory is internalizing it, and remembering or recalling it without telling anyone is keeping it private. For example, if a child is asked to give an "introspective" account of how she did subtraction in respect of some simple arithmetical problem, quite likely she will reply in terms of just such a replay. She will reply in terms of the moves she learned recently on her mother's lap, on the blackboard, or in her textbook. She will have stored in memory, on high-quality, nondecomposing "film," a "picture" of herself doing subtraction sums.

If the problem is to take 642 from 1397, we do it either on paper or in our head by "picturing" ourselves doing it. If the latter we might "see" ourselves writing down 1397, then placing 642 underneath it with the 6 under the 3, the 4 under the 9, and the 2 under the 7; then we might "see" ourselves subtract in single vertical columns beginning from the right, and so on. What is not stored are "pictures" of mothers' laps, blackboards, ruled exercise books, and ballpoint pens. What is stored is an abstraction from the myriad perceptual data we processed when learning subtraction. Also what is internalized is not a covert, reduced, and unemitted form of our doing subtraction sums in old school exercise books or of someone else doing it for us on a blackboard, nor is it some more mysterious "as if" or anticipation of the doing of subtraction sums. What I do when I "introspect" my subtracting one number from another is quite simple and unremarkable. I produce in the edited, "rounded off," internalized "replay" of visual memory and imagination a partly correctly recalled and, probably, a partly imaginatively constructed version or model of my or someone's doing a relevant subtraction sum.

We must not fall into the trap of thinking that when "introspection" is in the form of a perceptual "replay" in memory or "dramatization" in imagination or most likely both, it must always be in "pictorial" form, that is, always in terms of visual perception. The term "perception" in this context is meant to cover all the forms of perception, including kinesthetic sensations. I am not committed to the view that our internalized model of the performance of mental arithmetic or, in general, thinking to oneself, must be in the form of a "pictorial" replay. One of our perceptions—arguably the most important in this context because it is most intimately connected with speech—is hearing. We can hear ourselves or others do mental arithmetic out loud or ourslyes reading from a text out loud. Another form of modeling in terms of edited, tidied-up, perceptual replay of overt cognitive performances will be in terms of the heard spoken word. Our model of our thinking to ourselves might well be in the form of a replay of our own heard words once spoken but now imaginatively reconstructed. Our speech is internalized, not in literal movements of the mechanisms of speech as some behaviorists would have it but in an edited version of the memory of the heard speech or in an imaginatively constructed and recalled version of heard speech. For example, since I learned my arithmetical tables in English by bellowing them out loud in unison with the rest of the school class and in time with the primary teacher's fist thumping the desk, it is quite likely that if I am asked to multiply eleven by twelve, I will "hear myself" say "Eleven twelves are one hundred and thirty-two" or, more likely, I might have to start a bit farther back at, say, "Seven twelves . . . " and so approach "Eleven twelves . . . " smoothly and at speed.[23]

Few, I imagine, will be convinced by my skepticism with respect to all the versions of the orthodox account of introspection, for a belief in introspection is basic to our culture. Moreover introspection seems fundamental to both our knowledge of and our concept of our self, for introspection is held to give us direct knowledge of the self at work, especially in its higher, truly human, cognitive functions, and part of the concept of a human ego is that it is self-inspecting. The belief in introspection will not be easily given up. Indeed it is quite frightening to think that others might know more about our self and our mind than we ourselves do. To admit that they do might seem to some to be a way of assassinating the self.[24]

But the picture is not as gloomy as it seems. "Introspection," as I have explained it, has an important, probably crucial part to play in our lives. In the course of the discussion of this point I will refer to additional material from normal and abnormal psychology, which, I believe, further strengthens the account I have given of "introspection" in terms of the "replay" of perceptual memory and imagination.

Chapter 8
The Point of "Introspection"

---

1 "Introspection" Furnishes Us with Knowledge of Other Minds

In *Consciousness Regained*, Nicholas Humphrey argued that evolutionally the point of consciousness, and in particular introspective consciousness (or what it is that consciousness enables the conscious animal to do that it would not otherwise be able to do), lay in the fact that it enabled each person "to use a privileged picture of his own self as a model for what it is like to be another person," and so to gain a better understanding of other persons.[1] Introspecting our own mental activities, in other words, gives us, by analogy, knowledge of minds in general. With respect to this view Humphrey refers to (and partly quotes) Hobbes's proclamation with approval:

> But there is another saying not of late understood, by which they might learn truly to read one another, if they would take the pains; and that is, *Nosce teipsum, Read thy self* . . . [which is meant] to teach us, that for the similitude of the thoughts, and Passions of one man, to the thoughts, and Passions of another, whosoever looketh into himself, and considereth what he doth, when he does *think, opine, reason, hope, feare,* &c., and upon what grounds; he shall thereby read and know, what are the thoughts, and Passions of all other men, upon the like occasions. . . . And though by mens actions wee do discover their designe sometimes; yet to do it without comparing them with our own, and distinguishing all circumstances, by which the case may come to be altered, is to decypher without a key.[2]

Thus, Humphrey argues, this ability to gain an insight into human psychology by developing the capacity to inspect directly one's own mental activities constitutes the most sophisticated achievement in the evolution of the human mind. It is the catalyst that enables humans to fuse together successfully into societies. It enables one human to calculate or predict what others will do, as well as the consequences of his own behavior, and so to understand and in consequence be able to adjust to what others desire and do, whether the adjustment is one of outmaneuvering others or of cooperating with them.

Although Humphrey's view of the nature of introspection is that it is a process that amounts to the "examination of the contents of consciousness," in other words more or less an introspectionist view of introspection, this does not automatically invalidate his thesis about the usefulness or point of introspection.[3] Even if "introspection" is other than he supposes it to be—as I have argued—it may still serve the purpose of informing the "introspector" about human cognitive life or at least the cognitive life of those around about him. This I shall argue for shortly. What is much more difficult to establish is that information about the cognitive life of those around us will enable us to live more easily with them and so in general fuse together more successfully into societies or at least more successfully than we would otherwise do. Later in this chapter I shall attempt to bring forward some evidence in support of some aspects of this contention as well. What I shall not attempt here is to give reasons for supposing that evolutionally humans gain greater benefits from living together in society than in not doing so. Arguably they do gain some benefits. For example, a person in society gains support in times of need. He (or she) probably lives more peacefully and less stressfully than he might otherwise do, and he achieves certain aims that only cooperative collective activity could achieve. But whether this would be outweighed by equivalent losses, I do not know, and it is too far from my central concerns to go into here.

In a review of *Consciousness Regained*, Mark Ridley pointed out that Humphrey had not made good his case that in order to evolve the ability to model human mental life and so to anticipate better the behavior of others, we need consciousness, including the conscious introspection of conscious events.[4] All that we need, Ridley suggested, is the ability to make models of human cognitive life and the ability to employ such models in order to predict human behavior. This modeling and prediction could go on at a nonconscious level just as, for example, the adjustment of our respiration rate takes place by means of the activity of receptors in our blood vessels nonconsciously monitoring oxygen levels in our blood and sending signals to the part of the brain that controls respiration. More generally it seems that anything that can be done consciously could be done just as effectively in an automatic wired-in way. As an argument that in order to achieve the result of providing an organism with a mechanism or ability for understanding other similar organisms, the resulting mechanism or ability need not include the provision of consciousness and self-consciousness, Ridley's argument seems to be cogent. But again the residue of Humphrey's position remains: the point of the mechanism or ability "to introspect" is in fact to provide humans (and perhaps other higher animals) with a model of both their own and others' cognitive activities and of human cognitive activities in general as a means of achieving a better understanding of other humans.

Leaving aside his introspectionist account of introspection and his claim that the point of "introspection" demands that the process be conscious, I think that Humphrey's account of the usefulness of having an ability to produce cognitive models is nevertheless of interest. It would certainly fit well with my suggested account of "introspection" as the perceptual "replay," in terms of perceptual memory and imagination, of highly interpreted, edited, and selected accounts or models of particular cognitive activities as discovered in and abstracted from overtly performed cognitive and cognition-imbued activities, for to do this is ipso facto to engage in the modeling of human psychology. So our cognitive models are useful but not because, as Humphrey and the introspectionists would say, they are the product of a special privileged access to the workings of our own mind, which in turn enables us to extrapolate the findings to the minds of others; they are useful because in the very "introspective" process of producing models of particular cognitive behavior, we are producing models of cognitive activities that by derivation are clearly applicable to other people. The data from which the models are constructed are the behavior of ourselves and other people as filtered through the "folk psychology" of our culture, which itself is a general view of human psychology. Insofar as our brains are connected to our behavior in much the same way as others' brains are connected to their behavior and our behavior is a product of the cognitive activities of our brains, it can be presumed that others' behavior is a product of the cognitive activities of their brains. Thus any model of cognitive activity or series of models drawn from something approaching a general survey of available intelligent behavior will go some way in the direction of providing an account of human cognitive activity in general.

Some research by developmental psychologists in the United States suggested that children from at least one area of the country—when they had developed what could be called a clear concept of mind— initially associated the mind in particular with the sensory by-products, dreaming and imagination, and only secondarily with thinking, deciding, making plans, and solving problems.[5] Even so, thinking and cognate activities were often associated with inner speech or inner voices. Feelings were sometimes also associated with the mind. In general it seemed that the mind "appeared" as a source of "inward fantasy" in contrast to the brain's role of control center for bodily movement and personal action. Only much later did the concept of mind come to be associated with the concept of the self, a development that seemed to coincide roughly with the development of the quite sophisticated ability to form an abstract concept or model of the mind with a clear set of faculties and activities or, in general, mental events. Along with this more abstract model came the employment of it in talk about others, as well as oneself.

In short the underlying moves in the development are that children abstract the concept of mind from concepts of the elusive, immaterial, or at least ethereal aspects of dreaming, imagination, and internally heard speech. This in turn becomes solidified into a concept of a mind, which is the source of these activities, and finally this is used to communicate with others about our inner cognitive life and to come to an understanding of the inner cognitive life of others. Perhaps this latter stage should be put in reverse so that we generate an abstract, sophisticated concept of mind under pressure of the need to develop an explanation of our actions and the actions of others that includes reference to internal cognitive activities. I suspect that parents in particular may contribute to this pressure when they ask such questions as "Why did you do that?" and are not satisfied until they get answers that refer to acceptable or at least understandable beliefs, evaluations, wants, hopes, and so on. The child defends her action of climbing up on to the shelf in terms of 'I was hoping to find Teddy' and 'I thought that this was where Daddy hid the biscuits' or merely 'I wanted to see what was up there.' Then the child learns to ask such questions as "Why did you smack me?" and to receive explanations in terms of her parents' beliefs, values, demands, or wishes. A child also constructs a cognitive life for her cat, doll, and the menacing dog next door.

2 "Introspection" and Understanding Other Cultures

In proposing, along with Humphrey, that a major part of the point of "introspection" is to build models of cognitive activity as an aid to understanding, predicting, and planning behavior, I want to draw particular attention to its part and its importance in helping us predict the behavior of others so as to come to understand them and in that sense at least make them less alien, for—and this follows from my suggestion that our models of cognitive activity are culture-based and -biased— it is notorious that we can fail to understand the "mind" of people from another culture. We have not observed them or observed them often enough or perceptively and so have not formed a model (or at least an adequate model) of their mind. A good illustration of this occurs in the experiences of those who were the prisoners of war of the Japanese. The following extract is from the second of two BBC radio programs about what it was like to be a prisoner of war in the Far East and is based on the remembered experiences of those who were such prisoners:

> Such a background [of Japanese militarism and resentment of colonial empires] on its own is quite enough to account for a large part of Japanese behaviour, but in the actual day-to-day encounter of captor and prisoner there were other elements still. Perhaps these were best summed up by a survivor of the infamous Burma–Siam Railway, who remarked to me: "We simply couldn't understand the reasoning processes behind the things they did. We never could and never did; there was just something completely different, they were totally unpredictable, in our view."[6]

What is more, there was little possibility of quickly building up models of the Japanese way of thought (or cognitive life). For a start there was the language barrier. Few of the Japanese soldiers spoke any English, and few of the Allied prisoners spoke any Japanese, and there were usually no interpreters on hand. Those who were, were "interpreters" in name only. In addition, as the cliché has it, the Japanese seemed inscrutable in a literal sense; one could not read their faces. Gesture and facial expression—though generally they have their effect more or less unnoticed by us—are almost as powerful a medium as language for expressing beliefs, thoughts, desires, and values. When we frown or laugh or smile, or show sorrow or disgust or perplexity or anger, we do so at something or other and in doing so often reveal our outlook or standpoint. But if someone cannot "read" another's face or gestures—another race's face and gestures—a huge gulf in comprehension develops between the two. The "unread" face appears expressionless, inscrutable, impassive, cold, and unheeding. Or when it suddenly and unaccountably erupts into a recognizable laugh or display of anger, the result is frightening and baffling:

> They [Japanese faces] seemed expressionless . . . you couldn't make out how the owners were reacting or what they might do next. It may well be, of course, that the guards experienced the same problem with the prisoners: some had never seen a European in the flesh before they found themselves in charge of large numbers of them. The result was, in one opinion, that each side was always making the most terrible mistakes in interpreting the other and this provoked the most profound insecurity in the Japanese, who were in any case inclined to be jumpy and hysterical. They also constantly suspected they were being laughed at—as indeed they occasionally were: there is something deeply comic in the sight of

such very small soldiers dwarfed by their own rifles and fixed bayonets. In fact, it is likely that neither side had much idea of what made the other side laugh, while what the Europeans observed was often anything but reassuring: a Japanese factory girl, for instance, lost one foot in a machine and her workmates giggled. All these circumstances paved the way to violence.[7]

3 "Introspection" and Our "Self-Concept"

So far I have concentrated on what might be called the social purpose of "introspection" whereby, by a process of forming a general model of that sort of person's mind from observation of that sort of person's behavior, speech and gesture, one person gains insight into his or her character, views, values, needs, and behavior. But part of the purpose of "introspection" is connected with the formation of what in psychology is often called our own "self-concept." Just as we have a model of our body such that, if a foot is amputated, we have to learn by degrees not to locate our present pain in the nonexistent foot, so we concoct a model of our own character that is related to the way we think and behave, what we believe and care about, or in general what we are like. Only by degrees do we come to form such a model and only by degrees can we adjust it to new information. We can learn, say, that we hold views we did not believe or could not even imagine that we held. To our horror, we can realize that we are racist or sexist or selfish or mean or patronizing or neglectful. Often this realization creeps over us gradually, but it can dawn on us suddenly and traumatically. In neither case is such knowledge gained by instant access to some inner self giving private performances for our own benefit; rather the process is of garnering information from available hints and clues and then putting it together, perhaps imperceptibly or perhaps suddenly and dramatically. Certainly the gathering and garnering will quite likely involve replaying incidents or imagined incidents in perceptual memory or imagination and in that sense involve "introspection," but there is no internal peering at some internal inhabitant suddenly caught in the spotlight and recognizable as the "Self." The concept of one's own character or person is the result of making something reasonably continuous and coherent in the biographical sense and something reasonably consistent and integral in the logicopsychological sense, out of the mélange of our knowledge of our own everyday acts, reactions, and knowledge of others' actions and reactions to ourselves.

The "introspective" processes of perceptual memory and imagination help to produce a self-concept in an evaluative sense as well. We do not merely need to build up a holistic concept of our self—a descriptively coherent and consistent concept of our self—but we also need to build up a healthy self-concept, which in turn implies some self-esteem or self-respect. Although a healthy self-concept does not necessarily imply blindness to one's faults or shortcomings but may result from one having come to terms with them, nevertheless the process of "coming to terms," at least for some people, may involve an underestimation of one's faults in relation to those of others or even a disinclination to think in terms of faults much at all.[8] An idealized view of the self may be necessary for the psychological health of some people; in some cases in regard to the self, ignorance may be more likely to lead to bliss.

Although we need some self-consciousness and self-respect in order to maintain psychological health, the proportions must be right. If we err in either direction and have too much self-consciousness or self-absorption, or too little, we are in trouble. R. D. Laing has described such breakdowns in both directions in the following way:

> Self-consciousness comes to be relied upon to help sustain the individual's precarious ontological security. . . . For instance, whereas the hysteric seems only too glad to be able to forget and to "repress" aspects of his being, the schizoid individual characteristically seeks to make his awareness of himself as intensive and extensive as possible.[9]

The schizoid seems to be overaware of himself but has also got himself into a frame of mind such that he feels insecure in a profound way if he does not preoccupy himself with his own mental and bodily life and with a "reality" that is far more than normal dominated by his self. Laing likens this aspect of the schizoid personality to a child's wanting the light on in his bedroom at night and sometimes wanting his parents to sit with him until he falls asleep, in the belief perhaps that if the child can see himself or be seen by someone he loves and trusts, then he—his self—is secure. Although this may be a questionable interpretation, Laing suggests that falling asleep is frightening to a child because it is the losing of self-consciousness: "In sleep the inner light that illumines one's own being is out."[10]

If we translate this account of schizophrenia (of some types of schizophrenia) into the terms of my hypothesis about what is going on when we claim to "introspect," then it would mean that psychological illness or incapacity can consist in being hyperactive in employing our perceptual memory or imagination in regard to mulling over our abstracted models of our own self and its motives and values, or in being hyperactive in replaying real or imagined episodes in our lives, and so in becoming overly ruminative and introverted. I do not know whether in general psychiatric research would support this speculation, though there does seem to be a considerable body of evidence that visual and especially auditory hallucinations, delusions, and obsessions of various sorts (or, in general, what might be called the imagination "run wild") are often associated with some sorts of schizophrenia, depression, and obsessional states.[11] Thus psychiatrists have sometimes used the hallucinogenic effects of mescaline and LSD as approximations or artificially produced schizophrenic states.[12] But it is not clear whether these delusions, hallucinations, and obsessions are generally of an excessively self-searching and self-centered nature.[13]

Jung was the first to delineate and label the two psychological types of introvert and extravert. Although he associated mental health with a certain essential core of both introversion and extraversion, he also associated schizophrenia (or dementia praecox at least) with exaggerated introversion, pointing out that the schizophrenic person is associated with the "loss of adaptation to reality, a peculiar phenomenon consisting in the special tendency of these patients to construct an inner fantasy world of their own, surrendering for this purpose their adaptation to reality," for the inner dream world becomes more real to them than external reality.[14] Conversely, Jung associated exaggerated extraversion with a lack of an inner life of imagination or fantasy or of ruminative self-absorbed thought, which in turn he associated with hysterical neuroses and what is now called psychopathy. But Jung's account of psychological types was much more complex than these comments might suggest, for he also produced an account of the four basic psychological or psychic functions—thinking, feeling, sensation, and intuition—that ran across the introversion-extraversion distinction, such that there could be an introverted feeling person or an extraverted thinking person and so on.[15] It seems fair to say, however, that Jung's accounts of mental illness in terms of introversion and extraversion,[16] with comparatively minor adjustments, still remain a central part of one of the accepted versions of the nature of mental illness.[17]

There is also the suggestion from sensory deprivation experiments that, for our mental health, we need always to maintain a certain level of sensory life and that perceptual memory and imagination are central to this. If our senses are deprived of stimuli, we recall or try to invent a sensory life in perceptual memory and imagination. For example, when immersed in a soundproof and lightproof room, a person will "hear" trucks rumble by or "hear" planes flying overhead or "see" windows and grates with people peering through them. But arguably one of the most revealing findings from such experiments was that it became very difficult even to think after a while. It seems that many of us need to talk, or listen, or put pen to paper from time to time in order to provide the "fuel" for the inner processes of thinking. Thinking to ourselves is often parasitic upon our sensory or perceptual life in a literal way, so that if the latter suffers, so eventually does the former:

> Those [of the subjects in the sensory deprivation experiments] who lost their ability to concentrate, about two out of three subjects, usually refused to admit it. They made excuses for their failures which placed the blame away from themselves, often claiming that they were capable of thinking but that it seemed pointless in the absence of anyone with whom to discuss their thoughts. Others insisted that for the first time they realised how important a paper and pencil were to their thinking process. One subject insisted that he was unable to think because he was not permitted to talk out loud.[18]

It is interesting to note also that, initially, being plunged into the isolation of the sensory deprivation chamber seemed to improve concentration. There were no distractions, a restful atmosphere, and plenty of time. But after a day or so, concentration and direction of thought became difficult to maintain and eventually disintegrated into random day-dreaming, repetitious thinking, or panic. There seems to be a strong, undeniable connection between the continuous activity of our senses and a healthy inner life, including a healthy "introspective" life.

4 "Introspection" and the Changing Face of Psychology

Although we do not need a Cartesian introspectionist model of the mind, as ordinary persons we may need some macromodel of the cognitive activities of the brain. Certainly we could not cope with direct access to the raw brain and its neuronal activities, for its vastness and complexity would overwhelm us. The brain works much better without interference from us. The brain is a way-station, a switching post that receives, sifts, stores, and sends off electrochemical signals, and all its energy is aimed at producing appropriate output (behavior) now or later. For us to know directly and immediately about the workings of our brain is about as useful as it is for a clock to have direct and immediate information about its own mainspring. If we had immediate access to and knowledge of the brain, we would be gaining knowledge about neuronal firings and the state of the neuron-protecting glial cells and in general the intricacies of cerebral processes and states—but we would learn nothing about our mental life.[19]

We may not be able to do without some sort of macro and admittedly inexact model or series of models of what the brain achieves cognitively. If we had no account, we could not even talk of ourselves or others in respect of our cognitive activities and achievements. We could not, for example, mention or make use of the cognitive antecedents of action, which in turn means that we could not operate with concepts of deliberating, deciding, choosing, evaluating, believing, hoping, wishing, wanting, desiring, planning, forecasting, predicting, intending, and so on. Probably we would be reduced permanently to very crude behaviorist explanations wherein one could make no mention of anything but present behavior and probabilities of future behavior computed by reference to correlations observed in respect of past behavior, for this is what happened when psychology gave up more or less at about the same time introspectionist, associationist, and faculty explanations and was unwilling to put anything of a centralist nature in their place. As we have seen, recent behaviorist and peripheralist theories and explanations have given way to centralist (brain-centered or mind-centered or cognition-emphasized) theories and explanations in philosophy and psychology because we seem to have a need to mention something other than behavior and its stimulus conditions in the environment. We need to mention something cognitive between environmental input and behavioral output if we are to produce adequate accounts of human psychology.

Macromodeling for use in ordinary social intercourse is just modeling in terms of concepts such as deliberating, deciding, wanting, and so on. On the other hand, psychology, at least in the future, may need to work with a macromodel or macromodels couched in more technical and more sophisticated terms, which psychologists will have to generate. The former ordinary person's macromodel may be data for the psychologist's model, and in turn the psychologist's model may influence the ordinary person's model and perhaps, in the distant future, may even come to replace it in whole or in part. The gap between ordinary amateur "folk" psychologizing and tested psychological explanations may be reduced to a crack.

What does seem clear with hindsight is that the view of "introspection" and of the "data of introspection" gained from the experimental practice of the introspectionists was bound to be highly misleading. "Introspection" was thought to be the method of finding out about mental events and their contents or, in general, "psychic facts," and in practice this amounted to the highly artificial scenario of a series of subjects "peering" inwardly into their own stream of consciousness in the deliberately isolated and manipulated conditions of the psychological laboratory. Far from "introspection" and its data being related in any way to behavior, the subject was made to sit still and confront simple perceptual stimuli, such as a green triangle, and to report according to well-defined rules to the tune of metronome, chronograph, and tachistoscope. Toward the end of the heyday of introspectionism, a disciple of William James put it thus:

> Of course, much of our incidental introspection is not scientific but in "remembering green" for example, we can "(1) keep distracting stimuli away, and (2) introspect the memory-green or the fancy-green in an even frame of mind. These are standard conditions. They can be accurately recorded by the psychologist who introspects and they can be repeated by other psychologists." Any experience, whatever the circumstances under which it occurs, can be scientifically introspected so far as distraction is eliminated, an "even frame of mind" is preserved, and accurate record is made.[20]

There was so much emphasis on laboratory or scientific conditions and the absence of distractions that the clues as to what introspection was really about became lost. Although the quotation quite clearly delineates "introspection" as taking place by means of perceptual memory ("memory-green") and imagination ("fancy-green"), these clues as to the real nature of introspection were lost in the haste to ensure that the paraphernalia of science were in order. Similarly the point of "introspection" became lost. As ordinary everyday "introspection" was discarded as hopelessly casual and unscientific, so the distorted view of "introspection" as scientifically certified, privileged access to a person's own inner conscious life was framed in gold. It became impossible to realize that "introspection" had to do with forming series of models of cognitive activity in terms of edited, culture-filtered versions of purposeful, intelligent behavioral activity and that this was to be done by means of perceptual memory and imagination. According to the introspectionists, memory, imagination, and other cognitive items along with the internal sense data of perception were the chief contents or targets of "introspection" and not the vehicle. "Introspection" was an internal microscope for studying such internal states as sensation, memory, imagination, and thought, not a process of modeling cognitive activity by means of perception, memory, and imagination in order to facilitate the understanding of past behavior, the planning of future action, and in general the nature of human endeavors. Put bluntly, introspectionism had not merely distorted psychological method; it had clouded the understanding of "introspection" itself for the next hundred years.

5 Some Misuses of "Introspection"

I have argued that what passes under the label of "introspection"—though it is not what it is generally thought to be—is nonetheless important in human life. "Introspection" is employed by us in the difficult process of gaining an insight into the mind and behavior of others, in the formation of our concept or concepts of ourselves as persons and of our personality, and in the precarious business of maintaining our psychological health. In short, "introspection" is not a psychological appendix or pineal gland but has many uses. I want to end this chapter by arguing that "introspection" should not be used in certain ways that it has been used and continues to be used in psychology and the brain sciences because it cannot provide the information it is supposed to provide.

In spite of the lessons to be learned by pondering on the history of theorizing about the nature of "introspection," some empirical researchers are still laboring to map in detail the brain and its operations by employing "introspection" as if it were in relation to brain processes what an auroscope is in relation to the interior convoluted pathways of the ear. "Introspection" is thought by some to be an efficient and ready-to-hand "instrument" for discovering the neurotaxonomy of the "hard-wired" processes in the brain. A recent investigator into the nature of human emotion writes that "the most efficient and reasonable way to obtain an initial neurotaxonomy of the hard-wired processes in the mammalian brain is through introspection."[21] On the other hand I have argued in detail that "introspection" is not a process whereby we gain privileged access to the brain but is the modeling of the hidden cognitive life of our brains by the roundabout process of perceiving, and editing, and elaborating, and interpreting, and "replaying" a large array of perceived performances of ourselves and others, where the recalling or imaginative reconstruction is done by means of nothing more mysterious than perceptual memory and imagination. If this is indeed so, then the data of "introspection" cannot be construed as details about brain processes and so cannot be the basis for even a first-glance neurotaxonomy of the "hard-wired" processes of the mammalian brain. What we gain access to by means of "introspection" is a private and personal storehouse of myriad public performances, edited and "replayed" according to largely stereotyped views about our cognitive life.

For similar reasons I think that those who invoke "introspection" as the ready means for investigating the functioning of the brain's doppelgänger, the mind, are mistaken. Take, for example, the following claim:

> Through watching how the program gets it wrong and making introspective guesses as to how we might get it right, he [the programmer in artificial intelligence] develops a conscious and

articulate sensitivity to the way the mind uses its knowledge and beliefs, and relates this to the working of his program.[22]

If this means that in any literal sense the programmer in artificial intelligence uses "introspection" as a means of checking how the "mind" solves a certain sort of problem so as to prepare in the light of this new information a better machine program for solving the same sort of problem, then this way of putting it is seriously misleading. "Introspection" will furnish us only with our current "folk psychological" model of how we think that we (our brains) solve certain sorts of problems, and such a model will be inferior to any rival model based on better information as to how our brains solve such problems (that is, as to how we really solve such problems) or to any model built up in terms of an ideally rational "artificial intelligence" solution to such sorts of problems based on the methods of some pure deductive or inductive logic. In short, ordinary "introspection" will quite likely furnish us on many occasions with only an ordinary and amateurish model for solving particular problems. To use it as a source of specialized logical or neurological knowledge is to misunderstand its nature.

Finally, there is something unconvincing, though for different reasons, in the following sort of appeal to introspection: "Questions as to whether all positive rewards lose their impact under neuroleptic treatment and whether both primary and secondary reinforcers are affected are best answered by human introspective report."[23] Neuroleptic drugs, such as chlorpromazine, haloperidol, and pimozide, are thought to modify behavior by a variety of effects, including especially the blocking of the dopamine-mediated arousal of the "pleasure centers" in the brain or the central areas of positive reinforcement in the brain. Other effects claimed in the literature are the blunting of memory and the susceptibility to stimuli, including pain, and a tendency to increase appetite while in other respects producing apathy and listlessness.[24] Now it seems to be suggested in the quotation that "introspection" gives us direct access to our motivation processes or at least, in the particular case of positive reinforcement, that "introspection" can tell us whether and when rewards have lost their impact. Thus it would seem to follow that if Smith is given neuroleptic drugs to inhibit his desire to have sexual intercourse with children, then a good way of checking on the efficacy of the drugs would be to ask Smith to "introspect" in order to discover whether he still has a desire to have sexual intercourse with children. This would seem to be a dangerously misleading procedure given the evidence that our "introspective" reports on our own motives (usually couched in terms of beliefs and desires) are notoriously unreliable.

On the other hand, the passage in question may amount to only a claim that we are the best source of information as to whether certain feelings we previously had in certain circumstances are present or absent now in just those circumstances. The person feeling (having the feeling) is the best source for the presence of feelings. But reports on feelings are not the result of an internal peering at feelings, for to be feelings they must be felt anyway and, if felt, then they can be reported (given the requisite linguistic ability and so on). We do not need to "introspect" in order to say what we are looking at, hearing, tasting, smelling, or feeling.

I would not want to deny that sticking electrodes into clearly marked points of human brains, passing electrical currents through the electrodes, and then asking the subjects or patients to report on their experiences is a useful way of mapping what experiences are associated with electrical interference at certain points of the human brain, and this in turn may eventually help us to work out how the brain achieves certain things that give rise to those experiences. This enterprise, however, must not be confused with using allegedly introspective data as a source of information about the brain. An experience of "seeing a blue flash," which has resulted from planting an electrode into a certain spot on the visual cortex, is not an introspective process. It is simply a perceptual process, for it is a similar experience to seeing a blue flash of lightning except that now the causal sequence is different. The experience is caused now by direct intervention in the brain's electrochemical processes rather than by photoelectric excitation through the eye's lens system, retina, and optic nerve.

In conclusion, although I have argued that what we are really doing when we claim to introspect is important and valuable to humans, it is not useful as an instrument for gaining direct knowledge about our brains, minds, or cognitive processes. To think otherwise is to misconstrue the nature and point of introspection.

Chapter 9
The View from Above and Beyond

1 Summing Up

From roughly the time of Augustine to William James, it had hardly been questioned that there were two fundamental sources of empirical knowledge: the world outside our epidermis and the world within. There were the objects of our external senses and those of our internal sense whose operation was variously referred to as reflection, internal sensation or observation or perception, or introspection. The status and usefulness of such an inner sense were seriously called into question by the behaviorists in psychology and philosophy, but the ensuing state of affairs was either a patent failure to solve the residual "problem of privacy" or, in the hands of their theoretical successors, a gradual substitution of accounts of introspection based ultimately on unconvincing mechanistic analogies—such as radar scanning and data retrieval—for the old accounts in terms of an inner sense or "mind's eye" and its objects. While introspection was dismissed as the method in psychology, it was usually kept on the sidelines though at most as a crude curtain raiser to serious scientific endeavor. On the other hand, when subsequently accounts were demanded of the nature of the process of introspection itself, at times it was described in such surprisingly robust mechanistic terms that it became unclear why it had been thought to be so untrustworthy and of so little use and sidelined so severely and completely. At other times, when it was depicted as a flawed and basically unreliable mechanism, it was unclear how such an unhelpful, if not positively harmful, mechanism could have developed as an essential part of those glories of human evolution, consciousness and self-knowledge. The provision of a convincing account of the nature and point of introspection remained as a major theoretical hazard to any explorer in psychology, philosophy, and the brain sciences rash enough to seek to map the nature of human consciousness and cognition.

From time to time, particularly in recent years, there have been some suggestions, hints, and a few blunt announcements that something is radically wrong with the core conception of introspection, which has managed to retain its health and vigor through various changes of theoretical climate and costume. There is a growing suspicion that to conceive of introspection as some sort of inner second-level process of observation or scanning of inner first-order cognitive and appetitive processes or events, or as some sort of monitoring of internal truncated miniature behavior, or as some sort of immediate retrieval of data about the brain's information processing, is a misconception. I have attempted to give substance to this growing skepticism by articulating the course of the critical debates about the nature and efficacy of introspection that have gone on, whether on stage or behind the props, for almost a hundred years and then by drawing together some cues and clues about the nature of introspection that can be garnered from the experimental and theoretical literature in the behavioral and brain sciences and in the critical literature of philosophy.

I have suggested that we should admit that the bulk at least of our causally efficacious inner mental (or brain) processes is not known directly by us, so whatever it is that currently goes on under the label "introspection," it cannot be an internal perceiving, sensing, or scanning of internal cognitive and appetitive brain processes or events—not even an immediate mechanistic retrieval of directly recorded information about them or their information processing. More positively I have surmised that—given that we are of a culture that makes such claims—what is occurring when we claim to be introspecting is often more like the formation of or reference to some already formed, stereotyped, culture-tinged model or version or rationalization of what we believe to be our inner cognitive and appetitive processes in particular circumstances. This model is constructed on the basis of data from our ordinary perceptual experiences of our own or others' intelligent, purposive, and public performances. The modeling is not carried out by any special faculty or sui generis organ but involves only the employment of mature analytical skills in regard to human behavior plus perceptual memory and imagination.

My views, then, are leaning decidedly in the direction of a "disappearance theory" of introspection. By this I mean not the disappearance of a mentalist account of introspection so as to leave in its place a brain process account but the view that we do not engage in any form at all of internal inspecting, monitoring, or data retrieval. We neither scan the brain nor inspect the mind when we claim to "introspect"; in fact what we do is fashion models of particular cognitive or appetitive episodes by abstracting them from perceived overt cognitive acts and "replay" them by means of perceptual memory and imagination. We do not introspect; we internally reconstruct—at least in outline or in edited or dramatized or surmised version—overt intelligent performances. These will usually be in terms of some language, code, or calculus but need not be. Playing chess is an intelligent activity; playing chess in imagination or "introspectively" poring over yesterday's game in one's mind (in one's perceptual memory and imagination) is an internal version of the same activity.

If any overall mind-brain view emerges from this, it is that our descriptions of humans in mental terms cannot be based on "eyewitness" or even first-hand accounts of internal mental or brain activities nor are they accounts of the brain's program (as the "true blue" functionalist would assert) but rough-and-ready "folk psychological" rationales (or rationalizations, or dynamic models or versions) of what the brain and the rest of the human parts that go toward producing intelligent purposive human action do when seen from a cognitive-appetitive point of view. The more immediate ancestors of this view are the behaviorists, for I share their radical skepticism about the existence of an internal process of observing, sensing, scanning, or anything cognate in regard to mental or brain events and their skepticism about the efficacy, as a source of immediate and accurate knowledge about human cognitive and appetitive processes, of whatever it is that is occurring when we claim to introspect. Where I depart from behaviorism is in rejecting both its account of "introspection" that does not acknowledge the involvement of any internal processes at all and its account of "introspection" that depicts it as involving the recording or registering of internal miniature or truncated muscular versions of ordinary overt intelligent acts. What the behaviorists should have done in order to preserve the link with behavior was to give an account of what goes on under the label "introspection" in terms of the construction of models of what in "folk psychology" we construe to be our behaviorally efficacious cognitive and appetitive acts (of our brain and other relevant bodily parts) by means of the internal, covert processes of perceptual memory and imagination that feed off the ordinary perceptions of overt, cognitively imbued behavior. This view preserves our intuitions that introspecting is an occurrent experiential conscious process and not just an inferential one, as some behaviorists and others have suggested, and at the same time acknowledges the cogency of the behaviorists' skepticism about accounts of introspection as internal perceivings or sensings in or at least of some internal arena.

The more distant ancestors of this view are the empiricists, for I have taken it as axiomatic that perception is fundamental to all our knowledge, whether of ourselves or of the world about us. In addition I have argued that our conscious experiential life either involves directly and immediately the exercise of our senses, including those in regard to our own bodily movements and physiological changes, or, as is the case with what goes on under the label "introspection," involves them at one remove in the exercise of those processes symbiotic with our bodily senses: perceptual memory and imagination. The rest, lying hidden in the dark, silent labyrinth of the brain, plays no part in our experiences and will remain more or less unknown to us until neuroscientists gradually unfold its mysteries for us. Even if my account of what is going on when we claim to be introspecting is rejected, I believe introspection cannot be explained as any sort of direct inspection of or even access to the functioning of the brain. Whatever "introspective reports" are supplying us with, they cannot be direct reports of internal occurrent cognitive and appetitive brain processes, whether the reports are couched in either mental or brain or functional terms. That sort of introspecting is a myth.

I am not denying the existence of consciousness or phenomenal qualia, as some recent functionalists have done, because I find unconvincing the accounts of perception, perceptual memory, imagination, dreaming, hallucination, and kindred experiences that do not make any reference to phenomenal experiences. In particular I cannot see how anyone can give a plausible account of these processes, from the point of view of the subject of them (the person in whom the processes take place), without acknowledging that at least on some occasions they involve such qualia as raw feels, tactile and visual experiences, smells, and the like. On the other hand I do deny that there are qualia in connection with any nonperception-based processes (where perception, recall, refers in the context to kinesthetic and proprioceptive experiences—"ceptions" of our inner functioning—as well as to sensations and perceivings of the world about us). I have argued that there is no stream of conscious cognitive and appetitive items or conscious access to them except insofar as cognition and appetition can be part of perception or perception-based processes (such as perceptual memory and imagination) experienced by the subject of them. On the other hand, we can "model" cognition and appetition by means of perceptual memory and imagination. To put this another way, there are no ideas floating in our heads or felt surges of the will, though we may consciously imagine ideas floating in some mental fluid or imagine we feel the rising tide of volition swelling over the seawalls of the mind.

2 Looking Ahead

Sometimes the "models" of our cognitive and appetitive life, which are produced by means of our skills of analysis and abstraction applied to the data of perception and employing the processes of perceptual memory and imagination, will be quite particular models of very circumscribed parts of our cognitive-appetitive life. For example, our internal stored version of how we do long division or recall our mother's maiden name will probably comprise nothing more than an edited, tidied-up version of heard or seen performances of doing long division or recalling our mother's maiden name. At other times, when the models in question are of a more generalized sort—such as models of motivation or emotion, including those of a particular type of motivation or of a particular emotion—the models will be in terms of items from what is often called our "folk psychology": in terms of beliefs, wants, desires, intentions, hopes, wishes, expectations, and all the other items in our common sense and more or less shared view of human psychology. But it need not always be so in regard to this latter sort of model. Indeed it is unlikely that it will always be so, as it is likely that our rather vague and generalized commonsense view of our own psychology will be altered gradually but radically. As we become more knowledgeable about human psychology—with knowledge drawn from such sources as the brain and behavioral sciences, social sciences, and artificial intelligence—our common generalized accounts of our cognitive-appetitive activities will employ more detailed and more sophisticated (because better informed) concepts as the basic building blocks in the modeling.

In piecemeal fashion, from a consideration of the behavior of ourselves and others in the light of environmental input and against the background of our culture's "folk psychology," which has changed little over the last thousand years or more, we fashion merely guessed-at and idealized accounts of our cognitive-appetitive life in terms of beliefs and desires and their close kin. In the future we may produce accounts of our cognitive-appetitive life that are based on the findings of the brain sciences. Terms such as "belief," "desire," "hope," "intention," and so on may be gradually replaced by if not neurophysiological terms then at least terms linked to psychoneurological hypotheses—that is, to hypotheses linking neuronal processes to human behavior by explaining the link between the two, though at present we can only guess at what the new "language" may turn out to be. Perhaps we may use explanations that refer to operations or processes in parts of the brain whose function is fairly well established or, more likely, to the functioning of known systems in the brain and cognate behavior-producing parts of our physiology. Is it too far-fetched to imagine, for example, a conversation that goes something like this? "I'm sorry I did that. It's my limbic system. It's always hyperactive in this sort of weather. I ought to take something for it." "Look. Don't worry. I understand perfectly. Besides, to tell you the truth, my sensory-motor system has been very volatile since my operation. I keep going off half-cocked like that. It's probably my fault." (Would we still be speaking of "fault" when such a time comes?)

There are, then, three main sources of information about our cognitive and appetitive acts or, in general, our mental life. The brain scientist can tell us about the electrochemical processes by which humans take in sensory information and the subsequent processes by means of which human speech, expression, gesture, and behavior are produced. The experimental psychologist can deduce what must have been our cognitive and appetitive processes—according to current terminology, borrowed from "folk psychology," what must have been our relevant knowledge, beliefs, values, motives, ideals, intentions, and so on—by patiently discovering which perceived environmental factors produce this or that sort of behavior in this or that sort of person. Finally the layperson can produce a "folk psychological" account of his cognitive-appetitive activity in terms of a model or, more likely, a series of highly interpreted and culture-tinged models ultimately based on a consideration of the overt cognitive performances of himself or others. These last accounts can and often are corrected in the light of the former accounts. The experimental psychologist will explain that according to careful experimental investigation, your behavior is most likely to be the result of the "so-and-so effect" and not the result of the belief-desire set in terms of which our "folk psychological" account would explain it. In the future, the neurophysiologist may be able to correct both accounts by saying that there is no neurophysiological support for either the experimental psychologist's or the commonsense account of why you or I did something or other this morning. Besides, in the future these three sorts of explanations may well overlap and eventually coalesce.

If one of the most profound changes in our concept of the self has been the gradual dethronement of the belief that we have within us a free-standing, self-moving initiator of human action called "Free Will," another may well turn out to be the gradually inculcated skepticism in regard to the common conviction that we can internally perceive, scan, or in some other way gain immediate knowledge of what in our present terminology we call the cognitive-appetitive acts of our brain or mind. The disappearance of introspection may lead some to believe that our hold on the "self" has become more tenuous, but equally it may lead others to realize that it is healthier, or at least more truthful, to view the "introspected self" as the human artifact that it is.

Notes

Chapter 1

1. D. O. Hebb, "The mind's eye," *Psychology Today* 2 (1969): 55.
2. K. V. Wilkes, *Physicalism*, Studies in Philosophical Psychology Series (Routledge and Kegan Paul, 1978), ch. 7.
3. Aristotle, *De Anima*, bk. 3, ch. 4, esp. 429b–430a.
4. Augustine, *De Trinitate*, bk. 10, sec. 7, Library of Christian Classics, vol. 8, *Augustine: Later Works*, trans. and ed. J. Burnaby (SCM Press, 1955), p. 80.
5. See Descartes's letter of 14 November 1640 to Andreas Colvius, Protestant minister at Dordrecht, in Descartes, *Philosophical Letters*, trans. and ed. Anthony Kenny (Blackwell, 1981), p. 83.
6. Augustine, *De Trinitate*, bk. 10, sec. 13, p. 85.
7. Aquinas, *Summa Theologiae* (Blackfriars in conjunction with Eyre & Spottiswoode and McGraw-Hill), vol. 12: *Human Intelligence*, ed. P. T. Durbin, la Question 87, article 1, p. 109.
8. F. C. Copleston *Aquinas* (Penguin Books, 1955), pp. 26ff. (esp. pp. 29–30).
9. E.g., Wilkes, *Physicalism*, p. 135.
10. R. Descartes, *Discourse on the Method of Rightly Directing One's Reason and Seeking Truth in the Sciences* (1637) in *Descartes: Philosophical Writings* ed. and trans. E. Anscombe and P. T. Geach (Nelson 1954), p. 20.
11. Ibid., p. 32. Also, in a letter of 16 October 1639 to Friar Marin Mersenne, Descartes explained that "the soul acquires all its information by the reflexion which it makes either on itself (in the case of intellectual matters) or (in the case of corporeal matters) on the various dispositions of the brain to which it is joined which may result from the action of the senses or from other causes." *Descartes: Philosophical Letters*, p. 66.
12. Thomas Hobbes, in "Author's Introduction," *Leviathan*, ed. C. MacPherson (Penguin, 1968), p. 82; see also Augustine, *De Trinitate*, bk. 10, sec. 7.
13. *A New English Dictionary on Historical Principles*, ed. J. A. H. Murray (Oxford, at the Clarendon Press, 1888), cites the prolific polymath Sir Matthew Hale's work *The Primitive Origination of Mankind, Considered and Examined According to the Light of Nature* (London, 1677) as the home of the first use of the term "introspection": "The actings of the Mind or Imagination it self, by way of reflection or introspection of themselves" (I, ii, 55).
14. For an account of the difficulties in discovering exactly what Locke and Hume meant by reflection, see J. Douglas Rabb, "Reflection, reflexion, and introspection," *Locke Newsletter* 8 (1977).
15. John Locke, *An Essay Concerning Human Understanding* (1690), ed. J. W. Yolton (Everyman-Dent, 2 vols., 1965); vol. 1, bk. 2, ch. 1, sec. 24.

16. Ibid., vol. 1, bk. 2, ch. 6.

17. David Hume, *A Treatise of Human Nature* (1739), bk. 1, pt. 4, sec. 2, Selby-Bigge ed., p. 212.

18. Franz Brentano, *Psychology from an Empirical Standpoint*, International Library of Philosophy and Scientific Method, ed. O. Kraus and L. McAlister, trans. A. C. Rancurella, D. B. Terrell, and L. McAlister (Routledge & Kegan Paul, 1973) bk. 1, sec. 1, p. 3.

19. Ibid., bk. 1, sec. 2.2, p. 29.

20. Wilhelm Wundt, "Selbstbeobachtung und innere Wahrnehmung," *Philosophische Studien* 4 (1888).

21. See E. G. Boring, "A history of introspection," *Psychological Bulletin* 50 (1953), and K. Danziger, "The history of introspection reconsidered," *Journal of the History of the Behavioral Sciences* 16 (1980).

22. Boring, "History," p. 172.

23. Danziger, "History," pp. 245–246.

24. William James, *The Principles of Psychology* (1890), 2 vols. (Dover, 1950), 1:192–193.

25. Danziger, "History," pp. 247ff.

26. From 1900 to 1920, Wundt published the ten volumes of his work on the psychology of culture, entitled *Volkerpsychologie* (Folk Psychology). There is a short version in English entitled, *Elements of Folk Psychology: Outlines of a Psychological History of the Development of Mankind*, trans. L. Schaub (George Allen & Unwin, 1916). In regard to Wundt's social psychology, see Robert Farr's excellent "Wilhelm Wundt (1832–1920) and the origins of psychology as an experimental and social science," *British Journal of Social Psychology* 22 (1983).

27. James, *Principles*, p. vi.

28. William James, *Text Book of Psychology (or Briefer Course)* (Macmillan, 1892), p. 1.

29. James, *Principles*, 1:185.

30. See James Mill, *Analysis of the Phenomena of the Human Mind*, 2 vols. (Baldwin and Cradock, 1829), esp. vol. 2, ch. 15, and Alexander Bain, *Mental and Moral Science: A Compendium of Psychology and Ethics* (1868, abridgement of *The Senses and the Intellect*, 1855, and *The Emotions and the Will*, 1859), 2d ed. (Longmans, Green, 1868) esp. ch. 1.

31. James, *Principles*, 1:182.

32. In Aristotle's *Parva Naturalia*, in *The Basic Works of Aristotle*, ed. R. McKeon (Random House, 1941).

33. J. S. Mill, *System of Logic*, bk. 6, ch. 4, §3.

34. A. Comte, *Cours de philosophie positive*, 1, 34–38; quoted in James, *Principles*, 1:188.

35. J. S. Mill, *Auguste Comte and Positivism*, 3d ed. (1882), p. 64; quoted in James, *Principles*, 1:189.

36. Robert Woodworth and Harold Schlosberg, *Experimental Psychology*, 3d ed. (Methuen, 1955), p. 90. See also D. E. Broadbent, *Perception and Communication* (Pergamon, 1958), and under "Attention," *Encyclopedia of Psychology*, ed. H. J. Eysenck, W. J. Arnold, and R. Meili (Fontana, 1975), vol. 1.

37. Recent work along these lines is D. A. Allpot, B. Antonis, and P. Reynolds, "On the division of attention: A disproof of the single channel hypothesis," *Quarterly Journal of Experimental Psychology* 24 (1972). Allport gives an "overview," at least from his point of view, in "Attention and performance," in G. Claxton, ed., *Cognitive Psychology: New Directions*, International Library of Psychology (Routledge & Kegan Paul, 1980).

38. Woodworth and Schlosberg, *Experimental Psychology*, p. 90.

39. Recent very sophisticated work that inclines to this sort of middle ground is W. Schneider and R. M. Shiffrin, "Controlled and automatic human information

processing: I. Detection, search, and attention" and "Controlled and automatic human information processing: II. Perceptual learning, automatic attending, and a general theory," *Psychological Review* 84 (1977). A good overview of this whole area, showing how difficult it is to come to clear-cut conclusions, is J. M. Wilding, *Perception: From Sense to Object* (Hutchinson, 1982), ch. 5.

40. James, *Principles*, 1:196–198.
41. Ibid., 1:1.
42. A. Comte, *Cours de philosophie positive*, 1:34–38, quoted in James, *Principles*, 1:188.
43. James, *Principles*, 1:191.
44. I owe this point to my former undergraduate student, Stephen Cowley.
45. James, *Principles*, 1:191–192.
46. Bertrand Russell, *The Analysis of Mind* (Allen & Unwin, 1921), lecture 6.
47. Derived, in abridged form, from H. B. English, "In aid of introspection," *American Journal of Psychology* 32 (1921): 406–410.
48. G. Humphrey, *Thinking: An Introduction to Its Experimental Psychology* (Methuen, 1951) p. 120; see also T. Okabe, "An experimental study of belief," *American Journal of Psychology* 21 (1910). Okabe was a disciple of Titchener at Cornell.
49. See Humphrey, *Thinking*, ch. 4. Edwin G. Boring described another famous debate that underlined the precarious and unconvincing nature of the data of introspection: "There is always to be remembered that famous session of the Society of Experimentalist Psychologists in which Titchener, after hot debate with Holt, exclaimed: 'You can see that green is neither yellowish nor bluish!' And Holt replied: 'On the contrary, it is obvious that a green is that yellow-blue which is just exactly as blue as it is yellow.' That impasse was an ominous portent of the fate of introspection." "Mind and mechanism," *American Journal of Psychology* 59 (1946): 176.
50. William James, "Does 'consciousness' exist?" *Journal of Philosophy, Psychology, and Scientific Method* (1904); reprinted in James, *Essays in Radical Empiricism* (1912), ed. F. Bowers and I. F. Skrupskelis (Harvard University Press, 1976).
51. He held that the world was made up of "pure experiences" that became differentiated into an inner psychological world and an outer physical one.
52. James, *Essays*, pp. 3–4.
53. Ibid., p. 19.

Chapter 2

1. Walter B. Pillsbury, *The Essentials of Psychology* (Macmillan, 1911). Pillsbury pursued his doctoral research under Titchener and was much influenced by his work. William McDougall, who was not a behaviorist, shared with later behaviorists the desire to rid psychology of its obsession with introspection. In his *An Introduction to Social Psychology* (Methuen, 1908), he defined psychology as "the positive science . . . of conduct or behaviour."
2. John Watson, *Psychology from the Standpoint of a Behaviorist* (Lippincott, 1919).
3. See, in particular, James McKeen Cattell, "The conceptions and methods of psychology," *Popular Science Monthly* 60 (1904); Adolph Meyer, "The role of the mental factors in psychiatry," *American Journal of Insanity* 65 (1908); and Max Meyer, *The Fundamental Laws of Human Behaviour* (Richard G. Badger—Gorham Press, 1911), and *The Psychology of the Other-One: An Introductory Text-Book of Psychology* (Missouri Book Co., 1921).
4. Cattell, "Conceptions," p. 180.
5. See K. Danziger, "The history of introspection reconsidered," *Journal of the History of the Behavioural Sciences* 16 (1980): 257–259, and Robert S. Woodworth, "The accuracy of voluntary movement," *Psychological Review Monographs* 3 (1899).

6. John Watson, "Psychology as the behaviorist views it," *Psychological Review* 20 (1913): 158; see also Knight Dunlap, "The case against introspection," *Psychological Review* 19 (1912).

7. A full account of the genesis of Watson's behaviorism can be found in David Cohen, *J. B. Watson: The Founder of Behaviourism* (Routledge & Kegan Paul, 1979), esp. ch. 3.

8. J. B. Watson "Is thinking merely the action of language mechanisms?" *British Journal of Psychology* 11 (1920): 94.

9. G. H. Mead, *Mind, Self and Society: From the Standpoint of a Social Behaviorist,* ed. C. W. Morris (Cambridge University Press, 1934), pp. 2–3.

10. See J. B. Watson, "The place of the conditioned-reflex in psychology," *Psychological Review* 23 (1916). It was an address by Watson, as president, to the assembled American Psychological Association, Chicago meeting, December 1915.

11. Ibid., p. 90.

12. Ibid., p. 91.

13. Perhaps the most famous name in regard to such methods for studying animals, at least in Watson's day, was that of Edward Lee Thorndike with his "problem cage." See, for example, his "Animal intelligence: an experimental study of the associative processes in animals," originally his dissertation at Columbia University under the supervision of J. McKean Cattell and published in *Psychological Review Monographs,* 2 (1898). The "cage" or "box" is described in detail on pp. 8–12. The classical reference in regard to this modified "Skinner box" or, as Skinner himself preferred to call it, "air-crib," is Skinner's article, "Baby in a box," first published in the *Ladies' Home Journal* (October 1945) and reprinted in Skinner's *Cumulative Record.* Skinner remarks that at the time of writing, "Several hundred babies have been reared in what is now known as an 'Air-Crib.'" But it should be pointed out that, contrary to rumor, infants were not placed in the "air-crib" for purposes of conditioning.

14. See, for example, William McDougall, "Prolegomena to psychology," *Psychological Review* 29 (1922). For a general account of the backlash, and the early behaviorist response to it, see Cohen, *J. B. Watson,* ch. 3, esp. pp. 72ff. The virulent nature of the controversy between introspectionists and behaviorists led J. R. Kantor to wonder, "Can it be to the advantage of psychology if the several psychologists indulge in such violent disagreements that they can question the value of each other's work and its scientific validity? And yet to the existence of such derogatory ideas of each other's work on the part of the psychologists the content of our psychological literature could hardly bear more persuasive testimony." In "Can the psychophysical experiment reconcile Introspectionists and Objectivists?" *American Journal of Psychology* 33 (1922): 481.

15. A. H. Jones, "The method of psychology," *Journal of Philosophy, Psychology and Scientific Method* 12 (1915): 467.

16. Ibid., p. 468.

17. Edward Chace Tolman, "A new formula for behaviourism," *Psychological Review* 29 (1922), p. 53.

18. "The behavioristic interpretation of consciousness II," *Psychological Review* 30 (1923): 332. There are some similarities between Lashley's account and that of Shallice in "The dominant action system: An information-processing approach to consciousness," in *The Stream of Consciousness: Scientific Investigations into the Flow of Human Experience,* ed. K. S. Pope and J. L. Singer (Plenum Press, 1978).

19. J. B. Watson, 'Is thinking merely the action of the language mechanisms?' *British Journal of Psychology* 11 (1920).

20. R. S. Woodworth and H. Schlosberg, *Experimental Psychology,* 3d ed. (Methuen, 1955), p. 816.

21. Ibid.
22. Ibid., p. 817.
23. "The behavioristic interpretation of consciousness II," *Psychological Review* 30 (1923): 337–338.
24. Ibid., pp. 338–339.
25. Ibid., p. 352.
26. For a critique of Ryle's attack, see William Lyons, *Gilbert Ryle: An Introduction to His Philosophy* (Harvester and Humanities Presses, 1980), ch. 7.
27. Gilbert Ryle, *The Concept of Mind* (Hutchinson, 1949), p. 166.
28. Ibid., p. 169.
29. Ibid., p. 170.
30. See, for example, Gilbert Ryle, *On Thinking*, ed. K. Kolenda (Blackwell, 1979), paper 2.
31. B. F. Skinner, *The Behavior of Organisms* (Appleton-Century-Crofts, 1938). It is interesting to note that he expressed a general suspicion of theoretical work in psychology in this early work. In chapter 2, "Scope and Method," Skinner wrote that "as to hypotheses, the system does not require them—at least in the usual sense" and went on to suggest that his own program of studying "the dynamic properties of operant behavior" would inject sufficient order into such research.
32. B. F. Skinner "Rules for behavior," review of R. S. Peters, *Psychology and Ethical Development*, in *Times Literary Supplement* (March 1975).
33. See, for example, "A case history in scientific method," *American Psychologist* 11 (1956), reprinted in B. F. Skinner, *Cumulative Record* (Appleton-Century-Crofts, 1959), p. 227.
34. B. F. Skinner, *About Behaviorism* (Jonathan Cape, 1974), p. 19.
35. B. F. Skinner, *Science and Human Behavior* (Collier Macmillan—Free Press, 1965), p. 258.
36. Ibid., p. 35. Skinner uses the term "function" to mean "covariant effect of," that is, as the word is used in mathematics, whereas later cognitive psychologists and philosophers (as we shall see) use the term to mean a "role, use or application of," that is, its use in the biological sciences. This is understandably confusing given that Skinner generally takes his cue from the biological sciences.
37. Ibid., p. 262.
38. Ibid., p. 264. On p. 287 Skinner writes, "The patient under psychoanalysis may become highly skilled in observing his own covert behavior."
39. Ibid., p. 257.
40. Ibid., p. 263.
41. Ibid., p. 289.
42. See esp. Gilbert Ryle, *Dilemmas: The Tarner Lectures, 1953* (Cambridge University Press, 1954), p. 108, but also see Gilbert Ryle, *The Concept of Mind* (Hutchinson, 1949), ch. 7, and for discussion William Lyons, *Gilbert Ryle: An Introduction to His Philosophy* (Harvester and Humanities Presses, 1980), ch. 8.
43. Skinner, *Science and Human Behavior*, p. 265.
44. Ibid., pp. 264–275, esp. pp. 273–275.
45. Ibid., p. 282. See also Skinner, *About Behaviorism*, pp. 17, 27.

Chapter 3

1. It is arguable, however, that Edwin G. Boring was a psychological precursor of philsophical materialism in both his book *The Physical Dimensions of Consciousness* (Century, 1933) and his article "Mind and mechanism," *American Journal of Psychology* 59 (1946). There are hints of eliminative materialism and functionalism in his work. For

example, he says, "I believe that robotic thinking helps precision of psychological thought, and will continue to help it until psychophysiology is so far advanced that an image is nothing other than a neural event." ("Mind and mechanism," p. 192.) The scene in psychology at this time might be best described by saying that materialism was a background assumption rather than a topic for debate.

2. Philosophy of mind might be described roughly as traditional philosophical problems concerning the nature of mind and the mental. Philosophical psychology, again roughly, might be described as philosophical problems arising out of work in psychology.

3. See Keith Campbell, "Materialism," *Encyclopedia of Philosophy*, ed. P. Edwards (Collier Macmillan—The Free Press, 1967), 5:180–181.

4. See Hobbes, *Leviathan*, pt. 1, "Of Man," esp. chs. 1–6.

5. See Hobbes's own introduction to *Leviathan*.

6. See, for example, Hilary Putnam's "Minds and machines," in *Dimensions of Mind: A Symposium*, ed. Sidney Hook (Collier, 1961), secs. 3, 6, 7. The concept of a simple automatic computing machine was described by A. M. Turing in terms of a linear tape with at least some symbols on it, a device for scanning the tape and writing in, altering, or erasing symbols, and a set of instructions governing the activities of the device in relation to the tape. The "logical description" of such a machine describes what the machine does only in terms of what it does with the input symbols and so what state or stages it goes through symbol-wise. It makes no mention of how the machine might work in practice or what sort of machine it might be (that is, whether it be an electronic or mechanical or some other sort of device).

7. Rudolph Carnap, "Psychology in physical language," in *Logical Positivism*, ed. A. J. Ayer (The Free Press and George Allen & Unwin, 1959), p. 168. "Psychology in physical language" was originally published in the house journal of the logical positivists of the Vienna Circle, *Erkenntnis* 3 (1932–1933). A logical positivist is a positivist— or someone who holds that the paradigm of correct method and of exact knowledge is that which is inherent in the positive sciences—who couched his positivism in terms of the verification principle and thus expounded positivism in logico-linguistic terms. A simple version of a verification principle claims that a statement is meaningful if and only if it is either empirically verifiable or it can be seen, or shown, to be true simply by the analysis of the meanings of the signs or symbols used in the statement.

8. Ibid., p. 181.

9. Ibid., pp. 191ff.

10. Campbell, "Materialism," p. 184.

11. U. T. Place, "Is consciousness a brain process?" in *The Philosophy of Mind*, ed. V. C. Chappell (Prentice-Hall, 1962), pp. 101–102; first published in *British Journal of Psychology* 47 (1956). Regarding the urgency to get beyond behaviorist analyses in the march away from dualism, see J. J. C. Smart, *Philosophy and Scientific Realism* (Routledge & Kegan Paul, 1963), pp. 88–92.

12. Ibid., p. 107.

13. Smart, "Sensations and brain processes," in *The Philosophy of Mind*, ed. V. C. Chappell; first published in *Philosophical Review* 68 (1959). There is also a slightly amended, rewritten version in Smart's *Philosophy and Scientific Realism*.

14. See also Putnam "Minds and machines," in *Dimensions of Mind*, ed. S. Hook, sec. 5, and David K. Lewis, "An argument for the identity theory," *Journal of Philosophy* 63 (1966): sec. 2.

15. The best account of David Armstrong's causal theory of the mind is in his (unjustly neglected) collection of papers, *The Nature of Mind and Other Essays* (Harvester Press, 1981). The first four papers are particularly recommended. Armstrong also directs the reader to Lewis, "Argument."

16. Armstrong, "The nature of mind," in *Nature of Mind*, p. 10.

17. David Armstrong, *A Materialist Theory of the Mind* (Routledge & Kegan Paul, 1968), esp. ch. 6, secs. 10, 11, and ch. 15.

18. Ibid., p. 328; see also D. M. Armstrong, 'Is introspective knowledge incorrigible?" *Philosophical Review* 72 (1963).

19. Ibid., pp. 100ff. This doctrine about the corrigibility of introspective reports is not shared by all materialists. See, for example, Michael E. Levin's *Metaphysics and the Mind-Body Problem*, Clarendon Library of Logic and Philosophy (Clarendon Press, 1979), ch. 5.

20. Ibid., p. 111.

21. Donald Broadbent, *Behaviour* (Eyre & Spottiswoode, 1961), ch. 1, p. 21.

22. Cf. D. C. Dennett, *Content and Consciousness* (Routledge & Kegan Paul, 1969), pp. 103–104.

23. Richard Rorty, "Mind-body identity, privacy, and categories," *Review of Metaphysics* 19 (1965). Rorty holds a "disappearance theory" of the mental.

24. Ibid., p. 40.

25. A. R. Luria, *The Working Brain: An Introduction to Neuropsychology* (Penguin Books, 1973), pp. 34–38. In her paper, "Functionalism, psychology, and the philosophy of mind," *Philosophical Topics* 12 (1981), K. V. Wilkes provides a number of examples of how apparently conceptually simple terms (such as "alexia") cover a bewildering array of brain structures and, when studied closely, behavioral functions as well.

26. Luria, *Working Brain*, p. 29. In his article, "Localization and distribution of function in the brain," in *Neuropsychology after Lashley: Fifty Years since the Publication of* Brain Mechanisms and Intelligence, ed. J. Orbach (Lawrence Erlbaum, 1982), Karl Pribram writes in similar vein of the state of affairs at the level of individual brain cells: "With the exceptions of color and species-specific vocalizations, the phenomenal-neural correspondence seems at best strained in view of the multiple selectivities of most cells and the fact that these multiple selectivities fail, for the most part, in any cell or cell assembly to map coherently phenomenally experienced psychophysical characteristics" (p. 281).

27. See also R. W. Sperry, "Neurology and the mind-brain problem," *American Scientist* 40 (1952).

28. Luria, *Working Brain*, p. 41.

29. See, for example, Colin Blakemore, *Mechanics of the Mind* (Cambridge University Press, 1977), ch. 2, esp. pp. 50ff.; John Eccles, *The Understanding of the Brain* (McGraw-Hill, 1973), ch. 3, esp. p. 101; and Carl Cotman and James McGaugh, *Behavioral Neuroscience* (Academic Press, 1980), ch. 14.

30. A good general coverage of the electrochemical nature of brain function can be found in J. Z. Young, *Programs of the Brain* (Oxford University Press, 1978), chs. 7, 8.

31. Campbell, "Materialism," p. 185.

32. Donald Davidson, "Psychology as philosophy," in *The Philosophy of Mind*, ed. J. Glover, Oxford Readings in Philosophy (Oxford University Press, 1976), p. 103; this article was first printed in *Philosophy of Psychology*, ed. S. C. Brown (Macmillan, 1974).

33. Ibid., p. 103.

34. In "Reports of immediate experiences," *Synthese* 22 (1971), J. J. C. Smart may have edged toward a functionalist physicalist stance whereby the mental is not eliminated or preserved in some etiolated emasculated form but preserved robustly at a theoretical level, for he writes that "we can think of the ache (or rather the having-an-ache) as a quasi-theoretical entity, which is typically caused by such things as strained muscles, bad teeth, too much beer, and so on, and so we can allow much more content to

the notion of an ache" (p. 354). However, since Smart also draws an analogy between such psychological theoretical entities as experiencing an ache and theoretical entities in physics, such as an electron, it begins to look as if experiencing aches is becoming an entity with causal powers or properties—powers like the electron's to cause tangible effects, such as water droplets in a cloud chamber. Presumably such experiences are not to be said to have mental powers or properties, but, on the other hand, it is no longer easy to ascribe to them to properties or powers of brain states. Smart does refer to experiencing aches as "hypothetical entities," so this may be a way of disconnecting the analogy between experiencing aches and electrons and so of shortcircuiting demands to know about the causal powers of experiences of aches. I am unclear as to what position Smart is adopting in his *Synthese* paper.

Chapter 4

1. See, for example, W. Penfield and T. Rasmussen, *The Cerebral Cortex of Man: A Clinical Study of Localization of Function* (Macmillan, 1957), and W. Penfield, *The Excitable Cortex in Conscious Man*, Sherrington Lectures No. 5 (Liverpool University Press, 1958).

2. What might be seen as prototypes of recent functionalism in philosophy can be discerned in some of the pragmatists—for example, in G. H. Mead, *Mind, Self, and Society: From the Standpoint of a Social Behaviourist*, ed. C. W. Morris (Cambridge University Press, 1934), pp. 191ff. On the other hand, contempoary functionalists do not make reference to or give acknowledgment to Mead or any of the other pragmatists of that period. Quite likely modern functionalism has been generated more or less entirely in response to contemporary concerns. Early work in this later tradition are Hilary Putnam, "Minds and machines," originally published in *Dimensions of Mind: A Symposium*, ed. S. Hook (Collier Books, 1961), and reprinted in Putnam's *Mind, Language and Reality*, Philosophical papers, vol. 2 (Cambridge University Press, 1975), and J. A. Deutsch, *The Structural Basis of Behaviour* (Cambridge University Press, 1960).

3. The classical papers by Putnam on functionalism are "Minds and machines" (1960), "Robots: Machines or artificially created life?" (1964), "Brains and behavior" (1963), "The mental life of some machines" (1967), "The nature of mental states" (1967), and "Philosophy and our mental life" (1973), all of which appear in Putnam, *Mind*.

4. Putnam, *Mind*, p. xiii.

5. Putnam, "Philosophy and our mental life," p. 291.

6. Ibid., p. 293.

7. The tabulation of the machine's outputs in terms of columns representing internal states and rows representing input instructions. The intersection of the input instruction and current state gives the output displayed in the square at the point of intersection. There is a good account of the concept of a "machine table" and, in general, a "Turing machine" in Andrew Hodges, *Alan Turing: The Enigma* (Burnett Books, 1983), pp. 96ff.

8. Putnam explains this analogy in most detail in "Minds and machines."

9. Putnam's account as to why these properties are "real and autonomous features of our world" is perhaps best displayed in "Philosophy and our mental life."

10. In ibid., p. 294, Putnam explains the notion of functional isomorphism by saying "that two systems are functionally isomorphic if there is an isomorphism that makes both of them models for the same psychological theory . . . they are isomorphic realizations of the same abstract structure."

11. Putnam deals with the drawbacks to the computer-human analogy in ibid., pp. 298ff., and "Minds and machines" sec. 3.

12. Putnam, "Philosophy and our mental life," p. 303.

13. Putnam, "Minds and machines," pp. 146ff.

14. Daniel Dennett, *Content and Consciousness* (Routledge & Kegan Paul, 1969), p. 40. Another more recent functionalist account of introspection is to be found in Stephen N. Thomas, *The Formal Mechanics of Mind*, Harvester Studies in Cognitive Science (Harvester Press, 1978), pt. 1, sec. 5. See also K. Anders Ericsson and Herbert A. Simon, "Verbal reports as data," *Psychological Review* 87 (1980).

15. Ibid., p. 79.

16. Ibid., p. 80.

17. Daniel Dennett, *Brainstorms: Philosophical Essays on Mind and Psychology* (Harvester Press, 1979). There are also arguments against Turing machine functionalism in N. J. Block and J. R. Fodor, "What psychological states are not," *Philosophical Review* 81 (1972): esp. pt. 3.

18. John Searle, "Minds, brains and programs," *Behavioral and Brain Sciences* 3 (1980). Hofstadter and Dennett take it seriously enough to reprint it and attempt a rebuttal of it in D. Hofstadter and D. Dennett, *The Mind's I: Fantasies and Reflections on Self and Soul* (Harvester Press, 1981).

19. In *Brainstorms*, p. xx, Dennett suggests that such items would not appear in a "mature psychology."

20. Ibid. The elaboration of the notion of an "intentional system"is in pt. 1, ch. 1.

21. The following account is culled from Dennett, *Content and Consciousness*, chs. 5–8.

22. Dennett also discusses consciousness$_1$ and consciousness$_2$ (sometimes awareness$_1$ and awareness$_2$) in his "Reply to Arbib and Gunderson" in *Brainstorms*, and remarks there that he still maintains the distinction (p. 31). It is interesting to note that the neuropsychologist Karl H. Pribram generates a similar two-level account of consciousness in "Mind, brain, and consciousness: The organisation of competence and conduct," in *The Psychology of Consciousness*, ed. R. J. Davidson and J. M. Davidson (Plenum, 1980), pp. 49–51. Pribram traces the origin of his account back to William James's two levels of attention in *The Principles of Psychology*.

23. The retraction occurs in Dennett, *Brainstorms*, p. 171.

24. The account is taken from ibid., pt. 3, ch. 9, and should be read in conjunction with Dennett's article, "On the absence of phenomenology," in *Body, Mind, and Method*, ed. D. F. Gustafson and B. L. Tapscott (D. Reidel, 1979). There is a model of introspection, somewhat like Dennett's (in *Brainstorms*), in Ericsson and Simon, "Verbal reports as data."

25. *Brainstorms*, p. 156.

26. Ibid., p. 152.

27. Ibid., p. 153.

28. Dennett refers to the experimental work of J. R. Lackner and M. Garrett, "Resolving ambiguity: Effects of biasing context in the unattended ear," *Cognition* 1 (1972), and D. Broadbent, *Perception and Communication* (Pergamon Press, 1958).

29. In Dennett's "Reply," p. 30.

30. *A Materialist Theory of the Mind* (Routledge & Kegan Paul, 1968), ch. 6, secs. 10, 11, ch. 15. Armstrong's causal theory cum physicalist account is here being considered as if it were merely a free-floating functionalist account.

31. William James *The Principles of Psychology* (Dover ed. 1950), 1:266ff.

32. On this point, see Samuel Porter, "Is thought possible without language? Case of a deaf-mute," *Princeton Review* 57 (1881). This was James's source for the Ballard case. In "Thought before language: A deaf-mute's recollections," *Philosophical Review* 1 (1892), William James gives an account of the prelanguage thoughts of another deaf-mute, Theophilus H. d'Estrella, who was first a patient and then an instructor at the California Institution for the Deaf, Dumb, and Blind.

33. In "Dennett on awareness," *Philosophical Studies* 23 (1972), Richard Rorty expresses related doubts concerning Dennett's use of the items "analyzer" and "speech center" in his models of consciousness and introspection. As Rorty points out, for example, the inputs and outputs of the "analyzer" are suspiciously like what was referred to by the old-fashioned mentalist term "thoughts," except that there is added, gratuitously, that they are now items locatable in the brain, at least in principle.

In " 'Functionalism' in Philosophy of Psychology," in *Proceedings of the Aristotelian Society* 80 (1979–1980), Norman Malcolm suggests that this is a symptom of a deeper problem—unavoidable circularity in explanation—inherent in this type of functionalism.

34. Daniel Dennett, "Artificial intelligence as philosophy and as psychology," in *Brainstorms*, p. 110.

35. Ibid., p. 122.

36. Ibid., pp. 123–124.

37. Dennett draws attention, for example, to Winograd's SHRDLU program in *Understanding Natural Language* (Academic Press, 1972): see *Brainstorms*, pp. 115–117, 124.

38. William G. Lycan, if I am not mistaken, sees this Janus-faced quality of Dennettian functionalism as a distinct advantage; see his "Form, function, and feel," *Journal of Philosophy* 78 (1981): 47ff. This paper as a whole is an excellent, sympathetic discussion of functionalism.

39. Searle is interesting on this aspect of functionalism; see his "Minds, brains, and programs," in *The Mind's I*, esp. pp. 371–372. See also Paul M. Churchland, *Scientific Realism and the Plasticity of Mind*, Cambridge Studies in Philosophy (Cambridge University Press, 1979), ch. 4, sec. 15, esp. pp. 112–113.

Chapter 5

1. One might note here that Paul and Patricia Churchland write of a "faculty of inner sense" in "Functionalism, qualia and intentionality," *Philosophical Topics* 12 (1981): 128ff., and Paul Churchland discusses a "faculty of introspection" in *Matter and Consciousness: A Contemporary Introduction to the Philosophy of Mind* (The MIT Press, 1984), p. 74. Anthony Quinton speculates about the "organ-like machinery of introspection" in his "In defence of introspection," *Philosophic Exchange* 2 (1977): sec. 3, though I take it that ultimately he rejects the suggestion.

2. I take this point from Colin McGinn, *The Character of Mind* (Oxford University Press–Opus Books, 1982), pp. 50–51. Wittgenstein makes a similar point in connection with remembering in *Philosophical Investigations*, trans. G. E. M. Anscombe (Blackwell, 1958), pt. 2, p. 231.

3. H. Ginsburg and S. Opper, *Piaget's Theory of Intellectual Development* (Prentice-Hall, 1979), esp. pp. 175ff.

4. See ibid., esp. pp. 175–177; E. A. Lunzer, "The development of consciousness," in *Aspects of Consciousness*, ed. Geoffrey Underwood and Robin Stevens (Academic Press, 1979), vol. 1; John Broughton, "Development of concepts of self, mind, reality, and knowledge," in *Social Cognition*, ed. W. Damon (Jossey-Bass, 1978); Monique Lefebvre-Pinard, "Understanding and auto-control of cognitive functions: Implications for the relationship between cognition and behaviour," *International Journal of Behavioral Development* 6 (1983).

5. Lunzer, "Development," p. 12.

6. Ginsburg and Opper, *Piaget's Theory*, pp. 176–177.

7. Ibid. The authors claim that Piaget does just that and that in general in his work there is "an overreliance on verbalizations as a source of evidence" (p. 177).

8. It has been argued recently by K. V. Wilkes, *Physicalism* (Routledge & Kegan Paul, 1978), ch. 7. Although, in regard to Aristotle, the passage in *De Anima*, bk. 3, ch. 4, 429b–430a, may be evidence against this view. In Plato, while there does not seem to be any explicit mention of any process like introspection, it could be argued that certain passages, such as *Theaetetus*, 187aff., *Philebus*, 38aff., and *Republic*, 435aff., 602c–608b, imply the recognition by Plato of some such process.

9. See Augustine, *De Trinitate*, bk. 10, sec. 7.

10. Clifford Geertz, " 'From the native's point of view': On the nature of anthropological understanding," in *Meaning in Anthropology*, ed. K. H. Basso and H. A. Selby, School of American Research Book (University of New Mexico Press, 1976).

11. See, for example, Catherine Lutz, "Ethnopsychology compared to what? Explaining behaviour and consciousness among the Ifaluk" (1982), unpublished manuscript. (The Ifaluk are the people of the Ifaluk atoll in the Western Caroline Islands in the Pacific Ocean.) See also Jean Smith, "Self and experience in Maori culture," in *Indigenous Psychologies: The Anthropology of the Self*, ed. P. Heelas and A. Lock, Language, Thought and Culture Series (Academic Press, 1981).

12. J. Prytz Johansen, *The Maori and His Religion in Its Non-Ritualistic Aspects* (I Kommission Hos Ejnar Munksgaard, Copenhagen, 1954), ch. 10, p. 249. Johansen suggests that there are possibly only two words that would be mental terms in our sense in the entire Maori vocabulary: *aroha* ("an internal emotion, which overwhelms people, often suddenly") and *wairua* ("The Spirit," which seems to be analogous to the Socratic *daimōn*).

13. Nicholas Humphrey, *Consciousness Regained: Chapters in the Development of Mind* (Oxford University Press, 1983), p. 8.

14. Ibid., p. 9.

15. Gilbert Ryle, *The Concept of Mind* (Hutchinson, 1949), p. 163.

16. The ensuing example is adapted from what might be considered one of the classical papers in this field: J. R. Lackner and M. F. Garrett, "Resolving ambiguity: Effects of biasing context in the unattended ear," *Cognition* 1 (1972), esp. pp. 359–363.

17. D. A. Laird gives an interesting case of this sort in regard to housewives' choosing among pairs of stockings, identical except for their scent, in "How the consumer estimates quality by subconscious sensory impressions: With special reference to the role of smell," *Journal of Applied Psychology* 16 (1932), and Richard E. Nisbett and Timothy DeCamp Wilson give a wealth of additional examples and references in "Telling more than we can know: Verbal reports on mental processes," *Psychological Review* 84 (1977). The latter discuss the "position effect" in regard to choice, pp. 243–244.

18. Nisbett and Wilson, "Telling more," p. 232.

19. Karl Lashley, "Cerebral organisation and behaviour," in *Proceedings of the Association for Research in Nervous and Mental Diseases*, vol. 36: *The Brain and Human Behaviour* (1958), ch. 1 (he coined the dictum); G. A. Miller, *Psychology: The Science of Mental Life* (Harper & Row, 1962), p. 56; U. Neisser, *Cognitive Psychology* (Prentice-Hall, 1967), p. 301; G. Mandler, *Mind and Emotion* (Wiley, 1975), p. 43; D. C. Dennett, *Brainstorms: Philosophical Essays on Mind and Psychology* (Harvester Press, 1979), p. 165 and "On the absence of phenomenology," in *Body, Mind and Method*, ed. D. F. Gustafson and B. L. Tapscott (Reidel, 1979); D. O. Hebb, *Essay on Mind* (Lawrence Erlbaum, 1980), p. 20.

20. Nisbett and Wilson, "Telling more," pp. 248ff. In regard to the "bystander effect," they refer on pp. 241–242 to B. Latané and J. M. Darley, *The Unresponsive Bystander: Why Doesn't He Help?* (Appleton-Century-Crofts, 1970).

21. See D. O. Hebb, "The mind's eye," *Psychology Today* 2, (1969); P. Raymond Dodge also made the point in "The theory and limitations of introspection," *American Journal of Psychology* 23 (1912): 223.

Chapter 6

1. The quote is from A. J. Ayer in *The Problem of Knowledge* (Pelican Books, 1956), ch. 3, where he gives a thorough and reasonably sympathetic account of sense data and allied theories of perception. Ayer gives a shorter account in *The Central Questions of Philosophy* (Pelican Books, 1973), ch. 4. See also Sydney Shoemaker, *Self-Knowledge and Self-Identity* (Cornell University Press, 1963), ch. 6; Wittgenstein, *Philosophical Investigations* (Basil Blackwell, 1958), pt. 1, secs. 416–417, p. 125; and Roderick Chisholm, "On the observability of the self," *Philosophy and Phenomenological Research* 30 (1969–1970): 14ff.

2. Gilbert Ryle, *The Concept of Mind* (Hutchinson, 1949), ch. 7. See also William Lyons, *Gilbert Ryle: An Introduction to His Philosophy* (Harvester and Humanities Presses, 1980), ch. 8.

3. See A. M. Quinton, "Ryle on Perception," in *Ryle*, ed. O. P. Wood and G. Pitcher, Modern Studies in Philosophy Series (Macmillan, 1970); and Lyons, *Ryle*, ch. 8.

4. Ayer, *Problem of Knowledge*, p. 86.

5. See the excellent surveys of empirical work on attention in R. S. Woodworth and H. Schlosberg, *Experimental Psychology*, 3d ed. (Methuen, 1955), ch. 4, and "Attention" in *Encyclopedia of Psychology*, ed. H. J. Eysenck, W. J. Arnold, and R. Meili (Fontana-Collins, 1975), vol. 1.

6. There is some good material on consciousness, realization, and attention in A. R. White, *Attention* (Blackwell, 1964), ch. 4.

7. See "Visual perception and illusions: Dialogue with Richard Gregory," in *States of Mind: Conversations with Psychological Investigators*, ed. Jonathan Miller (BBC Publications, 1983), p. 44.

8. Ulric Neisser, "The processes of vision," *Scientific American* 219 (1968): 206.

9. Miller, *States of Mind*, pp. 49ff. The Necker cube is named after L. A. Necker, the Swiss naturalist who developed it in 1832.

10. There is a good selection of optical illusions in "Visual perception," in *States of Mind*, and R. L. Gregory, *Eye and Brain: The Psychology of Seeing*, 3d ed. (Weidenfeld and Nicolson, 1977).

11. R. W. Sperry, "Neurology and the mind-brain problem," *American Scientist* 40 (1952): 301–2.

12. See R. L. Gregory, *Eye and Brain: The Psychology of Seeing*, pp. 161–162, who gives references to M. H. Segall, T. D. Campbell, and M. J. Herskovitz, *The Influence of Culture on Visual Perception* (Bobbs-Merrill, 1966), and J. B. Deregowski, "Illusion and culture," in *Illusion in Nature and Art*, ed. R. L. Gregory and E. H. Gombrich (Duckworth, 1974).

Chapter 7

1. Wittgenstein, *Philosophical Investigations*, 2d ed. (Blackwell, 1958), pt. 1, sec. 587, p. 154.

2. Gilbert Ryle, *The Concept of Mind* (Hutchinson, 1949), p. 247.

3. Ibid., p. 253.

4. See William Lyons, *Gilbert Ryle: An Introduction to His Philosophy* (Harvester and Humanities Presses, 1980), ch. 9.

5. This is building on the account I gave in ibid., ch. 9.

6. Daniel Dennett, *Content and Consciousness* (Routledge & Kegan Paul, 1969), pp. 136–137. My reply is a development of "The tiger and his stripes," *Analysis* 44 (1984).

7. Alastair Hannay, *Mental Images—A Defence* (Allen & Unwin, 1971), ch. 5, sec. 3.

8. J. A. Fodor, *The Language of Thought* (Crowell, 1975), pp. 187–191.

9. When discussing the "zebra and his stripes" in his paper "The mental image," *American Psychologist* 33 (1978): 131, Roger Shepard also seems to be suggesting something like this, for he writes, "In both the imaginal and perceptual conditions, my stripe-representing circuits may well be activated, but to determine the *number* of those stripes will require additional internal and, possibly, external operations. To be accurate, I may need to move my physical finger along the picture while counting—an operation that is more difficult with a purely internal image."

10. C. W. Perky, "An experimental study of imagination," *American Journal of Psychology* 21 (1910).

11. Roger N. Shepard, "Learning and recall as organisation and search," *Journal of Verbal Learning and Verbal Behaviour* 5 (1966).

12. Roger N. Shepard and Jacqueline Metzler, "Mental rotation of three-dimensional objects," in *Readings in Cognitive Psychology*, ed. M. Coltheart (Holt Rinehart & Winston, 1972), p. 109 (reprinted from *Science* 171, 1971). Shepard and Metzler claimed "that the average rate at which these particular objects can be thus 'rotated' is roughly 60 degrees per second" (p. 113). Further experiments of the same type are recorded in Lynn A. Cooper and Roger N. Shepard, "Chronometric studies of the rotation of mental images," in *Visual Information Processing*, ed. William G. Chase (Academic Press, 1973), and chronometric studies of "mental comparisons" are described in John T. E. Richardson, "Mental imagery in thinking and problem solving," in *Thinking and Reasoning: Psychological Approaches*, ed. J. St. B. Evans (Routledge & Kegan Paul, 1983).

13. See D. O. Hebb, "The mind's eye," *Psychology Today* 2 (1969): 56–57.

14. William G. Chase and Herbert A. Simon, "The mind's eye in chess," in Chase, *Visual Information Processing*. At a purely anecdotal level, there is an interesting passage in the second volume of A. J. Ayer's autobiography, *More of My Life* (Collins, 1984): "If I now play chess rather seldom it is partly because I have no regular opponent, partly because it vexes me that my game shows no improvement. I put this down chiefly to my lack of visual imagery. I cannot form a mental picture of the disposition of the pieces which would result from such and such a series of moves on either side. I have to reason it out: if I move my knight, then he will most probably move his bishop, and then I shall have to protect my queen, but won't that cost me a pawn? I find that I soon run into difficulties with this purely conceptual approach" (p. 119).

15. See Ulric Neisser, "The processes of vision," *Scientific American* 219 (1968): 210. In regard to the findings on dreams and eye movements, Neisser refers to the work of "William C. Dement and his collaborators." The best-known paper by this group is probably W. Dement and N. Kleitman, "The relation of eye movements during sleep to dream activity: An objective method for the study of dreaming," *Journal of Experimental Psychology* 53 (1957). Neisser also remarks that similar results were obtained in regard to the relation between eye movements and eidetic visual imagery (pp. 210–211).

16. On the "pictorial" qualities of imagination, consult Alan Richardson, *Mental Imagery* (Routledge & Kegan Paul, 1969); Ulric Neisser, "Changing conceptions of imagery," in *The Function and Nature of Imagery*, ed. P. W. Sheehan (Academic Press, 1972); Stephen M. Kosslyn, "Information representation in visual images," *Cognitive Psychology* 7 (1975); Peter W. Sheehan, "Mental imagery," in *Psychology Survey No. 1*, ed. B. M. Foss (George Allen & Unwin, 1978); and Ned Block, "Mental pictures and cognitive science," *Philosophical Review* 92 (1983). In his general survey of the field, Peter Sheehan remarks that "work on the nature of imagery, now, has come

to appeal rather specifically to the similarity in structure of perception of imagery" (p. 59) and claims that "the cumulative impact of the research that has been conducted in the last two decades affirms the reality of imagery in quite undeniable fashion" (pp. 67–68).

17. Thomas Hobbes, *Leviathan*, ed. C. B. MacPherson (Penguin Books, 1968), pt 1, ch. 2, p. 88.

18. Ibid., p. 90.

19. Ibid., p. 89.

20. Good general accounts of the psychology of memory are in D. S. Wright et al., *Introducing Psychology: An Experimental Approach* (Penguin, 1970), ch. 14, and Ulric Neisser, *Cognitive Psychology* (Prentice-Hall, 1967), ch. 11.

21. Cf. Ryle, *Concept of Mind*, ch. 6, esp. secs. 4, 5.

22. Ibid., p. 27.

23. After finishing the bulk of this manuscript, I came across Anthony Quinton's very interesting paper, "In defence of introspection," hidden away in *Philosophic Exchange* 2 (1977). There he gives the barest sketch of a view that, if I understand it correctly, has similarities to the one I have put forward. He puts forward an account of introspection "as the imaginative envisagement of probable behaviour" (p. 88) or what a person would say or do if the circumstances were appropriate for words and deeds. He also finds his inspiration in classical empiricism, suggesting that "to report one's imagery is, surely, what it has always been thought to be by the old empiricists who regarded so much of our mental life as the having of images, namely a kind of surrogate report of perception" (pp. 87–88).

24. See also Nisbett and Wilson, "Telling more than we can know: Verbal reports on mental processes," *Psychological Review* 84 (1977): 256–257.

Chapter 8

1. Nicholas Humphrey, *Consciousness Regained: Chapters in the Development of Mind* (Oxford University Press, 1983), p. 6.

2. Thomas Hobbes, *Leviathan*, ed. C. B. MacPherson (Penguin, 1968), pp. 82–83. Because Hobbes was a materialist, and most likely best interpreted as an eliminative materialist, his account of introspection—if he had elaborated one—would probably have amounted to brain scanning or something very like it and would have been beset by the problems which such an account is heir to.

3. Humphrey, *Consciousness Regained*, p. 30.

4. Mark Ridley, "The advantages of knowing," review of Nicholas Humphrey's *Consciousness Regained*, in *Times Literary Supplement* (September 1983): 1009.

5. See C. N. Johnson, "Acquisition of mental verbs and the concept of mind," in *Language Development* vol. 1: *Syntax and Semantics*, ed. S. Kuczaj (Lawrence Erlbaum, 1982), esp. pp. 468ff.

6. David Wade, "The ultimate offence: To be taken prisoner of war," *Listener* 109 (January 1983): p. 8.

7. Ibid., p. 9.

8. See, for example, Ruth C. Wylie, "The present status of self theory," in *Handbook of Personality Theory and Research*, ed. E. F. Borgatta and W. L. Lambert (Rand McNally, 1968), and Erich Fromm, "Selfishness and self-love," *Psychiatry* 2 (1939). (Perhaps Cicero is making a similar point with his dictum, "omne animal se ipsum diligere," in *De Finibus*, bk. 5, ch. 10, sec. 27.) In regard to our disclination to think in terms of our faults, see La Rochefoucauld, *The Maxims of the Duc de la Rochefoucauld*, trans. C. Fitzgibbon (Millington, 1974), maxims 397 and 442.

9. R. D. Laing, *The Divided Self* (Pelican, 1965), p. 112.

10. Ibid., p. 119.

11. W. L. Linford Rees, *A Short Textbook of Psychiatry*, 2d ed. (Hodder and Stoughton, 1976), pp. 164ff., 216ff.

12. Steven Rose, *The Conscious Brain* (Penguin, 1976), pp. 332ff.

13. The account in Bernard Hart, *The Psychology of Insanity*, 4th ed. (Cambridge University Press, 1930), ch. 11, suggests that they are of a self-centered (and usually "self-asserting") nature.

14. C. G. Jung, *Jung: Selected Writings* (Fontana, 1983), p. 55. The extract is from Jung's 1913 paper, "The theory of psychoanalysis," in *Freud and Psychoanalysis, Collected Works*, vol. 4, though the bulk of his account of psychological types is in his 1921 work, *Psychological Types, Collected Works*, vol. 6. His views on schizophrenia are contained in the series of papers of various dates collected in *The Psychogenesis of Mental Disease, Collected Works*, vol. 3.

15. Jung, *Jung: Selected Writings*, p. 18.

16. Introversion and extraversion are classifications of normal persons as much as of neurotics, at least for Jung.

17. See, for example, H. J. Eysenck, *You and Neurosis* (Fontana, 1977), pp. 21ff.

18. Jack Vernon, *Inside the Black Room: Studies of Sensory Deprivation* (Pelican, 1966), pp. 85–86.

19. More than thirty years ago, in "Neurology and the mind-brain problem," *American Scientist* 40 (1952): 294, R. W. Sperry concluded that "our general knowledge of brain structure and physiology has for many years been quite sufficient to rule out any possibility that cerebral processes duplicate, even remotely, the patterns of subjective experience." And even one of the most unrepentant Cartesians in the neuroscientific world, Wilder Penfield, grants that "what the mind does is different. It is not to be accounted for by any neuronal mechanism that I can discover." *The Mystery of the Mind: A Critical Study of Consciousness and the Human Brain* (Princeton University Press, 1975), p. 54.

20. Mary Whiton Calkins, "The self in scientific psychology," *American Journal of Psychology* 26 (1915): 501–502. The quotation within the quotation is from E. B. Titchener, *A Primer of Psychology* (Macmillan, 1899), pp. 33–35.

21. Jaak Panksepp, "Toward a general psychobiological theory of emotions," *Behavioral and Brain Sciences* 5 (1982): 408.

22. J. Laski and A. Laski, "Can machines think?" Review of D. R. Hofstadter and D. C. Dennett, *The Mind's I*, in *Listener* (April 1982).

23. R. A. Wise, "Neuroleptics and operant behaviour: The anhedonia hypothesis," *Behavioral and Brain Sciences* 5 (1982): 81.

24. See ibid., for example, and C. W. Cotman and J. L. McGaugh, *Behavioral Neuroscience: An Introduction* (Academic Press, 1980), pp. 326–332, L. S. Goodman and A. Gilman, *The Pharmacological Basis of Therapeutics*, 5th ed. (Macmillan, 1975), pp. 100–101; J. Crossland, *Lewis's Pharmacology*, 4th ed. (Livingstone, 1970), pp. 744–751; and W. C. Bowman and M. J. Rand, *Textbook of Pharmacology*, 2d ed. (Blackwell, 1980), pp. 12ff.

Bibliography

Adair, J. G., and Spinner, B. 1981. "Subject's access to cognitive processes: Demand characteristics and verbal report." *Journal for the Theory of Social Behavior* 2.

Allport, D. A. 1980. "Attention and performance." In *Cognitive Psychology: New Directions*, ed. G. Claxton. International Library of Psychology. Routledge & Kegan Paul.

Allport, D. A.; Antonis, B.; and Reynolds, P. 1972. "On the division of attention: A disproof of the single-channel hypothesis." *Quarterly Journal of Experimental Psychology* 24.

Anderson, John. 1929. "The non-existence of consciousness." Review of *Space, Time and Deity* by Samuel Alexander. *Australasian Journal of Philosophy and Psychology* 7. Reprinted in Anderson, *Essays in Empiricism*. Angus and Robertson, 1962.

Aquinas. 1968. *Summa Theologiae*. Vol. 12: *Human Intelligence*. Ed. and trans. Paul T. Durbin. Blackfriars, in conjunction with Eyre & Spottiswoode and McGraw-Hill.

Aristotle. 1941. *On Memory and Reminiscence*. In Aristotle, *Parva Naturalia* (The Short Physical Treatises) (4th century B.C.), in *The Basic Works of Aristotle*, Ed. R. McKeon. Random House.

Armstrong, D. M. 1963. "Is introspective knowledge incorrigible?" *Philosophical Review* 72.

Armstrong, D. M. 1968. *A Materialist Theory of the Mind*. International Library of Philosophy and Scientific Method. Routledge & Kegan Paul.

Armstrong, D. M. 1970. "The nature of mind." in *The Mind-Brain Identity Theory*. Ed. C. V. Borst. Macmillan.

Armstrong, D. M. 1981. *The Nature of Mind and Other Essays*. Harvester Press.

Augustine. 1955. *The Trinity* (c.410). In *Augustine: Later Works*. Vol. 8. Ed. and trans. J. Burnaby. Library of Christian Classics, SCM Press.

Aune, B. 1963. "Feelings, moods, and introspections." *Mind* 72.

Ayer, A. J. 1956. *The Problem of Knowledge*. Pelican Books.

Ayer, A. J. 1959. "Privacy," *Proceedings of the British Academy*, vol. 45. Reprinted in Ayer, *The Concept of a Person and Other Essays*. Macmillan, 1963.

Ayer, A. J. 1976. *The Central Questions of Philosophy*. Pelican.

Baars, Bernard. 1983. "Conscious contents provide the nervous system with coherent, global information." In *Consciousness and Self-Regulation: Advances in Research and Theory*, vol. 3. Ed. R. J. Davidson, G. E. Schwartz, and D. Shapiro. Plenum Press.

Baier, Kurt. 1962. "Smart on sensations." *Australasian Journal of Philosophy* 40.

Bain, Alexander. 1868. *Mental and Moral Science: A Compendium of Psychology and Ethics*. 2d ed. Abridgement of *The Senses and the Intellect*, 1855, and *The Emotions and the Will*, 1859. Longmans Green & Co.

Blackman, Derek. 1975. "Inner and outer man." Review of B. F. Skinner's *About Behaviorism*, in *Times Higher Education Supplement*, no. 180 (March).

Blakemore, Colin. 1975. "Central visual processing." In *Handbook of Psychobiology*, ed. Michael Gazzaniga and Colin Blakemore. Academic Press.

Block, Ned. 1983. "Mental pictures and cognitive science." *Philosophical Review* 92.

Block, Ned, and Fodor, J. A. 1972. "What psychological states are not." *Philosophical Review* 81.

Bode, B. H. 1913. "The method of introspection." *Journal of Philosophy, Psychology and Scientific Method* 10.

Boring, Edwin G. 1933. *The Physical Dimensions of Consciousness.* Century Psychology Series. Century Co.

Boring, Edwin G. 1946. "Mind and mechanism." *American Journal of Psychology* 59.

Boring, Edwin G. 1953. "A history of introspection." *Psychological Bulletin* 50.

Borst, C. V., ed. 1970. *The Mind-Brain Identity Theory.* Macmillan.

Bradley, M. C. 1963. "Sensations, brain-processes, and colours." *Australasian Journal of Philosophy* 41.

Bradley, M. C. 1964. "Critical notice of *Philosophy and Scientific Realism.*" *Australasian Journal of Philosophy* 42.

Brentano, Franz. 1973. *Psychology from an Empirical Standpoint* (1874). Ed. Oskar Kraus and Linda McAlister, trans. A. C. Rancurello, D. B. Terrell, and L. L. McAlister. International Library of Philosophy and Scientific Method. Routledge & Kegan Paul.

Bricke, John. 1980. *Hume's Philosophy of Mind.* Edinburgh University Press.

Broad, C. D. 1925. *The Mind and Its Place in Nature.* Kegan Paul, Trench, and Trübner.

Broadbent, Donald. 1961. *Behavior.* Eyre & Spottiswoode.

Broughton, John. 1978. "Development of concepts of self, mind, reality and knowledge." In *Social Cognition*, ed. W. Damon. New Directions for Child Development No. 1. Jossey-Bass.

Budd, M. J. 1969–1970. "Materialism and immaterialism." *Proceedings of the Aristotelian Society* 70.

Burton, Robert G. 1984. "B. F. Skinner's accounts of private events: A critique." *Journal for the Theory of Social Behaviour* 14.

Byrne, Richard. 1983. "Protocol analysis in problem solving." In *Thinking and Reasoning: Psychological Approaches*, ed. J. St. B. T. Evans. Routledge & Kegan Paul.

Calkins, Mary W. 1915. "The self in scientific psychology." *American Journal of Psychology* 26.

Campbell, Keith. 1967. "Materialism." In *The Encyclopedia of Philosophy*, ed. P. Edwards. Collier Macmillan–The Free Press.

Carnap, Rudolph. 1959. "Psychology in physical language." In *Logical Positivism*, ed. A. J. Ayer. The Free Press and George Allen & Unwin.

Cattell, James McKeen. 1904. "The conceptions and methods of psychology." *Popular Science Monthly* 60.

Chappell, V. C., ed. 1962. *The Philosophy of Mind.* Prentice-Hall.

Chase, William G., and Simon, Herbert A. 1973. "The mind's eye in chess." In *Visual Information Processing*, ed. William G. Chase. Academic Press.

Chisholm, Roderick. 1969. "On the observability of the self." *Philosophical and Phenomenological Research* 30.

Churchland, Patricia S. 1983. "Consciousness: The transmutation of a concept." *Pacific Philosophical Quarterly* 64.

Churchland, Paul M. 1979. *Scientific Realism and the Plasticity of Mind.* Cambridge Studies in Philosophy. Cambridge University Press.

Churchland, Paul M. 1981. "Eliminative materialism and the propositional attitudes." *Journal of Philosophy* 78.

Churchland, Paul M. 1984. *Matter and Consciousness: A Contemporary Introduction to the Philosophy of Mind.* Bradford Book. MIT Press.

Churchland, Paul M., and Churchland, Patricia S. 1981. "Functionalism, qualia, and intentionality." *Philosophical Topics* 12.

Cicero. 1914. *De Finibus Bonorum et Malorum* (1st century B.C.). Trans. H. Rackham, Loeb Classical Library, Heinemann and Macmillan.

Clack, J. R. 1973. "Chisholm and Hume on observing the self." *Philosophy and Phenomenological Research* 33.

Comte, Auguste. 1830–1842. *Cours de philosophie positive*. 6 vols. Bachelier.

Cooper, Lynn A., and Shepard, Roger N. 1973. "Chronometric studies of the rotation of mental images." In *Visual Information Processing*, ed. W. G. Chase. Academic Press.

Cornman, James. 1962. "The identity of mind and body." *Journal of Philosophy* 59.

Cotman, Carl, and McGaugh, James. 1980. *Behavioral Neuroscience: An Introduction*. Academic Press.

Crook, John H. 1980. *The Evolution of Human Consciousness*. Clarendon Press.

Crook, John H. 1982. "Imagined worlds: Programmed for insight?" *Listener* 107 (April).

Crook, John H. 1983. "On attributing consciousness to animals." *Nature* 303.

Culbertson, James T. 1983. *Consciousness: Natural and Artificial*. Libra Publishers.

Cummins, Robert. 1981. "What can be learned from *Brainstorms*?" *Philosophical Topics* 12.

D'Andrade, R. 1974. "Memory and the assessment of behaviour." In *Measurement in the Social Sciences*, ed. T. Blalock. Aldine Press.

Danto, A. 1960. "On consciousness in machines." In *Dimensions of Mind: A Symposium*, ed. Sidney Hook. Collier.

Danziger, Kurt. 1979a. "The positivist repudiation of Wundt." *Journal of the History of the Behavioral Sciences* 15.

Danziger, Kurt. 1979b. "The history of introspection reconsidered." York University, Department of Psychology Report no. 83; reprinted with slight modification in *Journal of the History of the Behavioral Sciences* 16 (1980).

Davidson, Donald. 1970. "Mental events." In *Experience and Theory*, ed. L. Foster and J. W. Swanson. University of Massachusetts Press and Duckworth; reprinted in Davidson, *Essays on Actions and Events*. Clarendon Press, 1980.

Davidson, Donald. 1974. "Psychology as philosophy." In *Philosophy of Psychology*, ed. S. C. Brown. Macmillan; reprinted in *The Philosophy of Mind*, ed. J. Glover. Oxford Readings in Philosophy. Oxford University Press, 1976.

Davidson, Donald. 1980. "The material mind." In Davidson, *Essays on Actions and Events*. Clarendon Press.

de la Rochefoucauld, F. 1974. *The Maxims of the Duc de la Rochefoucauld*. Trans. C. Fitzgibbon. Millington.

Dement, W., and Kleitman, N. 1957. "The relation of eye movements during sleep to dream activity: An objective method for the study of dreaming." *Journal of Experimental Psychology* 53.

Dennett, Daniel C. 1969. *Content and Consciousness*. International Library of Philosophy and Scientific Method. Routledge & Kegan Paul.

Dennett, Daniel C. 1971. "Intentional systems." *Journal of Philosophy* 68; reprinted in Dennett, *Brainstorms*. Harvester Press, 1979.

Dennett, Daniel C. 1979a. "Towards a cognitive theory of consciousness." In Dennett, *Brainstorms*. Harvester Press.

Dennett, Daniel C. 1979b. *Brainstorms: Philosophical Essays on Mind and Psychology*. Harvester Press.

Dennett, Daniel C. 1979c. "On the absence of phenomenology." In *Body, Mind and Method: Essays in Honour of Virgil C. Aldrich*, ed. D. F. Gustafson and B. L. Tapscott. D. Reidel.

Dennett, Daniel C. 1981a. "What is it like to be me?" *New Scientist* 91.

Dennett, Daniel C. 1981b. "Making sense of ourselves." *Philosophical Topics* 12.

Dennett, Daniel C. 1982–1983. "Styles of mental representation." *Proceedings of the Aristotelian Society* 83.

Dennett, Daniel C. 1983. "Intentional systems in cognitive etiology: The 'Panglossian paradigm' defended." *Behavioral and Brain Sciences* 6.

Deregowski, J. B. 1974. 'Illusion and culture." In *Illusion in Nature and Art*, ed. R. L. Gregory and E. H. Gombrich. Duckworth.

Descartes. 1954. *Discourse on the Method of Rightly Directing One's Reason and of Seeking Truth in the Sciences* (1637). In *Descartes: Philosophical Writings*, ed. and trans. E. Anscombe and P. T. Geach. Nelson.

Descartes. 1981. *Philosophical Letters*. Ed. and trans. A. Kenny. Blackwell.

De Soto, C. B.; London, M.; and Handel, S. 1965. "Social reasoning and spatial paralogic." *Journal of Personality and Social Psychology* 2.

Deutsch, J. A. 1962. "The Structural basis of behaviour." In Deutsch, *The Structural Basis of Behavior*. Cambridge University Press. Reprinted in *The Philosophy of Mind*, ed. J. Glover. Oxford Readings in Philosophy. Oxford University Press, 1976.

Dewitt, Larry W. 1975. "Consciousness, mind, and self: The implications of the split-brain studies." *British Journal for the Philosophy of Science* 26.

Dodge, Raymond. 1912. "The theory and limitations of introspection." *American Journal of Psychology* 23.

Dodge, Raymond. 1913. "Mental work: A study of psychodynamics." *Psychological Review* 20.

Dreyfus, Hubert, and Haugeland, John. 1974. "The computer as a mistaken model of the mind." In *Philosophy of Psychology*, ed. S. C. Brown. Macmillan.

Ducasse, C. J. 1936. "Introspection, mental acts, and sensa." *Mind* 45.

Dunlap, Knight. 1912. "The case against introspection."*Psychological Review* 19.

Eccles, John. 1967. "Evolution and the conscious self." In *The Human Mind: A Discussion of the Nobel Conference*, ed. J. D. Roslansky. North Holland.

Eccles, John. 1970. *Facing Reality: Philosophical Adventures by a Brain Scientist*. Longman.

Eccles, John. 1973. *The Understanding of the Brain*. McGraw-Hill.

Edelman, G. M., and Mountcastle, V. B. 1978. *The Mindful Brain: Cortical Organization and the Group-Selective Theory of Higher Brain Function*. MIT Press.

English, H. B. 1921. "In aid of introspection." *American Journal of Psychology* 32.

Ericsson, K. A., and Simon, Herbert A. 1980. "Verbal reports as data." *Psychological Review* 87.

Evans, Jonathan St. B. T. 1980. "Thinking: Experiential and information processing approaches." In *Cognitive Psychology: New Directions*, ed. G. Claxton. Routledge & Kegan Paul.

Evans, Jonathan St. B. T. 1981. "A reply to Morris." *British Journal of Psychology* 72.

Evans, Jonathan St. B. T. 1983. *Thinking and Reasoning: Psychological Approaches*. Routledge & Kegan Paul.

Evans, Jonathan St. B. T., and Wason, P. C. 1976. "Rationalization in a reasoning task." *British Journal of Psychology* 67.

Eysenck. H. J. 1975. "Behaviourism, pro and contra—Skinner skinned?" *Encounter* 44 (July).

Eysenck, H. J. 1977. *You and Neurosis*. Fontana.

Falk, Arthur E. 1975. "Learning to report one's introspections." *Philosophy of Science* 42.

Fancher, Raymond E. 1979. *Pioneers of Psychology*. Norton.

Farr, Robert. 1980. "Homo socio-psychologicus." In *Models of Man*, ed. A. J. Chapman and D. M. Jones. British Psychological Society.

Farr, Robert. 1983. "Wilhelm Wundt (1832–1920) and the origins of psychology as an experimental and social science." *British Journal of Social Psychology* 22.

Farrell, B. A. 1950. "Experience." *Mind* 59. Reprinted in *The Philosophy of Mind*, ed. V. C. Chappell. Prentice-Hall, 1962.

Feigl, H. 1958. "The 'mental' and the 'physical.' " In *Minnesota Studies in the Philosophy of Science*, vol. 2: *Concepts, Theories, and the Mind-Body Problem*, ed. H. Feigl, M. Scriven, and G. Maxwell. University of Minnesota Press.

Feigl, H. 1961. "Mind-body, *not* a pseudoproblem." In *Dimensions of Mind: A Symposium*, ed. Sidney Hook. Collier.

Feyerabend, Paul. 1963a. "Mental events and the brain." *Journal of Philosophy* 60.

Feyerabend, Paul, 1963b. "Materialism and the mind-body problem." *Review of Metaphysics* 17.

Flavell, J. H. 1979. "Metacognition and cognitive monitoring: A new area of cognitive-developmental inquiry." *American Psychologist* 34.

Fodor, J. A. 1965. "Explanations in psychology." In *Philosophy in America*, ed. Max Black. Cornell University Press.

Fodor, J. A. 1975. *The Language of Thought.* Language of Thought Series. Crowell.

Fodor, J. A. 1981. "The mind-body problem." *Scientific American* 244.

Fromm, Erich. 1939. "Selfishness and self-love." *Psychiatry* 2.

Frost, Eliot Park. 1914. "Cannot psychology dispense with consciousness?" *Psychological Review* 21.

Gardiner, Martin. 1984. "Quiz kids." Review of *The Great Mental Calculators* by Steven B. Smith, in *New York Review of Books* 31.

Gazzaniga, Michael S. 1967. "The split brain in man." *Scientific American* 217.

Gazzaniga, Michael S., and Blakemore, C., eds. 1975. *Handbook of Psychobiology.* Academic Press.

Gazzaniga, Michael S., and Ledoux, J. E. 1978. *The Integrated Mind.* Plenum Press.

Geertz, Clifford. 1976. " 'From the native's point of view': On the nature of anthropological understanding." In *Meaning in Anthropology*, ed. K. H. Basso and H. A. Selby. School of American Research Book. University of New Mexico Press.

Ginsberg, Herbert, and Opper, Sylvia. 1979. *Piaget's Theory of Intellectual Development.* 2d ed. Prentice-Hall.

Gregory, Richard. 1983. *Mind in Science.* Penguin.

Hamlyn, D. W. 1953. "Behaviour," *Philosophy* 28. Reprinted in *The Philosophy of Mind*, ed. V. C. Chappell. Prentice-Hall, 1962.

Hamlyn, D. W. 1983. "Self-Knowledge." In Hamlyn, *Perception, Learning and the Self: Essays in the Philosophy of Psychology.* Routledge & Kegan Paul; reprinted from *The Self*, ed. T. Mischel. Blackwell, 1977.

Hannay, Alastair. 1971. *Mental Images—A Defence.* George Allen & Unwin.

Hart, Bernard. 1930. *The Psychology of Insanity.* 4th ed. Cambridge University Press.

Haynes, Peter. 1976. "Mental imagery." *Canadian Journal of Philosophy* 6.

Hebb, D. O. 1969. "The mind's eye." *Psychology Today* 2.

Hebb, D. O. 1972. *Textbook of Psychology.* 3d ed. Saunders.

Hebb, D. O. 1980. *Essay on Mind.* Lawrence Erlbaum.

Hebb, D. O. 1982. "Elaborations of Hebb's cell assembly theory." In *Neuropsychology after Lashley—Fifty Years since the Publication of* Brain Mechanisms and Intelligence, ed. J. Orbach. Lawrence Erlbaum.

Heelas, P., and Lock, A., eds. 1981. *Indigenous Psychologies: The Anthropology of the Self.* Language Thought and Culture Series. Academic Press.

Herrick, C. J. 1915. "Introspection as a biological method." *Journal of Philosophy, Psychology and Scientific Method* 12.

Herrington, R. N., and Schneidau, P. 1968. "The effect of imagery on the waveshape of the visual evoked response." *Experientia* 24.

Hobbes. 1968. *Leviathan or the Matter, Forme & Power of a Commonwealth Ecclesiastical and Civill* (1651). Ed. C. B. McPherson. Penguin.

Hodges, Andrew. 1983. *Alan Turing: The Enigma*. Burnett Books.

Hofstadter, Douglas R., and Dennett, Daniel C. 1981. *The Mind's I: Fantasies and Reflections on Self and Soul*. Harvester Press.

Holt, E. B. 1914. *The Concept of Consciousness* (1912). George Allen & Unwin.

Hook, Sidney, ed. 1960. *Dimensions of Mind: A Symposium*. Proceedings of the Third Annual New York University Institute of Philosophy, 1959. Collier.

Hudson, W. 1956. "Why we cannot witness or observe what goes on 'in our heads.' " *Mind* 65.

Hume, David. 1888. *A Treatise of Human Nature* (1739). Ed. L. A. Selby-Bigge. Clarendon Press.

Humphrey, George. 1951. *Thinking: An Introduction to Its Experimental Psychology*. Methuen–John Wiley.

Humphrey, Nicholas. 1982a. "What is mind? No matter. What is matter? Never mind." Review of *The Mind's I* by D. Hofstadter and D. C. Dennett. In *London Review of Books* 3.

Humphrey, Nicholas. 1982b. "Consciousness: A just-so story" *New Scientist* 95; reprinted in *Consciousness Regained*.

Humphrey, Nicholas. 1983. *Consciousness Regained: Chapters in the Development of Mind*. Oxford University Press.

Hyslop, A. 1969. "The plight of the inner process." *Australasian Journal of Philosophy* 47.

Jackson, F. 1973. "Is there a good argument against the incorrigibility thesis?" *Australasian Journal of Philosophy* 51.

James, William. 1892. *Text Book of Psychology* (*Briefer Course* in U.S.A.). Henry Holt.

James, William. 1899. *Talks to Teachers on Psychology*. Longmans.

James, William. 1950. *The Principles of Psychology* (1890). 2 vols. Dover Books.

James, William. 1976. "Does 'consciousness' exist?" In James, *Essays in Radical Empiricism*. ed. F. Bowers and I. F. Skrupskelis. Harvard University Press. Reprinted from *Journal of Philosophy, Psychology and Scientific Method* 1 (1904).

Jaynes, Julian. 1976. *The Origin of Consciousness in the Breakdown of the Bicameral Mind*. Houghton Mifflin.

Johansen, J. Prytz. 1954. *The Maori and His Religion in Its Non-Ritualistic Aspects*. I Kommission Hos Ejnar Munksgaard.

Johnson, C. N. 1982. "The acquisition of mental verbs and the concept of mind." In *Language Development*. Vol. 1: *Syntax and Semantics*, ed. S. Kuczaj. Lawrence Erlbaum.

Johnson, C. N., and Wellman, H. M. 1982. "Children's developing conceptions of the mind and brain." *Child Development* 53.

Johnson-Laird, P. N. 1981. "Mental models in cognitive science." In *Perspectives on Cognitive Science*, ed. Donald A. Norman. Ablex–Lawrence Erlbaum.

Johnson-Laird, P. N. 1983. *Mental Models: Towards a Cognitive Science of Language, Inference and Consciousness*. Cambridge University Press.

Jones, A. H. 1915. "The method of psychology." *Journal of Philosophy, Psychology and Scientific Method* 12.

Jung, C. G. 1957–1979. *The Collected Works of C. G. Jung*. 20 vols. Routledge & Kegan Paul.

Jung, C. G. 1983. *Jung: Selected Writings*. Selected and introduced by Anthony Storr. Fontana.

Kalke, W. 1969. "What is wrong with Fodor and Putnam's functionalism?" *Nous* 3.

Kantor, J. R. 1922. "Can the psychophysical experiment reconcile Introspectionists and Objectivists?" *American Journal of Psychology* 33.

Kenny, A. 1968. "Cartesian privacy." In *Wittgenstein: The Philosophical Investigations*. ed. G. Pitcher. Doubleday-Macmillan.

Kirk, Robert. 1971. "Armstrong's analogue of introspection." *Philosophical Quarterly* 21.

Kneale, W. 1949–1950. "Experience and introspection." *Proceedings of the Aristotelian Society* 50.

Koffka, K. 1924–1925. "Introspection and the method of psychology." *British Journal of Psychology* 15.

Köhler, Wolfgang. 1947. *Gestalt Psychology: An Introduction to New Concepts in Modern Psychology*. Mentor Book. New American Library.

Kosslyn, Stephen M. 1975. "Information representation in visual images." *Cognitive Psychology* 7.

Kosslyn, Stephen M. 1980. *Images and Mind*. Harvard University Press.

Kraut, Robert E., and Lewis, Steven H. 1982. "Person perception and self-awareness: Knowledge of influences on one's own judgments." *Journal of Personality and Social Psychology* 42.

Lackner, J. R., and Garrett, M. F. 1972. "Resolving ambiguity: Effects of biasing context in the unattended ear." *Cognition* 1.

Laing, R. D. 1965. *The Divided Self*. Pelican.

Laird, D. A. 1932. "How the consumer estimates quality by subconscious sensory impressions: With special reference to the role of smell." *Journal of Applied Psychology* 16.

Laird, J. 1919. "Introspection." *Mind* 28.

Landesman, C. 1967. "Consciousness." In *The Encyclopedia of Philosophy*, ed. P. Edwards. Collier-Macmillan.

Lange, Friedrich A. 1950. *The History of Materialism* (1865), trans. E. C. Thomas. Humanities Press.

Lashley, Karl. 1923. "The behaviouristic interpretation of consciousness." *Psychological Review* 30.

Lashley, Karl. 1958. "Cerebral organization and behaviour." *Proceedings of the Association for Research in Nervous and Mental Diseases*, 36.

Latané, B., and Darley, J. M. 1970. *The Unresponsive Bystander: Why Doesn't He Help?* Appleton-Century-Crofts.

Lefebvre-Pinard, Monique. 1983. "Understanding and auto-control of cognitive functions: Implications for the relationship between cognition and behaviour." *International Journal of Behavioural Development* 6.

Levin, Michael E. 1979. *Metaphysics and the Mind-Body Problem*. Clarendon Press.

Lewis, David K. 1966. "An argument for the Identity Theory." *Journal of Philosophy* 63.

Loar, B. F. 1982. *Mind and Meaning*. Cambridge Studies in Philosophy. Cambridge University Press.

Locke, John. 1965. *An Essay Concerning Human Understanding* (1690), ed. John Yolton. 2 vols. Everyman–Dent.

Locke, Don. 1968. *Myself and Others*. Clarendon Press.

Lucas, John. 1972. "Consciousness without language." In A. Kenny, H. C. Longuet-Higgins, J. Lucas, and C. H. Waddington. *The Nature of Mind*. Edinburgh University Press.

Lunzer, E. A. 1980. "The development of consciousness." In *Aspects of Consciousness*, vol. 1: *Physiological Issues*, ed. Geoffrey Underwood and R. Stevens. Academic Press.

Luria, A. R. 1966. *Human Brain and Psychological Processes*, trans. B. Haigh. Harper & Row.

Luria, A. R. 1973. *The Working Brain: An Introduction to Neuropsychology.* trans. B. Haigh. Penguin.

Lutz, Catherine. 1982. "Ethnopsychology compared to what? Explaining behaviour and consciousness among the Ifaluk." Unpublished manuscript.

Lycan, William G. 1981a. "Psychological laws." *Philosophical Topics* 12.

Lycan, William G. 1981b. "Form, function and feel." *Journal of Philosophy* 78.

Lycos, Kimon. 1965. "Images and the imaginary." *Australasian Journal of Philosophy* 43.

Lyons, William. 1980. *Gilbert Ryle: An Introduction to His Philosophy.* Harvester and Humanities Presses.

Lyons, William. 1983. "The transformation of introspection." *British Journal of Social Psychology* 22.

Lyons, William. 1984a. "The tiger and his stripes." *Analysis* 44.

Lyons, William. 1984b. "Behaviourism and 'the problem of privacy.' " *Behavioural and Brain Sciences* 7.

Lyons, William. 1985a. "Dennett, functionalism, and introspection." *Canadian Journal of Philosophy,* supplementary vol. 11. "New Essays in the Philosophy of Mind," series 2.

Lyons, William. 1985b. "The behaviourists' struggle with introspection." *International Philosophical Quarterly* 25.

McDougall, William. 1908. *An Introduction to Social Psychology.* Methuen.

McDougall, William. 1922. "Prolegomena to psychology." *Psychological Review* 29.

Mace, C. A. 1950. "Introspection and analysis." In *Philosophical Analysis,* ed. Max Black. Cornell University Press.

McGinn, Colin. 1982. *The Character of Mind.* OPUS–Oxford University Press.

MacKay, D. M. 1966. "Cerebral organization and the conscious control of action." In *Brain and Conscious Experience,* ed. J. C. Eccles. Springer.

Mackie, J. L. 1963. "Are there any incorrigible empirical statements?" *Australasian Journal of Philosophy* 41.

Malcolm, Norman. 1979–1980. " 'Functionalism' in Philosophy of Psychology." *Proceedings of the Aristotelian Society* 80.

Manser, A. R. 1967. "Images," "Imagination." In *The Encyclopedia of Philosophy,* ed. P. Edwards. Collier Macmillan and Free Press.

Marr, David. 1977. "Artificial intelligence—a personal view." *Artificial Intelligence* 9.

Marr, David. 1982. *Vision: A Computational Investigation into the Human Representation and Processing of Visual Information.* W. H. Freeman.

Matthews, Gareth B. 1969. "Mental copies." *Philosophical Review* 78. Reprinted in *Ryle,* ed. O. P. Wood and G. Pitcher. Modern Studies in Philosophy. Macmillan.

Maudsley, Henry. 1916. *Organic to Human: Psychological and Sociological.* Macmillan.

Mead, G. H. 1934. *Mind, Self and Society: From the Standpoint of a Social Behaviourist,* ed. C. W. Morris. Cambridge University Press.

Medlin, Brian. 1967. "Ryle and the Mechanical Hypothesis." In *The Identity Theory of Mind,* ed. C. F. Presley. University of Queensland Press.

Meyer, Max F. 1921. *Psychology of the Other-One: An Introductory Text-Book of Psychology.* Missouri Book Co.

Mill, James. 1829. *Analysis of the Phenomena of the Human Mind.* 2 vols. Baldwin & Cradock.

Mill, J. S. 1882. *Auguste Comte and Positivism* (1865). Trübner.

Mill, J. S. 1905. *A System of Logic* (1843). Routledge & Sons.

Mill, J. S. 1878. *An Examination of Sir William Hamilton's Philosophy* (1865). Longmans, Green, Reader & Dyer.

Miller, George. 1966. *Psychology: The Science of Mental Life.* Pelican.

Miller, Jonathan, ed. 1983. *States of Mind: Conversations with Psychological Investigators.* BBC Publications.

Mischel, T. 1970. "Wundt and the conceptual foundations of psychology." *Philosophy and Phenomenological Research* 31.

Misiak, H., and Sexton, V. S. 1966. *History of Psychology: An Overview.* Grune & Stratton.

Morris, P. E. 1981. "Why Evans is wrong in criticizing introspective reports of subjects' strategies." *British Journal of Psychology* 72.

Murdoch, Iris. 1953. *Sartre: Romantic Rationalist.* Yale University Press.

Nagel, Thomas. 1965. "Physicalism." *Philosophical Review* 74.

Nagel, Thomas. 1970–1971. "Brain bisection and the unity of consciousness." *Synthese* 22.

Natsoulas, Thomas. 1970. "Concerning introspective 'knowledge.'" *Psychological Bulletin* 73.

Natsoulas, Thomas. 1977. "Consciousness: Consideration of an inferential hypothesis." *Journal for the Theory of Social Behaviour* 7.

Natsoulas, Thomas. 1982. "Conscious perception and the paradox of 'blind-sight.'" In *Aspects of Consciousness*, vol. 3: *Awareness and Self-Awareness*, ed. Geoffrey Underwood. Academic Press.

Neisser, Ulric. 1967. *Cognitive Psychology.* Prentice-Hall.

Neisser, Ulric. 1968. "The processes of vision." *Scientific American* 219.

Neisser, Ulric. 1972. "Changing conceptions of imagery." In *The Function and Nature of Imagery*, ed. P. W. Sheehan. Academic Press.

Neisser, Ulric. 1976. *Cognition and Reality: Principles and Implications of Cognitive Psychology.* W. H. Freeman.

Nerlich, Graham. 1967. "If you can't be wrong, then you can't be right." *Philosophical Quarterly* 17.

Newell, Allen. 1973. "Artificial intelligence and the concept of mind." in *Computer Models of Thought and Language*, ed. Roger C. Schank and Kenneth M. Colby. W. H. Freeman.

Nisbett, R. E., and Wilson, T. De C. 1977. "Telling more than we can know: Verbal reports on mental processes." *Psychological Review* 84.

Norman, Donald A., ed. 1981. *Perspectives on Cognitive Science.* Ablex–Lawrence Erlbaum.

Oatley, K. 1981. "Representing ourselves: Mental schemata, computational metaphors, and the nature of consciousness." In *Aspects of Consciousness*, vol. 2: *Structural Issues*, ed. G. Underwood and R. Stevens. Academic Press.

Okabe, T. 1910. "An experimental study of belief." *American Journal of Psychology* 21.

Orbach, J., ed. 1982. *Neuropsychology after Lashley: Fifty Years since the Publication of Brain Mechanisms and Intelligence.* Lawrence Erlbaum.

Oster, Gerald. 1970. "Phosphenes." *Scientific American* 222 (February).

Pappas, George S. 1975. "Defining incorrigibility." *The Personalist* 56.

Peacocke, Christopher. 1983. *Sense and Content: Experience, Thought, and Their Relations.* Clarendon Press.

Penfield, Wilder. 1958. *The Excitable Cortex in Conscious Man.* Sherrington Lectures No. 5. Liverpool University Press.

Penfield, Wilder. 1975. *The Mystery of the Mind: A Critical Study of Consciousness and the Human Brain.* Princeton University Press.

Penfield, Wilder, and Rasmussen, T. 1957. *The Cerebral Cortex of Man: A Clinical Study of Localization of Function.* Macmillan.

Pepper, Stephen. 1918. "What is introspection?" *American Journal of Psychology* 29.

Perky, C. W. 1910. "An experimental study of imagination." *American Journal of Psychology* 21.

Pillsbury, Walter B. 1911. *The Essentials of Psychology.* Macmillan.

Place, U. T. 1956. "Is consciousness a brain process?" *British Journal of Psychology* 47. Reprinted in *The Philosophy of Mind*, ed. V. C. Chappell. Prentice-Hall, 1962.

Place, U. T. 1966. "Consciousness and perception in psychology." *Proceedings of the Aristotelian Society*, supplementary vol. 40.

Porter, Samuel. 1881. "Is thought possible without language? Case of a deaf-mute." *Princeton Review* (January).

Posner, M. I. 1980. "Mental chronometry and the problem of consciousness." In *The Nature of Thought: Essays in Honour of D. O. Hebb*, ed. P. W. Jusczyk and R. M. Klein. Lawrence Erlbaum.

Prado, C. G. 1977. "Reference and consciousness." *Australasian Journal of Philosophy* 55.

Prado, C. G. 1978. "Reflexive consciousness." *Dialogue* 17.

Pribram, Karl H., ed. 1969. *Moods, States, and Mind.* Penguin Modern Psychology—Brain and Behaviour I. Penguin.

Pribram, Karl H. 1976. "Problems concerning the structure of consciousness." In *Consciousness and the Brain*, ed. G. C. Globus, G. Maxwell, and I. Savodnik. Plenum.

Pribram, Karl H. 1982. "Localization and distribution of function in the brain." In *Neuropsychology after Lashley: Fifty Years since the Publication of* Brain Mechanisms and Intelligence, ed. J. Orbach. Lawrence Erlbaum.

Puccetti, Roland. 1974. "Physicalism and the evolution of consciousness," *Canadian Journal of Philosophy*, supplementary vol. 1.

Puccetti, Roland. 1976. "The mute-self: A reaction to Dewitt's alternative account of the split-brain data." *British Journal for the Philosophy of Science* 27.

Puccetti, Roland. 1977. "Sperry on consciousness: A critical appreciation." *Journal of Medicine and Philosophy* 2.

Puccetti, Roland. 1978. "Ontology vs. ontogeny: A dilemma for Identity Theorists." *Dialogue* 17.

Putnam, Hilary. 1961. "Minds and machines." In *Dimensions of Mind: A Symposium*, ed. Sidney Hook. Collier Books. Reprinted in Putnam, *Mind, Language and Reality.* Cambridge University Press, 1975.

Putnam, Hilary. 1964. "Robots: Machines or artificially created life?" *Journal of Philosophy* 61. Reprinted in Putnam, *Mind, Language and Reality.* Cambridge University Press, 1975.

Putnam, Hilary. 1963. "Brains and behavior." In *Analytic Philosophy*, vol. 2, ed. R. J. Butler, Oxford University Press. Reprinted in Putnam, *Mind, Language and Reality.* Cambridge University Press, 1975.

Putnam, Hilary. 1967. "The mental life of some machines." In *Intentionality, Minds and Perception*, ed. H. N. Castañeda. Wayne State University Press. Reprinted in *The Philosophy of Mind*, ed. J. Glover, Oxford University Press, 1976, and in Putnam, *Mind, Language and Reality.* Cambridge University Press, 1975.

Putnam, Hilary. 1973. "Philosophy and our mental life," presented as part of a Foerster symposium, "Computers and the Mind," University of California, Berkeley. Reprinted in Putnam, *Mind, Language and Reality.* Cambridge University Press, 1975.

Putnam, Hilary. 1975a. "The nature of mental states." In Putnam, *Mind, Language and Reality.* Cambridge University Press, 1975; published as "Psychological predicates" in *Art, Mind and Religion*, Proceedings of the Oberlin Colloquium in Philosophy 1965, ed. W. H. Capitan and D. D. Merrill, University of Pittsburgh Press, 1967.

Putnam, Hilary. 1975b. *Mind, Language and Reality.* Philosphical Papers vol. 2. Cambridge University Press.

Pylyshyn, Zenon. 1973. "What the mind's eyes tells the mind's brain: A critique of mental imagery." *Psychological Bulletin* 80.

Pylyshyn, Zenon. 1974. "The symbolic nature of mental representation." Paper presented at a symposium "Objectives and Methodologies in Artificial Intelligence," Australian National University.

Pylyshyn, Zenon. 1980. "The 'causal power' of machines." Commentary on Searle, "Minds, brains, and programs." *The Behavioral and Brain Sciences* 3.

Quine, W. V. O. 1966. "On mental entities." In Quine, *The Ways of Paradox and Other Essays*. Random House.

Quinton, Anthony. 1970. "Ryle on perception." In *Ryle*, ed. O. P. Wood and G. Pitcher. Modern Studies in Philosophy Series. Macmillan.

Quinton, Anthony. 1977. "In defence of introspection." *Philosophic Exchange* 2.

Rabb, J. Douglas. 1977. "Reflection, reflexion, and introspection." *Locke Newsletter* 8.

Radford, John. 1974. "Reflections on introspection." *American Psychologist* 29.

Rakover, Sam. 1983. "Hypothesizing from introspections: A model for the role of mental entities in psychological explanation." *Journal for the Theory of Social Behaviour* 13.

Rees, W. L. Linford. 1976. *A Short Textbook of Psychiatry*. Hodder and Stoughton. 2d ed.

Rey, Georges. 1983. "A reason for doubting the existence of consciousness." In *Consciousness and Self-Regulation: Advances in Research and Theory*, vol. 3, ed. R. J. Davidson, G. E. Schwartz, and D. Shapiro. Plenum Press.

Richards, Norvin. 1973. "Depicting and visualising." *Mind* 82.

Richardson, Alan. 1969. *Mental Imagery*. Routledge & Kegan Paul.

Richardson, John T. E. 1983. "Mental imagery in thinking and problem solving." In *Thinking and Reasoning: Psychological Approaches*, ed. J. St. B. T. Evans. Routledge & Kegan Paul.

Richardson, Robert C. 1981. "Internal representation: Prologue to a theory of intentionality." *Philosophical Topics* 12.

Ridley, Mark. 1983. "The advantages of knowing." Review of N. Humphrey, *Consciousness Regained*, in *Times Literary Supplement* (September).

Rorty, Richard. 1965. "Mind-body identity, privacy and categories." *Review of Metaphysics* 19.

Rorty, Richard. 1972. "Dennett on awareness." *Philosophical Studies* 23.

Rose, Steven. 1976. *The Conscious Brain*. Penguin.

Russell, Bertrand. 1921. *The Analysis of Mind*. George Allen & Unwin.

Ryle, Gilbert. 1949. *The Concept of Mind*. Hutchinson.

Ryle, Gilbert. 1971. *Collected Papers*, vol. 2: *Collected Essays: 1929-1968*. Hutchinson.

Ryle, Gilbert. 1979. *On Thinking*, ed. K. Kolenda. Blackwell.

Schneider, W., and Shiffrin, R. M. 1977. "Controlled and automatic human information processing: I. Detection, search, and attention" and "Controlled and automatic human information processing: II. Perceptual learning, automatic attending, and a general theory." *Psychological Review* 84.

Searle, J. R. 1980. "Minds, brains, and programs." *The Behavioral and Brain Sciences* 3. Reprinted in D. R. Hofstadter and D. C. Dennett, *The Mind's I: Fantasies and Reflections on Self and Soul*. Harvester Press, 1981.

Searle, J. R. 1983. *Intentionality: An Essay in the Philosophy of Mind*. Cambridge University Press.

Segall, M. H.; Campbell, T. D.; and Herskovitz, M. J. 1966. *The Influence of Culture on Visual Perception*. Bobbs-Merrill.

Sellars, Wilfrid. 1965. "The identity approach to the mind-body problem." *Review of Metaphysics* 18.

Shaffer, Jerome. 1961. "Could mental states be brain processes?" *Journal of Philosophy*. Reprinted in *Body and Mind*, ed. G. N. A. Vesey. George Allen & Unwin, 1964.

Shaffer, Jerome. 1963. "Mental events and the brain." *Journal of Philosophy* 60.

Shallice, T. 1978. "The dominant action system: An information-processing approach to consciousness." In *The Stream of Consciousness: Scientific Investigations into the Flow of Human Experience*, ed. K. S. Pope and J. L. Singer. Plenum.

Sheehan, Peter W. 1978. "Mental imagery." In *Psychology Survey* No. 1, ed. B. M. Foss. George Allen & Unwin.

Sheehan, Peter W., and Neisser, Ulric. 1969. "Some variables affecting the vividness of imagery in recall." *British Journal of Psychology* 60.

Shepard, R. N. 1966. "Learning and recall as organization and search." *Journal of Verbal Learning and Verbal Behavior* 5.

Shepard, R. N. 1978. "The mental image." *American Psychologist* 33.

Shepard, R. N., and Metzler, J. 1971. "Mental rotation of three-dimensional objects." *Science* 171. Reprinted in *Readings in Cognitive Psychology*, ed. M. Coltheart. Holt Rinehart & Winston, 1972.

Sheridan, G. 1969. "The electroencephalogram argument against incorrigibility." *American Philosophical Quarterly* 6.

Shoemaker, Sydney. 1963. *Self-Knowledge and Self-Identity*. Cornell University Press.

Shoemaker, Sydney. 1968. "Self-reference and self-awareness." *Journal of Philosophy* 65.

Shoemaker, Sydney. 1975. "Functionalism and qualia." *Philosophical Studies* 27.

Shoemaker, Sydney. 1981. "Some varieties of functionalism." *Philosophical Topics* 12.

Shorter, J. M. 1952. "Imagination." *Mind* 61. Reprinted in *Ryle*, ed. O. P. Wood and G. Pitcher. Modern Studies in Philosophy Series. Macmillan, 1970.

Simon, Michael A. 1970. "Materialism, mental language, and mind-body identity." *Philosophy and Phenomenological Research* 30.

Skinner, B. F. 1938. *The Behavior of Organisms: An Experimental Analysis*. Appleton-Century-Crofts.

Skinner, B. F. 1956. "A case history in scientific method." *American Psychologist* 11. Reprinted in Skinner, *Cumulative Record*. Methuen, 1961.

Skinner, B. F. 1961. *Cumulative Record*. Enlarged ed. Methuen.

Skinner, B. F. 1965. *Science and Human Behavior* (1953). Collier Macmillan–Free Press.

Smart, J. J. C. 1959. "Sensations and brain processes." *Philosophical Review* 68. Reprinted in *Body and Mind*, ed. G. N. A. Vesey, George Allen & Unwin, 1964, and in *The Philosophy of Mind*, ed. V. C. Chappell, Prentice-Hall, 1962.

Smart, J. J. C. 1963a. "Materialism." *Journal of Philosophy* 60.

Smart, J. J. C. 1963b. *Philosophy and Scientific Realism*. Routledge & Kegan Paul.

Smart, J. J. C. 1971. "Reports on immediate experiences." *Synthese* 22.

Smith, E. R., and Miller, F. D. 1978. "Limits on perception of cognitive processes: A reply to Nisbett and Wilson." *Psychological Review* 85.

Smith, Jean. 1981. "Self and experience in Maori culture." In *Indigenous Psychologies: The Anthropology of the Self*, ed. P. Heelas and A. Lock. Language, Thought, and Culture Series. Academic Press.

Sperry, R. W. 1952. "Neurology and the mind-brain problem." *American Scientist* 40.

Sperry, R. W. 1964. "The great cerebral commissure." *Scientific American* 210.

Sperry, R. W. 1968. "Hemisphere deconnection and unity in conscious awareness." *American Psychologist* 23.

Sperry, R. W. 1977. "Forebrain commissurotomy and conscious awareness." *Journal of Medicine and Philosophy* 2. Reprinted in *Neuropsychology after Lashley: Fifty Years since the Publication of* Brain Mechanisms and Intelligence, ed. J. Orbach, Lawrence Erlbaum, 1982.

Squires, J. E. R. 1968. "Visualising." *Mind* 77.

Stich, Stephen. 1981. "Dennett on intentional systems." *Philosophical Topics* 12.

Stich, Stephen. 1983. *From Folk Psychology to Cognitive Science: The Case against Belief*. Bradford Book—MIT Press.

Stout, G. F. 1929. *A Manual of Psychology* (1898), 4th ed., ed. and rev. G. F. Stout, C. A. Mace, and W. B. Clive. University Tutorial Series.

Strong, C. A. 1939. "The sensori-motor theory of awareness." *Journal of Philosophy* 36.

Thomas, Stephen N. 1978. *The Formal Mechanics of Mind*. Harvester Studies in Cognitive Science. Harvester Press.

Titchener, E. B. 1899. *A Primer of Psychology*. Macmillan.

Titchener, E. B. 1909a. *A Textbook of Psychology*. Macmillan.

Titchener, E. B. 1909b. *Lectures on the Experimental Psychology of the Thought Processes.* Macmillan.

Titchener, E. B. 1912. "Prolegomena to a study of introspection." *American Journal of Psychology* 23.

Titchener, E. B. 1914. "Psychology: Science or technology?" *Popular Science Monthly* 84.

Titchener, E. B. 1921. "Wilhelm Wundt." *American Journal of Psychology* 32.

Tolman, E. C. 1922. "A new formula for behaviourism." *Psychological Review* 29.

Tormey, A. 1973. "Access, incorrigibility and identity." *Journal of Philosophy* 70.

Valentine, E. R. 1982. *Conceptual Issues in Psychology*. George Allen & Unwin.

Vernon, Jack. 1963. *Inside the Black Room: Studies in Sensory Deprivation*. Pelican.

Vesey, G. N. A., ed. 1964. *Body and Mind*. George Allen & Unwin.

Wade, David. 1983. "The ultimate offence: To be taken prisoner of war." *Listener* 109 (January).

Watson, J. B. 1913. "Psychology as the behaviourist views it." *Psychological Review* 20.

Watson, J. B. 1916. "The place of the conditioned-reflex in psychology." *Psychological Review* 23.

Watson, J. B. 1919. *Psychology from the Standpoint of a Behaviourist*. J. B. Lippincott.

Watson, J. B. 1920. "Is thinking merely the action of language mechanisms?" *British Journal of Psychology* 11.

West, Michael. 1982. "Meditation and self-awareness: Physiological and phenomenological approaches." In *Aspects of Consciousness*, vol. 3: *Awareness and Self-Awareness*, ed. Geoffrey Underwood. Academic Press.

White, Alan R. 1964. *Attention*. Basil Blackwell.

White, P. 1980. "Limitations on verbal reports of internal events: A refutation of Nisbett and Wilson and of Bem." *Psychological Review* 87.

Wilding, J. M. 1982. *Perception: From Sense to Object*. Hutchinson.

Wilkes, K. V. 1978. *Physicalism*. Studies in Philosophical Psychology. Routledge & Kegan Paul.

Wilkes, K. V. 1981. "Functionalism, psychology, and the philosophy of mind." *Philosophical Topics* 12.

Wilson, T. D., and Nisbett, R. E. 1978. "The accuracy of verbal reports about the effects of stimuli on evaluations and behaviour." *Social Psychology* 41.

Wittgenstein, L. 1958. *Philosophical Investigations* (1953), trans. G. E. M. Anscombe. Blackwell.

Woodworth, Robert S. 1899. "The accuracy of voluntary movement." *Psychological Review Monographs* 3. no. 13.

Woodworth, R. S., and Schlosberg, H. 1955. *Experimental Psychology*. 3d ed. Methuen.

Woodworth, R. S., and Sheehan, M. R. 1964. *Schools of Psychology*. Methuen.

Wright, D. S., et al. 1970. *Introducing Psychology: An Experimental Approach*. Penguin.

Wundt, Wilhelm. 1888. "Selbstbeobachtung und innere Wahrnehmung." *Philosophische Studien* 4.

Wundt, Wilhelm. 1912. *An Introduction to Psychology* (1911), trans. R. Pintner. George Allen & Unwin.

Wylie, Ruth C. 1968. "The present status of self theory." In *Handbook of Personality Theory and Research*, ed. E. F. Borgatta and W. H. Lambert. Rand McNally.

Young, J. Z. 1978. *Programs of the Brain*. Oxford University Press.

Young, R. M. 1970. *Mind, Brain, and Adaptation in the 19th Century*. Clarendon Press.

Index

⅃Ŀ Bradford Books